Raymond L. Welty
Memorial Collection in History

Sustaining Patron

in the field of

Near Eastern History

Given by

Phi Alpha Theta

WITHDRAWN

WORLD AFFAIRS
National and International Viewpoints

WORLD AFFAIRS
National and International Viewpoints

The titles in this collection were selected
from the Council on Foreign Relations' publication:
The Foreign Affairs 50-Year Bibliography

Advisory Editor
RONALD STEEL

Memoirs of HALIDÉ EDIB

Halide Edib Adivar

ARNO PRESS
A NEW YORK TIMES COMPANY
New York • 1972

956.102092
A235m
1972

Reprint Edition 1972 by Arno Press Inc.

Reprinted from a copy in The Newark Public Library

World Affairs: National and International Viewpoints
ISBN for complete set: 0-405-04560-3
See last pages of this volume for titles.

Manufactured in the United States of America.

Publisher's Note: The frontispiece has been reproduced in black and white for this edition.

Library of Congress Cataloging in Publication Data

Adıvar, Halide Edib, 1885-1964.
  Memoirs of Halide Edib.

  (World affairs: national and international viewpoints)
  Reprint of the 1926 ed.
  1. Turkey--History--Mohammed, 1909-1918.
2. Turkey--History--Revolution, 1918-1923.
I. Title. II. Series.
DR592.A43 1972   956.1'02'0924 [B]   72-4272
ISBN 0-405-04568-9

Memoirs of
Halidé Edib

Alexandre Pankoff

COLORFUL CONSTANTINOPLE

Memoirs of
HALIDÉ EDIB

With a frontispiece in color by
ALEXANDRE PANKOFF
and many illustrations from photographs

THE CENTURY CO.
New York   London

Copyright, 1926, by
THE CENTURY CO.

PRINTED IN U. S. A.

CONTENTS

PART I

BETWEEN THE OLD AND THE NEW TURKEY, 1885–1908

CHAPTER		PAGE
I	THIS IS THE STORY OF A LITTLE GIRL	3
II	WHEN THE STORY BECOMES MINE	30
III	OUR VARIOUS HOMES IN SCUTARI	113
IV	THE WISTERIA-COVERED HOUSE AGAIN	155
V	COLLEGE FOR THE SECOND TIME	190
VI	MARRIED LIFE AND THE WORLD	207

PART II

NEW TURKEY IN THE MAKING

VII	THE PERIOD OF POLITICAL REFORM: THE TANZIMAT, 1839–76	235
VIII	THE YOUNG TURKS	246
IX	THE CONSTITUTIONAL REVOLUTION OF 1908	252
X	TOWARD REACTION: THE ARMENIAN QUESTION	273
XI	REFUGEE FOR THE FIRST TIME	285
XII	SOME PUBLIC AND PERSONAL EVENTS, 1909–12	295
XIII	PHASES AND CAUSES OF NATIONALISM AND PAN-TURANISM IN TURKEY	312
XIV	THE BALKAN WAR	329
XV	MY EDUCATIONAL ACTIVITIES, 1913–14	345
XVI	THE WORLD WAR, 1914–16	377
XVII	HOW I WENT TO SYRIA	389
XVIII	EDUCATIONAL WORK IN SYRIA	431
	EPILOGUE	472

ILLUSTRATIONS

COLORFUL CONSTANTINOPLE	*Frontispiece*
	FACING PAGE
FAMILIAR OLD SCENES	17
THE CEMETERY WHERE I PLAYED AS A CHILD	32
MOSQUE OF SULEYMANIE	65
THE MAIN ROAD IN ISTAMBOUL	80
THE YARD OF THE EYOUB MOSQUE WHERE I FED THE PIGEONS AT EVERY YEARLY VISIT	97
ENTRANCE TO EYOUB MOSQUE	112
A SELAMLIK IN ABDUL HAMID'S TIME	129
SULTAN TEPÉ	144
ISTAMBOUL	161
THE HILL OPPOSITE OUR HOUSE IN SULTAN TEPÉ	176
A TOUCH OF THE PAST	200
JENI-JEMI MOSQUE, AND THE DRESS OF THE TURKISH WOMAN OF NINETEEN HUNDRED	225
LANDING-PLACE IN SCUTARI	240
A VERY OLD STREET IN SCUTARI	257
IN ISTAMBOUL	272
THE MOSQUE OF FATIH	305
TURKISH WOMEN IN NINETEEN EIGHTEEN	320
ON THE WATERSIDE	360
WHEN THE MOSQUES WERE FULL THE FAITHFUL PRAYED OUTSIDE	385
CARPENTERING CLASS IN AINTOURA	400
MONTESSORI CLASS IN AINTOURA	417
A GROUP OF GIRLS IN AINTOURA	432
THE ARMENIAN CHILDREN WERE GOOD MUSICIANS	449
SHOEMAKING CLASS IN AINTOURA	464

PART ONE

BETWEEN THE OLD AND THE NEW TURKEY, 1885–1908

MEMOIRS OF HALIDÉ EDIB

CHAPTER I

THIS IS THE STORY OF A LITTLE GIRL

SEVERAL instances of sudden consciousness of herself flash into her memory as she muses on her first self-acquaintance. There is the background: the big house in Beshiktash, on a hill overlooking the blue Marmora at a distance, and near at hand the hills of Yildiz with the majestic white buildings surrounded by the rich dark green of pines and willows which are pointed out to her as the residence of his Majesty Abdul Hamid.

She is not, however, interested in what the distance held, for the old wisteria-covered house, peeping through the purple flowers, with its many windows flashing in the evening blaze, is dominating her. The garden is on terraces, and there are tall acacias, a low fruit orchard with its spring freshness and glory, and a long primitive vine-trellis casting an enchanting green light and shade on the narrow pathway beneath it. This is the place where she moves and plays. There is a little fountain too, with a pair of lions spouting water from their mouths in the evening hours—making the only music in the twilight there. In the early morning, pigeons, ever so many pigeons, walk round her, and she quietly watches granny feeding them with crumbs. The wonderful smell, the wonderful color-scheme, and the wonderful feeling of stepping into the world for the first time in that garden.

There is another flash, which faintly lights up another house, not granny's any longer, but her father's own house near-by. . . . An intense uneasiness and an obscure feeling, perhaps of undefined fear. The woman whom she calls "mother" is lying in semi-darkness beside her, in a large bed, clad in her white gown. There are those two long, silky plaits, which seem to coil with the life of some mysterious coiling animals, and that small, pale face with its unusually long, curly black lashes resting on the sickly pallor of the drawn cheeks. This mother is a thing of mystery and uneasiness to the little girl. She is afraid of her, she is drawn to her, and yet that thing called affection has not taken shape in her heart; there is only a painful sense of dependence on this mother who is quietly fading out from the background of her life. The only act of that mother which the little girl remembers is when she finds herself sitting on the rather specially comfortable lap and the pale face with its silky lashes is lighted by the tender luster of the dark eyes while the woman dexterously plays with the little girl's tiny hands and takes each finger and cuts the nails—rather low—for it hurts. But no howling is possible as long as that low voice, with, as it seems, some warm color caught from the eyes, murmurs, "There is a

THIS IS THE STORY OF A LITTLE GIRL

little bird perched here" (this is said to the palm); "this one caught it" (this is to the thumb); "this one killed it; this ate it; and this little one came home from school and cried, 'Where is the bird? Where is the bird?' " Oh, the soft tickle of that touch and the hidden caress in that voice!

Another incident, but this time it is one of unrelieved misery. That soft mother dressed in white, with those wonderful eyes, has a dreadful habit of playing on a queer musical instrument. The little girl hated it passionately. She had not yet learned to bear ugly sounds and sights. A little girl from a poor neighbor's had come in and begged to hear the musical box, and the mother, indulgently, sweetly, no doubt, had begun turning the handle, producing the distorted music, whereupon the little one began to howl and kick and scream with all her might. She was really agonized by the horrible noise, and she had not yet realized that one is often alone in one's likes and dislikes, and one has just to learn to tolerate other people's false notes. But the little woman in white slapped her on her cheeks, locked the door so that she could not escape, and turned the handle of the hated thing on and on. How long it lasted before sheer exhaustion sent the little girl to sleep, she has no idea.

The next thing that appears in her memory is a sedan-chair with yellow curtains, carried by two men. The fading woman, dressed as always in white, is sitting inside, and they are taking her to a house in Yildiz. The little girl walks by the side of the horrible thing, her hand held by her father's tall groom. As they are going along she pulls open the yellow curtains and peeps in and sees there such a wan face with two such strange dark lights under their silky fringes that to this day she can see it clearly, painfully still. To this day too the little girl hates yellow. It gives her a sickly pain in her stomach.

The new house in Yildiz was large, but only three servants and that fading woman inhabited it—the father appearing only of an evening and riding away on his horse the first thing in the morning.

The light is once more turned down, and now there is no mother. The little girl stupidly wanders about, understands nothing, knows nothing, feels lonely and abandoned. Every evening the father sits by a small round table. One single candle flickers, and his tears fall on the candle-tray, while the servants walk about on tiptoe and pull the little girl away by the hand.

Ali is the man-servant who takes care of her; he is her *lala,* that indispensable personage in every old Turkish household, for which no English, no European, equivalent can exist, for it arose from roots wholly foreign to them, wholly Oriental. The *lala* was the natural outcome of the marked separation between the indoor and outdoor life of that day and world. Indoors was the delicate, intimate rule of women; out of doors was the realm of men. They could play there their proper rôle of protector, and one felt happy and secure in their presence. As child, and as child only, one could share to the full the freedom of the two worlds, and one's *lala* was one's natural companion into all the open-air places of experience. Then too he brings with him into memory that *je ne sais quoi* of the old-world service —devotion, attachment, pride, possession even—which the modern Turkish world has forgotten but which made so much of the warmth and color of the old household life. In the *lala's* strength one was secure; on his devotion one could rely—tyrannously—and from his innocent familiarity one could learn the truths and fables which only fall from the lips of primitive affection. But to return. The little girl's *lala* is Ali, a quiet big man with a great deal of affection if she could specify that strange feeling yet. He is kind and grave and buys her colored sweets in the street, a thing which is strictly forbidden by her father. The woman who cooks and serves the meals is called Rassim, a dark and ugly creature with a face entirely covered by marks of small-pox. Rassim is in love with Ali, and Ali's brother Mustafa is the other man-servant. After the mother disappears the little one is in the men's sitting-room most of the time, and this is the way they must have talked, although she only realized the meaning of their words much later:

Rassim: "The old lady is lost to everything in her mourning. She cannot move or think, so now I can do what I like with the child."

ALI: "Stop that talk. I will make thy mother cry, if thou touchest a single hair of her head."

RASSIM: "But she's telling tales about us all the time. Thou knowest how she goes and mimics everything thou or I do so that every one knows what we are doing."

ALI: "What does *she* know? Poor little mite! Thou liest, Rassim.

RASSIM: *"Vallahi* [by Allah], I don't"—she grinds her teeth at the little girl—"if she lets out anything more about us two I will let the crabs loose on her."

ALI: "What are the crabs for?"

RASSIM: "They are good for consumption. We had them to grind and put on her back, but she died before we could put them on."

ALI: "How is Bey Effendi [the master]?"

RASSIM: "Still crying by the light of that single candle. It is the portrait of the other man that they found on her breast when she died which has done the mischief."

ALI: "Thou must have put it there, thou pig!"

RASSIM: "No, *vallahi!* If she had not had the portrait how could I have put it anywhere? O Ali . . . his name was Ali too. All the Alis are tyrants."

Then she sings the old song:

"Ali, my Ali, my rose, come thou to the rosebush; if thou comest not, give me a peach" (i. e., a kiss), "O Ali.

"My Ali is gone to market; the evil eye will touch him; he who wishes Ali dead, may he lie in the grave instead "

Then she puts her arms round Ali and kisses him, which action is always followed by shaking the little girl and looking into her wondering eyes:

"Halidé Hanim, thou art not to tell, never, never."

What is it that they do not want her to tell? When and how she has ever told anything she does not know, but she answers:

"I *will* tell, Rassim Dadi;[1] I *will* tell."

Then follows the usual fighting between Ali and Rassim because of the little girl, and Mustafa looks on, with that disagreeable grin on his face.

The next morning she runs down to the kitchen in her night-dress, her feet all bare. She has a queer quivering feeling down her back, and her mind is full of crabs, whatever they may be.

"I *will* tell, Rassim Dadi," she screams defiantly on the last step, and before she can run up-stairs again she is caught and set in the middle of the kitchen while a large basket full of something is poured out on the floor, and there the little creeping horrors are all round her feet.

The helpless terror, the speechless agony of fear, the hair damp on her forehead, the staring eyes that hurt! She has no remembrance of the end of this terrible event, but she knows well the stories her granny used to tell later about Rassim's cruelty to herself.

"I rescued the poor little creature," granny would

---

[1] In Turkish such appellations as nurse, princess, etc., are put after the personal name, and for elderly servants politeness demands that some such title must be given.

say; "I was coming to the house that morning, and from the garden I heard the child screaming. I rang, and Rassim never thought it was I, so she opened the door, and I found the child laid on the mat, her mouth filled with black pepper, which Rassim had been stuffing her with, and struggling to get away. I could have beaten Rassim, the wretch! But the little one continued defiant to the last. 'I *will* tell, Rassim Dadi,' she kept on screaming, while Rassim, wild with rage, kept on shouting, 'Say thou wilt not tell.' "

But all that is strangely forgotten, and the only thing that can be seen through the haze is a somehow connected vignette of the little Halidé sitting on the lap of a wonderful old man, with burning eyes and a flowing white beard, who caresses her hair with a gentleness so queer from those rough hands. "Poor little mite!" grandfather keeps saying.

Her next and last impression of the house in Yildiz is quite different. Rassim had been dismissed because of her cruelty, Ali and Mustafa had gone, and an old lady housekeeper and a young Circassian boy were living in the house, the housekeeper looking after her father and Halidé herself. Her father was going regularly to the palace again as in the old days. His tall groom with that lovely big bay horse used to stand by the door in the mornings, and the little girl would ride the horse before her father came out, her small feet dangling and the groom leading the horse by the bridle very gravely up and down the street. At last the father would come down-stairs and ride away followed by his groom on a white horse, while the little girl strained her eyes to get the last look of them as they disappeared round the turning of the long, stately road to Yildiz Kiosk.

She missed Ali badly, and even Rassim who had been so cruel she missed too. The atmosphere of excitement and disorder had gone. No one talked of a picture on a dead woman's breast and a man's tears. The father was mostly away in the palace, staying even at night, when it was his turn to be on duty.

It was now that the event which is somewhat like a symbol of her lifelong temperament occurred.

On the long divan, covered with white cloth, sat the old lady housekeeper, a kind and hard-working creature, leaning over her darning continually; the young Circassian sat at the table, lost in his books, for he was getting ready for a school education. (Her father had a mania for taking poor young men under his protection and sending them to school.) She, the little girl, was left to herself. There was no one scolding her or filling her mouth with black pepper for telling about things she did not know. There was complete silence. The father was no longer shedding tears by the flicker of a single candle. Her loneliness seemed suddenly to have taken the form of a tangible hardness in her throat. The woman with the long coiling plaits and wonderful eyes was no more. What was this silence about? Why had she no one to cuddle close to and go to sleep with? There was no answer to her unspoken questioning. Still only that dead silence. The next moment she stood in the middle of the room and spoke her mind out:

"I want my father!"

"He is at the palace."

"I want my father!"

"He will come back to-morrow."

"I want my father!"

"He cannot come, dear. The gates of the palace are closed at night, and the whole place is kept by guards."

"I want my father!"

Gradually the little voice rose and rose in hoarse and piercing howls of pain which she herself internally noted as strange. On and on it went, rising and howling till the Greek neighbors came in one by one to help the old lady housekeeper to calm and soothe her, their voices making a still greater noise than the little girl. The place was a Christian quarter—Armenians and Greeks were the only neighbors—and the Greeks of Constantinople talk louder than anybody else, especially if they are women. But there were twenty wild beasts ranging in the little girl's breast, making her howl and howl with pain till she caught sight of a pail of cold water brought by a Greek woman to stop her crying.

"She may catch cold."

"But she will burst if she goes on like that."

"O Panagia" (Holy Mother), "pour it on her head."

And pour it they did, which gave the old housekeeper the extra trouble of changing her clothes, but for the rest caused a sudden catch in her breath which stopped her for an instant only to begin louder and louder, wilder

THIS IS THE STORY OF A LITTLE GIRL

and wilder, the next moment. . . . It was the symbol of the force of her desires in later years, the same uncontrollable passion for things, which she rarely wanted, but which, once desired, must be obtained at all costs; the same passionate longing although no longer expressed by sobbing or howling.

Finally the old lady housekeeper and the Greek women beg the young Circassian to take the child to the palace.

It was almost midnight as the young man carried her in his arms through the guarded streets of Yildiz. He stopped at each tall soldier whose bayonet flashed under the street oil-lamps.

"Who goes there?"

And the young Circassian placed the little girl in the lamplight and showed her swollen face:

"It is Edib Bey's daughter. She would have died with crying if I hadn't promised to bring her to her father. Her mother died. . . ."

And the soldier, who probably had seen the mother's coffin pass not long ago, let them go on.

The little girl began to watch calmly and with pleasure the dimly lighted white road, the long shadows of the guards, while she heard the distant bark of the street dogs. She was not going to be knocked down by loneliness and dead silence any longer.

Before the gigantic portals which led immediately to the quarters where her father worked she and the Circassian youth were stopped once more. No one was allowed to pass the palace gates after midnight. . . .

But sometimes a little girl and her heart's desire are stronger than the iron rules of a great despot. The guards are human and probably have little daughters of their own in their villages. There is a long wait. A man in black dress comes to the door. He looks at the little girl by the lamplight and lets her pass on. At last they reach the father's apartment. He looks at her with astonishment and perhaps with pain. He has just jumped out of bed because there is a rumor of some little girl at the palace door crying for her father. . . . On a bed opposite the father's lies a fat man with an enormous head who is blinking at the scene. (He is Hakki Bey, later on the famous grand vizir.) Every one no doubt expects her to jump into her father's arms, but her attention is caught by the quilt on her father's bed. It is bright yellow . . . and the night is closed in her memory with that bright patch of the hated color.

Another short interval, and we are back in granny's wisteria-covered house again now. She sleeps in the large room where she was born, looking over that lovely garden. Three large windows open over the long, narrow divan, covered with the traditional clean white cloth of all Turkish divans. There is a red carpet on the floor and the curtains are white. Purple wisteria is in bloom, sunlight patches fall on the white cover under the open windows, a brilliant blue sky smiles over all, and the little girl is faint with color and beauty and the smell of it all. Before one window on a bright red cushion sits granny. She is in reality a very beautiful woman, but the little girl does not feel it. Her granny's eyes do not trouble her. In her little head and heart she is unconsciously aware of those people whose eyes make her uneasy, make her think; and the rest of human beings she ignores. Her granny has a very large white face. Her silky red hair waves and curls over her dazzlingly white shoulders and neck. Her eyes are pale gray and subdued. So are her small pink lips. Over a white transparent chemise she wears a light brown loose dress, a large white muslin collar, and sleeves rolled back over her gown. A Persian shawl encircles her waist. A light muslin print, worked with delicate Turkish embroidery, covers her head. The little girl is quieter and less afraid of unknown things when she sleeps in her little bed by her granny. The beds are Turkish beds, laid out every evening on the carpet and gathered up in the morning and put away.

There is one person whose eyes she is rather conscious of. He is a tall old man, and his eyes are dark and strong and stern. But they can be soft and tender too, and the Anatolian accent with which he tells her about the Russian wars in eastern Turkey she remembers because of those eyes. He is from Kemah and is illiterate but has been the chief of coffee-makers in the palace of Prince Reshad (the late Mohammed V). There are any amount of such chiefs in palace households—the chief of the tobacco-makers, the chief of the candle-bearers, the chief of the jug-holders, the chief of the royal dressers, the chief of the carpet-layers. And the chiefs do things which have nothing to do with their titles. They are mostly rich men with summer resorts and winter residences. But her grandfather is not rich. He has been too honest to be that, and the great sums he had legitimately gained had oozed away between the fair fingers of the white-faced, gray-eyed, golden-haired Constantinopolitan lady, my granny. He still regards his beautiful wife with wonder. He had taken her from an old ecclesiastical and aristocratic family of the sacred city of Eyoub. She was related to the keepers of the Holy Tomb there, and she had brought with her a very rich dowry of both goods and slaves. But both hers and his had passed out of her hands by the very simple system of giving more than she received all her life. He is perhaps embittered by her extravagance, for he talks of debts and money difficulties, which makes her uneasy in an indefinite way. It is like the love-affair of Rassim and Ali to the little Halidé. She suffers from it and does not know why.

In the old wooden house at this time too there is living a liberated "palace lady." [2] She is a small wizened Circassian and occupies the upper apartments of the house. She calls granny "mother." In former days granny had connections in the palace, and because of her husband's position she used to be quite a habitué there. So this palace lady had come to her when her services had ended at the Kiosk. She has wonderful jewelry, European furniture, a white slave, and gorgeous dresses. Her official post had been that of teacher of the women

[2] That is, one of those who formerly held a position in the sultan's palace but who have been retired.

FAMILIAR OLD SCENES

in the palace, and she is really a woman of learning and has a library. Mysteriously too she was the head dancer of the rabbit-dance. What this rabbit-dance is the little girl does not know but she remembers in winter nights the short skirts with gold fringes and gold sequins which the owner lays out and from which she strips off the gold, with the little girl's gay help, and sends it away to be sold.

There is a young uncle now also, and a little boy, the orphan of another uncle who is dead. The old housekeeper, the ruddy Circassian slave, the man-servant who is always a native of grandfather's country—Kemah—are the dramatis personæ of this interval. But the little girl has not formed human connections yet. All these people move outside her sphere. She knows two classes of people and two ages: "Children" are all little girls and continue to live in child-dom till they take the veil. . . . That happens when they are ten years old, and they then join the grown-ups forever after. All the grown-ups are the same and of the same age whether they are twelve or fifty. Boys are emphatically not children. They dress like men, or rather as they did at that time, and they are disagreeable and noisy. If there is anything in the world to dislike, for her, it is boys. They are almost like the ugly, noisy musical box which her mother played, still echoing in her brain as a continual false note. If there is anything in her heart that can be called a decided liking, it is for men, especially for those who have white beards and eyes that one feels and remembers.

One day an elder sister appeared at granny's. Where she had been and why she came all of a sudden the little girl did not know. They whisper round her that the sister's father, an aide-de-camp of Abdul Hamid's, had been exiled with all the rest of her family. Why her sister has another father and why she calls the little girl's father "father" only came to be understood much later. At present, there she simply is, a brilliant creature, with crimson cheeks, curly black hair, and burning eyes.

When she arrived she brought boxes of sweets for Halidé and for her little boy cousin. She kissed them both but all the same treated them like inferiors and ordered them about very freely. She was the very scourge of Allah in the house, as the uncle expressed it. She broke the little girl's toys, climbed trees like a little boy; she showed shocking disrespect to the palace lady and even made the poor quiet granny weep sometimes.

This period in the big wisteria-covered house came to an end with the visit of the young Circassian who had carried her to the palace on that strange midnight in his arms. He was now a regular student at a very big school, and as he was now called Mehmed Effendi by the household, the little girl realized that he was a personage to be respected and no longer a mere boy.

When the slave-girl Fikriyar one day called granny out to the selamlik (the men's side of the house) the little girl followed her, and standing by the door which shuts the women's apartments, she listened to the talk.

THIS IS THE STORY OF A LITTLE GIRL

She could not make out the conversation clearly but she knew that the meaning is this:

Her father has married again. His new wife is the young granddaughter of the old lady housekeeper who used to look after our home when Hassim's rule ceased. Granny cried softly on hearing the news, and Mehmed Effendi went on giving details.

What is marriage? Why does granny cry?

The little girl and the sister were carefully dressed. The little girl was kissed tenderly by every one as if they were taking leave of her by an open grave. And the two little girls walked away with Mehmed Effendi, to visit, so she understood, the new wife.

The house where her father was living was still in Yildiz but not in the old quarter. This was a smaller house, not so high up the hill and in rather a narrow street inhabited by Greeks and Armenians. The place was near the pine groves which are called Ihlamour, the Linden Grove. The large grove had a casino, and every Friday and Sunday there was music. Men and women went in crowds, the women sitting behind improvised lattices, which looked queer in an open place. But the little girl loved to go there later on when she occasionally escaped from home, and played on the pine-needles, listened to the soft hissing of the pines, gathered pine-seeds, and looked longingly across to the house with wisteria on the other side of the hills where the Moslem population and her granny dwelt.

But now the Circassian youth was leading them through the winding paths of the grove, holding both of them by the hand and telling the elder sister to behave and be polite.

"Her grandmother was a housekeeper," snapped she.

"How dare you? She was a lady with a house of her own," scolded the Circassian youth.

"She was a housekeeper."

"No, but anyhow *now* she is the mother-in-law of the Bey Effendi."

The little girl has heard this term "housekeeper" used by her own granny in disdainful tones when of late years the two houses had had a womanly feud, each accusing the other of witchcraft, backbiting, and plebeian origins.

They arrived at last. The door was opened by the old lady, and the little girl found herself in an atmosphere of the greatest tension. She became the central figure, and every one seemed to watch her with intense pity and curiosity. The house was in perfect order and very quiet. Up-stairs in the father's room sat the new wife sewing, while he was walking nervously up and down. The new wife was a creature of very pretty coloring, a pink face, a small pink mouth, blue eyes, and a long rich plait of pale golden hair. She was dressed in a dark blue costume (English fashion, as they call it), and over her pretty hair was a bright green silk Turkish kerchief. The little girl's first impression was that of sensuous pleasure in this pretty combination of colors. She felt just as she feels when she sees an almond-tree in blossom, and she jumped into the lady's lap and began to kiss her. The scene must have produced a surprising effect, for the father and the old lady began to wipe their eyes. The little girl learned much later that the father had agonized over the thought of this meeting, although the little girl was hardly four years old. The father supposed her to have an extraordinary sensibility, but the truth is that her sensibility to persons and nature or to things in general were just the same. If she cried when she saw any human being cry, she sobbed when she saw a poor street dog stoned by boys. But she did not know yet the meaning of mother, death, or other serious things. To her every phenomenon was of the same order. After all this might be the true meaning of life, although for her from this time forward nature and man appeared from very different angles.

In the evening when she saw that the sister was to go and she to stay she felt a painful pressure at her heart. She did not cry, but she felt heavy and shy in the new atmosphere. If she could have analyzed the acute suffering which timidity causes she would have known her true state.

Fortunately an old man with a white beard dropped on the scene and made things easier by the mere mild look of his blue and friendly eyes. He was the new wife's uncle, and he gave her nuts and pistachios—secretly, however, for she was allowed only milk in the evenings. He took her on his knees, talked to her, caressed her hair, and showed neither curiosity nor pity, treating her all the time as an equal. But the wife's mother and sisters, who arrived later to see the stepdaughter of their relative, studied and criticized her very freely. "What an unusual coloring! Would you call her dark?"

"No, stupid! Look what fair hair she has. It is yellow."

"Yellow! No indeed. Corn-colored I should say. Come here! What funny hair! It is almost white at the ends. Her nose is like a little potato; and what big lips she has!"

"Look at me, little girl! Oh, what eyes! They are not like a little girl's. They are quite uncanny." (There is whispering and much mysterious talking at this point.)

"They are too large! Oh, look away, little girl! I don't like her to look at me."

The humiliation and the torture of it! She is aware of her bodily self for the first time, and that with infinite distress. She feels that she must look like a toad, or an ugly bush with no pretty leaves, two things which have struck her as disagreeable. She realizes that her skin is not pink and her eyes not blue, and she begins to suffer from the presence of the people who have blue eyes and fair complexions. To this day she can feel the twinge and the stab in her heart which blue-eyed people with pink faces for years caused her.

Yet life in her father's home with the new wife is far from being disagreeable, for before long she has her first love-affair.

This all-important love-affair is preceded by the development of some other important likes and dislikes in her soul. The first of these is concerning her clothes.

THIS IS THE STORY OF A LITTLE GIRL

Now her father Edib Bey, secretary of his Majesty Abdul Hamid, had a strong admiration for the English and their way of bringing up children. He believed that the secret of their greatness was due to this, and so his method of bringing up his first-born was strongly influenced by English ways as he had read of them in books. He occupied himself personally with her dresses, underclothing, shoes, and stockings—even handkerchiefs. Turkey having, however, not yet entered the road of reform and modernism by a slavish imitation of English outward apparel, he did not make her wear a hat. As a matter of fact it would never have done for him even to express a desire to do such a thing, for hats were the outward and visible sign of Christians,[3] yet he only covered her head in winter with a kalpak (that snug Caucasian head-dress which for some subtle reason ranks with fezzes and tarbooshes rather than with hats and bonnets) and let her go bareheaded in the summer.

She wore short, dark blue frocks in winter, all English-made, and white linen in the summer. Her arms and legs were bare after the manner of English children, which shocked her granny and made her anxious lest she should catch cold.

But the little girl's objections were not as to the weather and its changes. She looked different from other children of her age and class. She attracted attention, and she was envious of the gorgeous-colored silk gowns, frills and ribbons, even jewels, with which other

---

[3] No good Mohammedan could wear the accursed things.

little girls were decked. To this day she feels occasional longings for gaudy colors and vulgar apparel although her true tastes are quite otherwise.

Next it was her diet. The Turkish children of her class were allowed to eat anything. They bought delicious red sugar cocks perched on sticks, licked hard sweetmeats of all shapes, colors, and tastes, while the little girl had a strict diet—some meat and vegetables, a very little fruit at meal-times and only milk in the evening. How she hated milk and loved fruit of all kinds! She longed to stuff herself with those wonderful cherries, raw cucumbers, and boiled corn that other people had, till she should not be able to move for very repletion. This severe régime left her with a great weakness for fruit, and a great hatred for milk and for the English system of bringing up children. Yes, if this diet, and the daily sponge-bath and the stuff they dropped into her eyes had been canceled, she would have been tolerably happy in her father's home.

If she were inferior to other human beings, and different in a sense which made her have more in common with a plant or a young animal, she was at any rate superior to them in heart affairs. Although she was under the influence of all kinds of beauty and her five senses were wildly alive to colored objects and beautiful sounds and so on, she was above men in her love as a real dog is above human beings.

Kyria Ellenie (Madame Ellen) was the head of the so-called kindergarten where little girls and some very small boys of the neighborhood were sent. It was kept by three Greek spinsters, Kyria Ellenie being the eldest. The children were mostly Greek and Armenian and the daughters of the Christian chiefs of Abdul Hamid, such as the chief of the bakers, the chief of the chemists, the chief of the booksellers, and so on. . . . The little girl was the only Turkish child there. She did not remember how she came to go first but she never forgot her intensest, sincerest, and perhaps longest love-affair. Its object was Kyria Ellenie. As the little girl was always laughed at because of the old lady's looks and her own weakness for them it is best to describe the old lady at once. Her large lips turned one up and the other down in a most unprepossessing way. Her small eyes were always running; her thin cheeks were all in lines and deep furrows. The limp gray hair hung on her temples; the wiry hard hands, with their toil-worn look, and her tall thin body in its loose black garments, completed the picture. Her outward ugliness was phenomenal but the little girl both with her natural and spiritual senses had perceived her inward beauty. No other human eyes had expressed that dog-like affection in its purest sense and beauty as did those blinking and watery ones. The cheeks must have got those deep marks through suffering for others, while that stooping posture of the body expressed a solicitude and eagerness to serve the forlorn little girls.

Till the little one came within the touch of that loving and humble old thing she was rather like a stranger in this funny world, like a dweller in Hades waiting to be initiated. All her impressions and joys were so far outward. In her inner self she was entirely isolated. She had no heart communication, which is what perhaps gives the real significance to human happiness. So far she had been internally in a lonely and expectant attitude, or rather patiently enduring her surroundings with the dumb and helpless feeling of a dog thrown into a world of different animals or of uncongenial human beings. I have seen little street dogs sitting in the sun in old Turkish quarters and blinking with just that look which expressed to me the little girl's state of heart. But that old teacher gave her the first life contact. She was no longer in Hades dozing in a sunless and strange atmosphere. There was a new life in her. She was no longer morbid and quiet. For the first time she made joyous movements, played happily with gestures which were not merely physical demonstrations but something more subjective and conscious. There was a wonderful security, a nameless delight in the old woman's presence. The little girl spoke, sang, and recited, happy to be able to give herself in humble gratitude for the other woman's warm heart.

But in this affair as in all similar ones the pangs and the drawbacks of love began. Kyria Ellenie had to go out sometimes to buy such things as vegetables and meat for her household. Then a demoniac howling would begin. It was either a repetition of that night when the portals of the palace were opened for her or a dumb wandering all over the house like some one searching for the beloved in her belongings, or like a little dog sniffing to discover the scent of its owner. The house was Turkish in its furnishings—the same immaculate white-covered divans and the large chest of drawers. The two traditional lamps and an old clock stood side by side in a row. The large quantity of dainty hand-made lace showed years of hand labor in the lonely life of the old spinster, while in a dim corner stood a panagia (icon of the Virgin Mary), an old oil-lamp flickering in front of it. Whenever the elder sister came to visit the little girls in the school she stealthily went up-stairs and tried to put the light out, whispering secretly to the little girl: "It is Christian. It is sinful." What did that all mean to the little girl? She had not entered yet that narrow human path where religion and language as well as racial differences make human beings devour each other. The little girl was still in a world where the joy of life is heart fusion and natural existence.

Her next attachment was the white curly dog Hector, who had running eyes like Kyria Ellenie. The dog licked her face and her hands twice daily, in the morning and in the evening.

This happy state of things went on for some time, she with her dolls and the dog and the joyous stimulus which her first taste of life had given her.

The Greek funerals passed by the door with priests in gorgeous garments and long trains held by little boys carrying candles in their free hands; the corpse on the coffin, decked in its best clothes, its face powdered and rouged, the low Byzantine chant hummed in cavernous tones "Kyrie Eleison." She used to put her dog in a swing, clothe herself in Kyria Ellenie's long black shawl, and march up and down the room singing in dead earnestness "Kyrie Eleison."

She is sometimes put on a table by Kyria Ellenie and asked to recite about the naughty cock that woke people in the morning. The little girl did not realize that she spoke two languages, one at school and one at home. Language to her was a mere gesture, and one used one or the other according to the person who understood this or that way of expression.

All this came to a rather sad end. She began to mope, to droop, and to feel desperately heavy; everything seeming to move round her in a slow and sickly swing. Every morning quite unconsciously she made a pretense of looking bright, so that she might not be kept at home, but every evening she walked home with a hammer beating in her brains. Every day she sat and gazed at Kyria Ellenie, but she did not imitate the Greek priests any more. When Kyria Ellenie put her on the table she still tried to recite about the naughty cock, but her voice as it came out of her mouth seemed to burn her like a flame.

One day as she painfully struggled upon the table to recite about the cock the swinging around became too sickly, and although she still went on, her eyes probably had a queer look, for Kyria Ellenie caught her in her arms and carried her home. This incident she remembered clearly years after, when she was addressing a public meeting with a temperature of 102 degrees; but on the second occasion naturally no one caught her. Thus ended her first love and her happy life at school.

She lay in bed for days with that dumb hot sickness and the nauseating swing of the furniture and the ceiling keeping tune with the hammering on her head.

For how many days and nights she knows not—it was endless—Greek neighbors came in and brought her sweets and talked in those high and shrill tones peculiar to Greek women of Istamboul. Men called doctors gathered round her bed and talked in low tones while the father openly cried and the new wife looked uneasy. Finally the doctors must have prescribed her a grandmother, for one morning this satisfactory remedy arrived in a closed carriage and took her away. Once more she was lifted in the arms of the Circassian youth; once more the wisteria-covered house entered her life vision.

CHAPTER II

WHEN THE STORY BECOMES MINE

THE brown childish orbs, brilliant and troubled in some unfathomable way, looked at me wonderingly. The next moment I had put a small hand over the mirror and covered those painful interrogation-points, leaving visible only the unformed round chin and the patch of red lips of the little girl. I realized then for the first time that this face, which people as a rule considered something unusual and unlike its environment, was mine. If I try to draw the portrait of the soul that belonged to the little face, I would describe it as two liquid, reddish brown eyes full of tragic anxiety and painful wonder at the funny species she belonged to, or asking such wordless questions as these: Who are they? Who am I? This white-faced woman whom I call granny and who is indispensable to me at night when I go to bed—she is a stranger; so are the others, so am I. What is a face? And what are eyes and these funny sensibilities? Does everybody feel the same? I have this internal smile which, translated into grown-up language, means humor. It makes me strangely aloof at times, and arouses a tiresome childish contempt, of which, only later, I learn the value and proper use. There is this internal catch too which squeezes one's throat and brings the water into one's eyes which people call tears. There is no reason why I should have these yet, for life is almost stagnant in its outside repose and quiet; nothing but the beautifully familiar setting and the familiar faces with their familiar looks.

Another vague feeling is taking shape and becoming dominant. It is the feeling with which I have had to fight the hardest and longest. It is fear. I cannot yet explain it in human terms, for in some way I feel that we share it, more than our other feelings, with the other kinds of creatures which people call animals. It defined itself for me first of all in a cemetery where one of our men-servants took us to play one morning. The low moan, the somber velvety sound, and the strange uncanny movements of the cypresses were all round us. We were playing in a hollow place with some other children, holding each other's hands, when the servant suddenly called out, "It is coming!" What was coming? I did not know, yet I felt distinctly the cold creepy tremor down my back and the dampness on my palms and head which coincided later with what we call fear. The children scattered and ran wildly about. The servant himself seemed very much upset and told us stories on the way home about the cypresses. "Although they look like trees," he said, "at night they turn into holy men in green turbans who haunt the gardens and rubbish-heaps. I just felt them move. I am sure they did not like our playing among their trunks."

I can trace the distinct emergence of these two feelings, fear and—later on—pity, besides that other queer twitch of the soul, or the internal smile. But this last sensation is interwoven with a great many others. Whenever I have had spiritual tension, extreme subjective consciousness, especially in the form of anxiety, then this smile has become an internal expansion and has prevented petrifaction. Otherwise I should have turned into a stone long ago on this uphill road of life, where, apart from my own loads to carry, a new people was being born; and the birth of any living thing, animal or human, is the supreme pain and the one significant event in this dried-up old world.

The story of the little girl is my own henceforth. As I go on painting my life at that time as sincerely as I possibly can, I realize that the me inside the almost strange body of mine is giving place to the external me, the flesh and blood me, and I am passing gradually out of that early inward consciousness into the common reality of life. I am no longer so distinct from other people. I am a part of the huge congregation of human beings, and I am doing as they do. So I may as well transfer the story entirely to the first person.

The wisteria-covered house in Beshiktash stands on one of the many bare hills which are now more or less built over. At that time they presented a large expanse of ground of many colors—the somber green of the vegetable-gardens and orchards, which took the place of parks, where women and children went to eat plums and cherries and cucumbers beside dark pools under

THE CEMETERY WHERE I PLAYED AS A CHILD

cool trees; the brilliant coloring of the hyacinth and tuberose gardens, stretching in brilliant patches of purple, yellow, white, and rich pinks and sending their rich perfumes in waves all over the place, while the dark shades of the pine-groves stood behind them as a natural background.

On Fridays the place would be full of children in bright-colored silk dresses, boys in long pantaloons, some ridiculously decked out in miniature generals' uniforms with golden epaulettes and driving about in grand carriages; the toy-sellers of Eyoub, carrying on their backs toys of the most glaring gilt and colors; the sweetmeat sellers shouting, and the water-carriers tinkling their glasses—whistles, rattles, bells—an infernal noise and the characteristic dust-cloud in which they all moved.

I think I should have enjoyed the bright dresses and the general gaiety of color and sound, although it was so vulgar, if an incident had not stamped the whole place and the whole show with a horrible memory for me.

Just as we were leaving the crowd one day, dragged by the man-servant along the winding road behind the hyacinth fields, we heard a long howl of a strange quality —so strange indeed that it made me shiver—and the servant looked right and left furtively, trying to locate it. Finally he plunged with us into a thorny by-path, pulling me and my sister so fast that we almost tore our clothes in the prickly bushes. I remember so well the unwholesome human curiosity he showed, just as crowds do at certain times for some spectacle of suffering. At the end of the path there was a ditch, and on the other side of the ditch an old wall had fallen on a dog, crushing half of its body under the stones.

It is full thirty years if not more since I saw and felt that scene. But I still distinctly see that yellow dog, with its clear yellow eyes, trying to get out with its fore paws, quivering, struggling in agony, and looking with that wonderful dumb appeal in its almost human eyes; while at intervals a pitiful howl escaped from its jaws, sending an incredibly painful note into the air, wolf fashion. The servant looked amused, while a few boys threw stones at it, delighted to see its helpless wriggle and to hear its howl.

This was a symbolic and ominous revelation for me of the ugly instinct which stains the human species. I hated to belong to it, in my childish and unconscious way, and I have realized since that no brute beast causes pain and commits cruelty for the simple pleasure of watching it. The cruelties which animals may commit in the course of their struggle for existence are too often done by us as a mere pleasure spectacle. I have seen this repeated in other times and in other ways, and each time it has given me the same physical horror and the same sickly pain as if a knife were cutting my body in two through my stomach. I hated the boys, the manservant, and the new revelation of life, which simply saturated me with an aching pain. My other self, the one who is distinct, and usually trying to make out the meanings of things intellectually, in such grave moments

WHEN THE STORY BECOMES MINE

becomes one with my physical self. If Allah had had mercy on me He would have stopped my life after this glimpse and spared me that queer, sharp, cutting pain so often repeated, that I have longed again and again to be anything except a human being. It is strange that whenever I have gone through this sensation of being cut in two, my dual personality has ceased, and I have become one raging revolting soul. This first glimpse, however, was too much for me. I don't know to this day how we got home, but I know that I was ill for a long time afterward. I lay quietly on granny's white sofa and she said to people: "She has been frightened by a dog. We are calling in the hodjas to cure her." I could not explain that it was not fright; I hardly knew what it was myself. I patiently lay where I was and let the holy men in green turbans come and read the Koran in undertones and breathe its holy virtue into my face.

It is now that I realized Arziè Hanum [1] for the first time. She burnt incense in my room, made queer gestures, and begged the fairies (peris) to set me free.

In the meantime father called daily, and, quite indignant at all this superstitious show, he brought in the famous German doctor called the old Mülich, who stuffed me with all sorts of disagreeable medicines.

With due respect to microbes and scientific explanations of human diseases, I must confess that most of my illnesses have coincided with some moral shock and

[1] *Hanum* is lady and corresponds approximately to either Mrs. or Miss.

that physical weakness has come with temporary loss of interest in life, while any new attachment or interest has made me leap back into life like a living arrow.

The long, dreary illness, with the vision of the misery of that half-crushed dog and its solitary howl of pain as well as the fiendish boys throwing stones at it, gradually receded before the more intimate initiation into the human atmosphere around me. People and scenes became more real, and I was grasping at meanings and groping for contacts.

I was having my first playmate too at this time. In fact perhaps she was the last also, for I never had any other friends in the same sense till my college years. She was the daughter of a *tablakèr*.[2] She was the same little girl who had made my mother play on that horrible instrument ever so long ago. Mother had somehow befriended the family, consisting of the mother, Ayesha Hanum, a Cæsarean woman who spoke a thick Anatolian dialect, her three daughters, one son, and her nice

[2] *Tablakèr* means tray-bearer. Hundreds of them belonged to the royal kitchen. One saw them moving about in great numbers in Yildiz, carrying enormous round trays, covered with black cloth, on their heads. Each tray was destined for some royal lady or some official or attendant of the sultan's. Although these men had low salaries, yet they were well to do; each had built himself a house in Beshiktash (a village on the Bosphorus near Yildiz) and kept their families in Constantinople. All this was done by selling the surplus food to Beshiktash people. Most of the houses bought their food from the royal kitchens through these people. As the royal kitchens were behind the bureau where my father worked in Yildiz Palace, I used to watch its colossal proceedings with intense delight. The enormous barrels of butter which they used to roll in, and roll out again when they were empty, attracted me most. I wondered how many little girls could be put in and allowed to play inside one of them; and to my childish imagination it seemed as if thirty small people could comfortably sit inside and do as they wished.

simple husband. The second daughter, who was always ill, came to be tended by my mother, who had lots of home-made medicines with which she helped the neighbors very generously, and she had a great reputation for household accomplishments and for her charitable aid. Shayesté, the youngest daughter of this family, was a hard, healthy, and somehow servile little girl, and my reasons for choosing her as a playmate seem selfish and almost ugly as I analyze them now. It is curious how the vain and the futile parts of a woman appear unconsciously in a little girl. She was the darkest little girl I knew, and having acquired an impression from my stepmother's relations that it is only fair people with blue eyes who are beautiful, and suffering from the belief that I was not fair enough for this, Shayesté's contrast to me gave me a foolish pleasure. Her neck was so dark, so like leather, her hands so brown, that I used to think she had never washed. I used often to put my hands near hers and feel a queer joy. The two looked like ivory and nutshell together. In fact there was something so much like a nutshell in her coloring altogether that my sister called her the Nut-rat (Funduk Faresi, i. e., the mouse).

She had a picturesque way of chattering, her small black eyes looking in all directions like a rat, and her hands moving violently. I hardly listened, but she went on all the same. One of her virtues was that she never questioned me, for there was nothing in life which put me out more than being questioned. Internally I was so locked up and so walled in by my own self that questions were an intrusion, a forcing open of the door of my soul against my will. Years later when I have been interviewed I have often thought of my childish days with sad amusement. Another reason for this sensibility was perhaps a timidity carried to a morbid degree. I felt, and still feel, spiritually undressed when some one is trying to peer into the inner life of my thought and feelings, although I can freely give myself at times to other people or to the public without being asked. Later, when I have been brought into prominence by the papers, either in the way of exaggerated praise or of attack, I have felt that Allah must certainly have an ironical turn of mind to enjoy striking people thus in their weakest points.

Shayesté's other virtue perhaps was her stupidity. Intellectual companionship is indispensable to me like food at intervals, but the constant presence of a highly active mind is a constant fatigue. One is conscious of another life too intensely all the time. Little Shayesté and I certainly did not tire each other. I hardly talked to her, and I remember our housekeeper constantly saying, "Halidé Hanum, have n't you got a tongue? Why do you only shake your head?" But I did talk to myself a great deal when I was alone, and Shayesté was the only person in whose presence I lived on as if I were entirely by myself.

We played in a large rectangular marble hall which opened upon the garden on one side and the selamlik on the other. From the middle of it old-fashioned double flying staircases went up to granny's apartment, and on the stairs enormous windows, all wisteria-muffled, opened on the neighbors' gardens. The light through the purple blossoms, and through the garden door from which vines crept up to the top windows, combined and made a delicious and cheerful sense through the place.

I had another companion, an imaginary one, whom I called Alexi. It is a Greek name, and perhaps it was a reminiscence of Kyria Ellenie days. I talked mostly to this personage, sang to him sometimes so sadly that I had a lump in my throat and tears in my eyes, sometimes so cheerfully that I laughed and danced in pure glee. The memory of those strange performances makes me think that if I had been born in a European country I might have been an actress, although I should have been a queer sort of actress, performing only when the spirit moved me and when I was free from self-consciousness and was persuaded that I had some beautiful message to give to the audience.

Shayesté took no notice of my antics. When I went from the acting mood into the contemplative and silent one, I would sit on one of the steps and think to myself, while she quietly went on playing with my dolls on another. If it were cold we would go into the housekeeper's room, where I kept all my toys. Dolls I loved; not the European-looking ones which my father brought me from the Pera shops but only those I made myself in my own way. With these I played till I was "too old to play" and had to do it in secret. It was in a way my embryonic novel-writing, for I made elaborate plots which the dolls enacted, all inevitably of a tragic and melancholy turn.

Shayesté was I believe being haunted by the dim realization of sex brought about by the marriage of her eldest sister, who gave rather full descriptions to her friends, especially to my sister, who was nine years old at the time. Shayesté talked of marriages all the while. Marriages frightened me because my uncle Kemal would say whenever I was sullen or stubborn (my personal method of being naughty), "Fikriyar, go and call the imam" (the priest); "I will marry her."

Another charm of Shayesté's was her strength and energy, in contrast with which I was painfully delicate and physically lazy in the extreme. She did all the fetching and carrying for me. I so disliked any kind of physical movement that I almost objected to having a body at all. I did not see any necessity for it, and no physical movement in those days did I do voluntarily, not even eating or drinking. Next to timidity, this physical laziness was my dominating trait. Even now, although I work hard—often almost furiously—I feel this tendency very strongly.

After dinner at sunset granny used to sit in her corner and read translated novels of adventure, while we were sent down to Hava Hanum's room to pass a few hours before we went to bed.

Those were the evenings which gave me glimpses into the inner lives of the people around me.

The central figure was Hava Hanum, my grandmother's housekeeper and helper. Although she did the cooking she would never allow herself to be called a cook. "I cook because I love the lady," she would say. But she was regularly paid as long as granny could afford it.

Her face was like wrinkled leather, but she had very bright energetic eyes and wore the trimmest and cleanest head-dresses and gowns imaginable. She affected slightly granny's pretty touch in dress and tried to imitate her grande dame manners, but in her heart she detested anything that was not bourgeois, and her real self was worth watching.

In social standing she would be below granny, who had an old aristocratic family name, Nizami-zadé, which, though she never used it, she was nevertheless proud of. She had married grandfather, who was below her in social status but who was both rich and honorable. Hava Hanum was of different origin. She was a merchant's daughter and a merchant's wife. They were very well to do till, according to her account, her husband married for the second time the widowed wife of his brother, and said that it was out of kindness. Polygamy being rare in the families who had no slaves, this brought bad luck to the household. Their house too was burnt down soon after in one of the big fires in Istamboul, and he lost his money besides. Hava Hanum never told us if she was jealous of the second wife, but she had withdrawn her wise and thrifty management from her husband's house. All of that belonged to the past now. He had divorced his second wife after his final misfortune and retired to a Turkish monastery with his son, who was delicate. He asked Hava Hanum's forgiveness and confessed that all his domestic calamity was due to having made her suffer. This she told with a certain triumph in her voice. After this she had drifted into poverty and loneliness. It was now that Arzié Hanum, who had known her previously, pitied her and took her to her own house, promising to find something for her to do which would not injure her self-respect.

Arzié Hanum had a story of her own too. Whenever Hava Hanum spoke of her I felt a lively curiosity, for Arzié Hanum was in Istamboul circles what Madame Thèbes is in Parisian ones. Besides I have vivid memories of her at our sick-beds.

Arzié Hanum had been initiated into seeing the future at the birth of her first-born. When a Turkish woman had a baby in those days it was well known that for forty days she was dangerously exposed to peri influence. In fact it was not safe for her to be left alone for a moment, and if she was poor and had no servants a neighbor would come in to stay in her room and would leave a broom behind the door if called out in an emergency; this keeps the spirits away. The woman has a Koran on her pillow and wears a red ribbon on her hair, and every evening incense is burned beside her to keep the evil ones at a distance.

Some of these necessary details must have been omitted in Arzié Hanum's case, for she had a fit and the peris took possession of her spirit and she became a clairvoyant and went to all the fashionable houses, as well as the poor ones, in sickness, childbirth, or other calamity, such as when people were under the influence of witchcraft, sorcery, or the evil influence of those who are called Themselves. She seemed familiar with Rüküsh Hanum, the chief young peri woman, and Yavrou Bey, a sort of *jeune premier* of the peris and probably the lover of Rüküsh Hanum.

Arzié Hanum lived in a charming tumbledown wooden house in a lost quarter of Scutari surrounded by a wild garden. She received her patients, or those who wanted her opinion on different things, in this house.

She had a round good-natured face, with two brilliant black eyes which twinkled with humor and squinted when she went into a trance, that is, got in contact with Themselves. She would sit on a low cushion on the floor, incense burning in a silver cup before her, her fingers hurriedly going through a rosary, and her eye fixed on one particular spot of the ceiling.

She talked and winked at the ceiling as naturally as she would to some familiar person.

"Thou art not going to keep that child in thrall. No, don't be nasty now. Thou shalt have thy cock and a nice one. Get out of the way, Rüküsh. Let me have it out with him." This to the ceiling.

Now to the patient:

"The man in question is living in a blue house. The street is narrow. Poor fellow, he bumps his head against the eaves. He is tight in the clutches of Yavrou Bey. He must have defiled some haunted rubbish-heap.[3] Let me see—no, it is a haunted fig-tree that he has offended. Yavrou! Now, now, you bring a cock that will appease him. And Rüküsh will be pleased with red sugar in a red scarf."

The demands of these young peris went up to lambs or gold pieces according as the station of the family became higher in the social scale. Marriages, divorces, family grievances and secrets all came to Arzié Hanum's house. A throng of people waited in the garden taking their turns patiently. She would do all this sometimes for nothing for the poor, and she helped old and bereaved people and orphans in her quarter. She must have given sound and reasonable advice I presume, or there would have been more divorce cases among her clients than there were.

Whenever granny went there, which was often in those days, I used to go with her to have Arzié pray over me and breathe her healing breath into my face. Then I would be sent out into the garden. Out there I always felt a tremor down my back. There used to be a dumb child with wild eyes, an orphan protégé of hers. It had a shaven head and wore girl's clothes, so I could not make out what its sex was. It looked after the lambs which were always about in the garden, marked with red henna to please Yavrou Bey, to whom they were ostensible offerings. And there were beautiful cocks too which the queer child ran after, making

[3] Rubbish-heaps and fig-trees were the special haunts of the peris and one did well to avoid them entirely, but more especially at night. If one were obliged to intrude it was best to murmur, "May They be in good hour"; i. e., may this be a time when They are in good mood.

all kinds of gestures and producing unearthly sounds. To me it was really Yavrou Bey's child, and the lambs were bewitched as well as the whole garden. Nothing would induce me to go under a fig-tree or upon a rubbish-heap in the place, lest I might step on the incalculable *jeune premier* and get a crooked mouth or a paralyzed tongue. Apart from her professional relations and her professional life Arzié Hanum seemed a sincere and friendly person with admirable discretion and an understanding heart. Was her kind heart perhaps pitying the credulity and ignorance of those who came to her? I cannot to this day be sure whether she entirely believed in what she was doing or whether she was consciously playing a part.

She had befriended old Hava Hanum and had kept her in her house till granny came across her there. She must have spoken to granny in this sort of way:

"You know, Hanum Effendi, she is a real lady and could not be a servant. But she is an excellent housekeeper; she cooks well, and you need not tell the world that you pay her and buy her clothes and her tobacco. She will do well and mother the children tenderly."

And granny, who could not afford a man cook any longer and had married all her old slaves off, needed a housekeeper. Very probably she who had seen such much grander days was able to understand the pitiable condition of another who had come down in the world; so she always treated her with consideration and indulgence.

"I met your granny," Hava Hanum used to say,

"when she was looking for a suitable ladylike old lady for your father's house. Having refused to take her son-in-law in her house, your grandmother wanted him to have proper care. She asked Arzié Hanum's advice about this, and she finally took Gülly Hanum, who was in the same position as I. When a little later I got to know your granny and told her all about myself, she immediately took me and has been like a sister to me ever since. May Allah reward her!"

She felt real gratitude to granny, but nevertheless it was through her evening discourses that I learned of granny's weak points. Hava Hanum dined with the family, received granny's guests, and always took care to sit in the place of honor, actually in a higher place than granny herself. But granny ignored all this benevolently and always maintained her charming manners toward her.

Hava Hanum used to tell a vivid story about the first night of her marriage which I can never forget. She would forget that her audience consisted of two little girls and a foolish Circassian slave, and would get into a dramatic mood.

"We used to have our hair plaited and left hanging down our backs in my young days," she would begin. "I had forty plaits; they were like a fringed shawl reaching from one shoulder to the other." (In fact, old as she was, she still had two thick plaits, henna-colored, wound over her soft head-dress.) "I had such beautiful teeth!" (Her mouth was like an empty black hole, but she ate wonderfully, managing the hardest morsels.) "My cheeks were like two bright peaches." (They were loose wrinkled leather now.) "My husband when led to my bridal chamber saw everything through my veil. He asked me three times to lift my veil,[4] but of course he opened it himself, offering me the face-seeing present.[5] But he had hardly looked at me before he called in the woman attendant.

"'Undo one of these plaits,' he ordered her.

"'O Effendi, her hair has been plaited by the professional bath hair-dressers. She only goes once a fortnight because it is such a tremendous business each time. How can I undo it?'

"'Undo it quickly. It cannot be real hair. It isn't possible she should have such a quantity. I must be sure that it is not false.'

"Two professional hair-dressers from the bath she used to go to were accordingly called in, and they undid my plaits while he wetted his handkerchief in his mouth and rubbed my cheeks."

"Why did he do that, Hava Hanum?" I would ask.

And my sister nudged me angrily for interrupting the story.

"To see if the paint would come off of course, you stupid!"

Well, finally the gentleman made sure that none of the beauteous attributes of his wife were false, and he shook his head over the possibility of such hair and such coloring.

---

[4] This is the ceremonial performance of old Turkish marriages.
[5] A bracelet, necklace, etc., according to the wealth of the bridegroom.

For years and years the first night ceremonial of marriages meant for me a repetition of this particular scene. As I had not acquired a femininistic turn of mind, I did not in the least object to any gentleman who tested the physical virtues of his wife as if he were examining any other property such as slaves or cows. I made a moral out of this story, after I had heard other versions of first night ceremonies from other ladies, which were more or less alike; and I concluded sadly that a bride could never cheat a Turkish husband by paint or false hair if her hair was thin and her cheeks pale. The evenings in Hava Hanum's sitting-room were in their way as instructive as a French salon before the Revolution.

Every evening we found her fire-brazier in the middle of the room with floor-cushions and her coffee-tray round it. With her cigarette in her mouth she would make her first cup of coffee, taking pains that it should be as frothy as possible, and then she would sip it boiling hot, her old eyes squeezed up ecstatically before she opened the evening's proceedings. After an hour's interval she would repeat the pleasant operation, sometimes giving me a little in a tiny saucer, which I licked up like a kitten.

My sister, hardly nine years old, already smoked in secret, but here in Hava Hanum's room she enjoyed her cigarette openly, bringing the smoke out from her nostrils like a grown-up; and feeling proud of this performance, she would begin fiercely to order me about, to which I so much objected that I would threaten her with, "I will tell granny if you make me fetch your things."

"Wilt thou?" she would blaze. "Come along then. It is I who will tell. Dost thou think I am afraid of any one? Besides we all know thou art a telltale. Thou hast Gipsy milk."

The accusation of having Gipsy milk and mixed milk was a common one in those days. As my mother had been too delicate, father had hired wet-nurses for me. It was believed that the milk a baby drinks affects its character, making it like the woman who nurses it. My first milk-mother, as we call a foster-mother, was an Albanian, and my sullen moods were put down to her. Granny would say, "Now it is the milk of that cross Albanian which is working in thee." The next was the wife of an onion-seller, a supposed Gipsy. Hence anything in me different from a conventional Turkish child was her fault. For three months fortunately a good and beloved person had nursed me, and this gave the explanation of certain good traits. Whenever I was docile, gentle, or unselfish it was attributed to my Nevres Badji,[6] a black slave of my granny's who had married in Istamboul. In spite of her black face she had a milk-white heart and had really nice manners. She had a respected position, and granny visited her often and allowed her to take us one at a time to her house for long visits in Ramazan. This holy month was a wonderful time in those days. The quarter where

[6] *Badji* is the appellation for a negro nurse.

it was most brilliantly celebrated was Istamboul, near the famous mosques; and Nevres Badji's house was in Suleymanié in the very center of this part of the city. But of these wonderful doings I have more to tell later, and for the moment I must return to our evenings in Hava Hanum's room.

We did not often have these little skirmishes, for most of the time she kept our minds absorbed in highly seasoned gossip about the inmates of the house. In some subtle way she liked to criticize granny, and mostly as regards her weakness for the palace lady. This subject was wickedly enjoyed by my sister.

"I can't understand," Hava Hanum would say, "her weakness for palace women. From what I can see the creatures have no sense. First she must needs have Haire Bey (my grandmother's eldest son)—may Allah's grace be on his soul!—marry that consumptive palace woman, Trigül Hanum. Everybody round about still remembers how fair and tall and stout he was; just like your granny herself, and not a bit like your uncle Kemal Bey or Kütchük Hanum." (Kutchuk Hanum means young lady, and every one belonging to granny's household always spoke of my mother in this way.) Although Trigül Hanum was tall and fair and very beautiful according to Kava Hanum, still she was so thin that she had her legs padded with cotton-wool, especially when she went out with the lady who had such beautiful plump legs, that is, granny. After giving birth to a boy, Refet, she had died. "Who knows?" Have Hanum would continue with shrewd discernment; "it may be true that consumption is contagious, for Haire Bey got ill too. But, poor fellow, he did not escape from palace ladies on his death-bed. He was married to Nevber Hanum, that frightful-looking woman who often comes to the house, when he was almost dying. It is true that she was a good nurse, but each time she left the room he used to say to his mother: 'Do marry me to a pretty woman. That woman's face makes me miserable.' Very soon after he died, and he was soon followed by his lovely boy—such a favorite as he was with Büyük Effendi" (the gentleman of the house, my grandfather). "But it was not in your granny to learn a lesson from this. Now she is trying to get Kemal Bey to marry that palace lady, who must be at least thirty, while he is only twenty-two. You see how stern and sad he looks. I know he will never marry her; never!"

Then the palace lady's Circassian slave would chime in:

"He locks his door whenever he goes into his room, and the blinds of his back windows opposite the red brick house are always drawn. Such a good Moslem as he is! If he were to smile at times you could n't find fault with him."

Then sister would snap out, "He does n't smile because he hates your lady."

"What has my lady done to him?"

"They want him to marry her, and she wants it too."

"She does not."

"She does, you idiotic Circassian! Why does she

wear those hard, starched, embroidered dresses one after the other, that make a crackly noise like a toad, so that every cat runs after her? She tries to swell up and look fat, and I know she paints her face white and red." (Beauty consisted in those days for the most part in plenty of white flesh.)

"But those are her palace dresses. Are n't they beautiful? Each one takes three hours to starch and iron."

"What do you say to her false tail of hair then?"

"It is not false, *Vallahi*."

Hava Hanum would stop them both. "It's no use talking. He would n't marry her even if she were the youngest and loveliest woman in the world. I will tell you why not; but swear that you won't repeat it."

After due oaths from my sister and Fikriyar she would begin. (She did not think me important enough to make me swear.)

"The red brick house opposite his room was taken by a Circassian family last year, and there was a pretty girl there."

A wonderful incident flashed into my mind as she told the story. One morning my uncle Kemal had called me into his room. He was very stern-looking and had a he-never-smiled-again expression on his face. A regular and hard-working secretary in the finance ministry, living as quietly as an old man, he was in reality perhaps older than his old father in heart and temperament. His leisure time he spent shut up in his room, drawing and making all sorts of bright-colored birds out of silk and wool, making models of houses, wonderfully designed down to the smallest detail, and doing lovely paintings. He had had no education and was obliged to hide all this from his father, who would have considered it heathenish. But no doubt he needed self-expression, as all of us do, and probably he had a talent for drawing. My sister's son, who is a painter and designer, probably has his talents from the same source.

Anyway, Uncle Kemal enjoyed this childish art, and enjoyed too our frank admiration of his work, the only admiration and sympathy he could get.

It was one of these Friday mornings in his room, and the blind of the back window was up. The window opened upon a row of tall acacias in our back garden, behind which one could see bits of the red brick house. Between the white flowers and the green leaves I caught sight of a dazzling something, like a golden fringe or a yellow shawl hanging from one of its windows. From this patch of bright gold catching the rays of a blazing sun leaned a round, freckled, white face, red lips, and the same gold over the head. That splendid shawl I discovered to be her hair let loose, for the reason which I can only now make out. The face was gazing right into the golden glory of the sun, catching its vivid splendor. The sheer blinding color and the animal magnificence of the picture dazzled me. I have never been so strangely and emotionally surprised by any face since.

"Ah!" I gasped. "How beautiful! Look, Uncle Kemal!"

I felt two nervous arms catch me by the shoulders

and pull me in with a jerk, as he closed the blinds hurriedly.

"It is rude to look at people like that. Fikriyar must have left the blinds up, I am afraid." It was half emotion and half apology for being found with an open blind with that apparition just opposite.

After that morning I very often stood under the acacias and watched the windows of the red brick house till my eyes ached. Only once again did I see the beautiful vision. It was probably another Friday morning, and she was once more looking at the sun in the same attitude and with the same loose hair.

Hava Hanum's story completed for me the meaning of the golden image and its apparently intentional pose.

"He called me to his room one evening when the ladies were out at the neighbors'," she said. "He was very sad, almost crying. 'I am dying for the girl in the red brick house,' he said. 'I entreat you to save my life.'

" 'What can I do, Kemal Bey?' I said.

" 'You must go and ask her in marriage for me, Auntie Hava.'

" 'And your mother's consent, my son?'

" 'You are never to tell my mother. She will never consent.'

"He kissed my hands and begged so hard that I promised, but after I left his room I began to think it over and be afraid of your granny. She might very likely dismiss me if she found me out doing anything without asking her consent. It might be disastrous for me, I knew. So late in the night I went to her room and woke her. She had her heart so set on that palace lady as a daughter-in-law that it was impossible to persuade her. But after a lot of talk she said to me, 'Don't say anything to him for a few days, and then pretend that you have been to her house and that she is already engaged.'

"The next few days my conscience kept pricking me. He passed the kitchen door with an expressionless face and never asked me once about the affair which he seemed to have had so at heart only a few days ago. Finally, however, I went to the young woman's house and inquired about her. There were only Circassians, and not one of them could talk decent Turkish, but they made me understand that she had been married to the swarthy, bearded man whom we used to take for her father, and only very recently.

"That very night I went up to his room and told him the news. He took it quietly and was in such a hurry to get me out of his room that one might have believed he did n't care if one did not know him. Before a fortnight had passed your granny called me to her room. He had grown so pale and despondent that she was at last anxious about him. 'Hava Hanum,' she said, 'go and ask that girl's hand for Kemal; he is simply fading away.' Then I told her that I had already been there and that it was too late."

"Well, that young man won't last much longer," a German doctor at his sister's funeral said. "He'll die before he's twenty-five."

As a matter of fact Uncle Kemal died before he was twenty-four. But there is something else to tell before

I come to that unhappy event which made such a turning-point in my childish history, for after it granny left the wisteria-covered house and never entered it any more.

We were getting ready for Ramazan, the "unique sultan of eleven months," as the watchman used to sing of that holy month in his street perambulations. Granny was in the kitchen most of the time making jams and syrups for Ramazan, an art in which she really excelled. Her father had been the chief sweet-maker of Sultan Abdul Medjid, the Dweller of Heaven. He could make syrups of three colors, white, red, and yellow—so she would tell us—and put them all in the same bottle without letting them mix, which sounded little short of miraculous to me in those days. I realized as she told us such exploits that granny did not care for her dead father as much as for her mother; one realized that his position must have been something like my own grandfather's in the house, a rich man but inferior in station to his wife, herself the daughter of a learned and holy personage.

"My father was not even virtuous like your grandfather," she would say. "Why, even before mother died he was after all the pretty slaves I used to buy. I had so many pretty white slaves, but Effendi" (her own husband) "never looked at one of them out of the corner of his eyes."

She sat on a chair stirring in regular order the three boiling and steaming dishes on braziers before her, Hava Hanum moving about and grumbling all the time.

WHEN THE STORY BECOMES MINE

This was a spring Ramazan,[7] and Hava Hanum was in the habit of making all sorts of health-reviving and youth-restoring lotions for herself, boiling black currants and queer spices together in earthenware dishes. As she was disturbed by all this bustle and noise in the kitchen, she criticized granny's extravagance, saying that the time for such fancies had passed. But granny did not heed her. She was determined to have a proper Ramazan with feasts and good things to eat in plenty. Every evening in those thirty days things looked somewhat sad. Uncle Kemal was losing flesh and color and grandfather getting cross and moody, always talking of debts and unpleasant happenings.

Uncle Kemal came into the kitchen on his return from the office, watched his mother's jam-making for a time, but escaped hastily if grandfather or the palace lady appeared on the scene. He did not get on with either, though for different reasons.

The difference between my grandparents' tempers and characters I also began to note at this period. She was refined, polite to the extreme even with the servants, never raising her voice or losing her temper. Whenever she was intensely annoyed the strongest language she used was, "What mint-honey art thou eating?" while in similar cases grandfather's powerful voice would roar out in its thickest Kemah accent, "What abomination art thou eating?" But he only scolded the servant and never interfered in the harem part of the house, and

---

[7] Turkish months, being lunar, do not constantly recur at any fixed part of the solar year.

his quarrels with his wife probably took place when the rest of the house was sleeping.

If my grandmother suffered from her stomach she had mint-leaves and lemon-peel boiled together and drank them; if she had a headache she used rose-leaves steeped in vinegar. He in the first case ate raw onions, breaking them with his fists, for he believed that a knife spoiled their juice; in the second case, he applied peeled potatoes to his forehead, tying them up in a white cloth. There was something varied and strong and very full-bodied about everything he told us. His voice was remarkable, a real sound of nature, with wonderful color and volume, and entirely expressive of the emotion he felt at the moment. Somehow I was more attracted by his onions and swearing than by my granny's mint-honey and perfumed vinegar.

He must once have loved granny with a wild passion, and he evidently loved her still; while she, although very feminine and sweet, did not seem to care for her husband in the way that most other women did. She was the only woman in my childhood who never spoke of sexual relations, and she seemed indeed utterly unconcerned with the other sex. Evidently she was a woman without passion, but she could be attached to people to such a degree that it often made one pity her; such devotion and unselfishness as she showed without ever asking any return or heeding the ridicule of the world. She never kissed or caressed any one so far as I can remember, not even the children of the palace lady, for whom she had the kind of attachment that is difficult to account for. There is only one caress of hers which I remember. She was on her death-bed, and she called me to her with her eyes, patted me with the one hand which she could still use a little, and delicately drew in her breath, as her lips touched the cheek which I laid against hers to be kissed. She did it longingly, tenderly; and this single touch of love physically expressed by her has left something like an open wound of memory which aches sweetly whenever I think of it. She gave herself quietly to those she loved, with no demonstration, no need of contact. I, who for years had grandfather's boiling nature and could have kissed my children continually and carried them in a pouch attached to my body like a kangaroo, often felt a childish irritation at her apparent lack of temperament.

Yet she undoubtedly influenced me, and I recognize that I have inherited from both my grandparents to an extraordinary degree. Undoubtedly my writing is hers. Her little education and her time had not allowed her to express herself in public, but her happiest moments were those when she could sit down and write crude love-stories and very old-fashioned verse. Yet all that she wrote was so silly and contrary to her own nature that it is evident she was led to write by the same internal motive as I was, namely to free herself from her dull existence. After the publication of my novel "Handan," which undeservedly took the public fancy almost to the point of hysteria, she came to me with an old copy-book under her arm and asked me timidly if she could publish the stuff and get some money out of it. She was badly in debt and harassed by her creditors. I read the whole crude story, so silly and sentimental and so different from her own humorous and original talk. When I tried to make her understand the impossibility of offering her book to a publisher she looked pained.

"Why," she said, "yours sell more than any one's."

"It is rather different, granny."

"Different? Where is the difference? It is all love stuff. I have tried to put more love in than you have. I have even put in a piano, and the lovers talk through the window, which is as far as I could possibly go; I could not make them make love to each other in a room like yours, even for the sake of my creditors or the publishers."

She had found out "Handan" in a way which no critic had. One story was as silly as the other, although for different reasons: hers because of its weak sentimentality, her refined nature not being able to recognize the sins of the flesh; while the silliness of "Handan" came from the over-strong dose of passion. It reeked with passion indeed, and grandfather was surely responsible for its physical side. Yet it is those silly types who have such long lives in literature. If granny had known how to use her hidden desires she would have produced a Turkish "Jane Eyre" not one bit less silly or sentimental than the English one. We somehow love to create the types farthest away from us, the types which our sense of humor or lack of a certain kind of courage prevents us personally from ever becoming.

WHEN THE STORY BECOMES MINE

Those interviews with granny have left regret and shame in my heart. I used to finish by lecturing her on her habit of running into debt. How crude and futile I must have appeared!

"Why make debts, granny?" I used to say. "You need not give presents to so many people."

"Child," she would answer, "shall I not buy the Bairam [8] clothes for my old slaves' children? So few are alive. I have ceased to do so for my friends' children. I have no personal desire, no more *ferajes* [9] according to the color of the flowers of the seasons, no more feasts. No, I have only three more days to live, and I'm not going to change now, debts or no debts."

"What would you do if you had your old fortune?"

"Do the same things over again."

She would have tears in her eyes in the end and repeat that she had only three days more to live, and stick stubbornly but sweetly to her last extravagance.

On the whole, however, it is clear to me that granny really did restrict her lavish tendencies somewhat as she grew older. The legends of the great doings before I was born pointed to something even more splendid than anything I was familiar with. As far as I am able to judge, her really last extravagant period, something like the old days, was the Ramazan I have already referred to—the Ramazan after which her last child and the old husband, who had sweated himself to death to have her wishes realized, grumblingly but loyally, died.

[8] Festival after Ramazan, when every one has new clothes.
[9] An out-of-door mantle, worn formerly by Turkish ladies.

When the cellar was looking like the hyacinth-fields, all yellow, red, and purple, but with syrups and jams in transparent glass jars instead of flowers; and when it had a smell as pungent and as varied as the spice-market, when the house blazed with dazzlingly white curtains, white divan-covers, and clean windows, and two women were working at two machines making new dresses for us children, my Nubian milk-mother Nevres Badji appeared on the scene.

As she kissed granny's dress, and when the mutual inquiries after the families' healths were over, she respectfully intimated that she had come to take me for the promised Ramazan visit. Sister's turn would come next, but this time it was thought better for her to go to another married slave of granny's, a tall and fair Circassian, whose forcible nature made her more able to control Mahmouré than the mild Nubian.

So on this memorable day before Ramazan I started with Nevres Badji on my way to Istamboul. I don't know how we got to the bridge, but the indignity she exposed me to after we had crossed it is branded as with fire in my memory. She evidently thought the steep hill from Merjan to Suleymanié would be too much for my childish legs, and so she hired a porter to carry me. The shame of it! The insult of it! It is true that I was not a stout walker, but it was either a carriage or a tram which granny always took when we went on expeditions of this kind, and the sight of the children of the poorer classes carried by porters had always filled me with disdain. From that day they had my full sympathy.

It was a tall Kurdish porter with a dark face and a tender heart, as they all usually have. He caressed my hair, patted my cheeks, laughed and tried to be friendly, tried his best to make me speak. He wanted to stop and buy me sweets out of his own poor purse if Nevres Badji had allowed such familiarity. Such an unpleasant penetrating smell attacked my nostrils from his body, and his face was so fond and foolish, and I was in such an irritated state of mind, feeling the Istamboul crowd to be an audience gathered to watch my humiliation, that I hated him violently at that moment; but I have changed my mind since, and I love him and his kind.

The first night at Nevres's house was not pleasant. The first night anywhere is unpleasant for a child, but it was more so in her house for two special reasons: first she made me sleep in her bed, and she had the incurable smell of colored people, so hard for a sensitive white nose to bear, however that nose may love the owner of the smell. Secondly she put out the light, and I was used to sleeping with an oil-lamp, a soft shaky light which bathed the furniture, as well as granny's face, in a dim and golden haze; whereas this darkness in Nevres Badji's room seemed to thicken so as to solidify Nevres Badji into a hard black mass, so hard that one could bite it, as Mark Twain says, but never be able to chew it without breaking one's teeth. I perspired with anguish and felt that the unmoving time too was solidified and fixed like the darkness.

But morning did come, as it always does. I heard her mild voice, mixed with the wonderful bass of a man making fond efforts to tone his voice down to the softest whisper; though somehow I felt that really he very much wanted me to wake up. It was Ahmet Aga, my milk-father, Nevres' second husband, a blond giant from Trebizond with a leonine red head, all hair and beard, and two delightful blue eyes—a captain of a custom-house launch which pursued smugglers at sea. He and his launch must have worked havoc in the hearts of the law-breakers, yet his heart was perhaps more childish than mine. As he had come in late the night before, I only found him on the sofa in his *gejelik* [10] in the morning, waiting for me like a little boy for his playmate.

I would spring from the floor-bed into his lap, and locking me in his arms, he would kiss my hair and call out playfully, "Milk-mother, bring our coffee and milk." Then with the coffee-cup on one of his knees and me on the other, we would drink our coffee and milk together. He began the morning with a joyful song. Although I have a poor ear and memory for music, I still hear the songs—both words and music—that I heard in my childhood, as sung by the people dead so long ago:

"My girl, my girl, my henna-painted lamb, a hodja wants to marry thee; what answer shall I say?"

"Mother, O mother, he'll make me wind his turban.

---

[10] A long padded coat worn as a sort of negligée, whether in the bedroom, house, or even mosque.

MOSQUE OF SULEYMANIÉ

WHEN THE STORY BECOMES MINE

Oh, tell the hodja, mother, thy daughter says him nay!"

"My girl, my girl, my henna-painted lamb, a soldier wants to marry thee; what answer shall I say?"

"The soldier has a cruel sword which he may use to kill me. Oh, tell the hodja, mother, thy daughter says him nay."

Thus the song went on, with proposals for marriage with every kind of profession, but the girl refuses till it comes to a scribe, whereupon she accepts with joy. Scribes were the favored husbands and lovers in those days, at least so said a multitude of people's delightful songs. Ahmet Aga always wanted me to sing the answers, and he sang them with me, so we must have sounded rather queer.

Meanwhile Nevres Badji used to move about the room, softly tidying everything with her eternal and internal smile which seemed to make no facial disturbance on her broad, bland, black face.

"Come, milk-mother, sing thou too," he used to roar, and she hummed the same thing in her sweetly humorous tones:

"I look at the meat in the butcher's shop and the melons on the stall, but never dost thou give me one thing to eat at all. Nor art thou fair and handsome, hast no good looks at all. A fine strong husband I could love, but thou art dwarfish small. So if I go and leave thee, make love to some poor black, and thou canst keep my *nikah;* I will not ask it back." (The *nikah* is the sum the husband has to pay the wife in case of divorce. If she demands the divorce, she usually gives up her right to the money in order to persuade him.)

They would wink at each other and enjoy some fun the meaning of which I did not catch, but I have never seen a happier and more loving couple since. They had a perfect mutual understanding and mutual contentment.

The second night in Nevres Badji's room was pleasanter. The young moon which started the Ramazan rejoicings had been seen by some one late in the night. Just as I was feeling immured by the rocky hardness of the lightless room, soft lights from outside lit up the white curtains as boys and men passed along the street with lanterns in their hands, singing and beating a tremendous drum. This made milk-mother get up, make a light, and begin to bustle round, getting ready for the first *sahur* (the night meal which is eaten after midnight in Ramazan in preparation for the next day's fasting), which every one would begin the next day.

The next morning when I woke, milk-father was snoring in his bed. Only milk-mother was up, probably to prepare my morning milk; and I had to have a lonely meal listening to the extraordinary silence which seemed to fill the house as well as the streets. It was only at three in the afternoon that the world began to wake up and we got ready for the visit to the mosques.

This part of Istamboul is a vast burnt waste, islanded with patches of charming dark wooden houses with shadowy eaves. Between these we passed, she holding my hand fast, that I might not get lost. The streets were full. Groups of women, in *charshafs* of many colors, moved along, the young with thick veils but the old with their faces uncovered, all with rosaries in hand and tight lips occasionally whispering a prayer. Every one carried a rosary, beautifully and fancifully colored, each mosque having had a fair where one could buy rosaries, pipes, women's trinkets, dried fruit, and all imaginable delicacies, especially spices. Men from all over the empire stood there, picturesquely dressed, crying their goods in musical tones and in their own languages. Arabs predominated in numbers, their stalls full of henna and kohl in pretty red leather tubes, which they pretended to have brought from Mecca, and which made their goods considered almost like holy relics and therefore to be much sought after. Besides holy tradition said that it was pleasing to Mohammed for women to dye their eyes with kohl and their fingers with henna.

Finally Suleymanié mosque was reached, where we were to hear preaching or *mukabelé*.[11] The sight of that gray and imposing group of buildings made me almost drunk with pleasure. I seemed to be composed of myriads of open cells through which penetrated this gray mass rising in the blue air. The feeling inside me was of a fluid motion, flooding and moving in a divine harmony through my little body. I have often thought since that a child's perception of beauty is superior to

[11] Every family had a *hafiz*, a man who knows the Koran by heart and the musical rules of the chanting. He has to chant the Koran for the soul of the dead. One heard them in every mosque, some being famous and more sought after for beauty of voice or rendering.

that of a grown-up. It is not a beauty of words. It is color; it is sound, it is harmony and line all combined yet producing a single sensation.

A moment's pause at the door to give one's shoes to the old man,[12] the lifting of the corner of the huge worn curtain, beside which one looked like a tiny rabbit, and then the entrance!

A gray endless upward sweep of dome, holding a hazy gray atmosphere in which hung the constellation of the tiny oil lamplets.[13] The light through the colored windows must have added a rosy hue, but the warmth of its pinkish shade was rather felt than seen. It was diffused in that gray air and added a faint tone which prevented the gray from being sad and somber, as it usually is on sea and sky. The magic of genius has given the mosque of Suleymanié the proportions which make one fancy it the largest building one has ever seen, so imposing is the sense of space and grandeur reduced to its simplest expression. Near the *mihrab*,[14] under different groups of lamps, sat various men in white turbans and loose black gowns, swinging their bodies in rhythm with the lilt of their minor chants. Everything seemed part of the simple majestic gray space with its

[12] No one may pollute a mosque by walking in it with shoes dirty with the impurities of the street. Huge padded curtains hang over the mosque doorways.

[13] Until recently all mosques were lit by tiny lamps, each lamp consisting of a small, cup-like glass filled with oil on which floated a wick. From the ceiling of the dome an iron framework was hung by heavy chains, and in this framework the lamps were placed; but so slight and delicate was it that when the lamps were lit the framework was unseen and the impression was of stars hanging in the sky of the dome.

[14] The part of a mosque which shows the direction of Mecca.

invisible rosy hue and its invisible pulsations. In the pulpits sat men in the same dresses as the chanters. They were preaching and waving their arms in more passionate rhythm than the chanting ones, but everything became toned down and swallowed up in the conquering silence, in the invisible pulsation of the air. Nevres sat down where she could listen to some man who was chanting for the souls of the dead. Some of these chanters were old and some young, but all had the transparent amber pallor and the hectic eyes of those who are fasting. In no time I felt caught up into the general sway and began moving my body unconsciously to and fro in the same harmonious manner as the rest. I became a part of the whole and could not have moved otherwise than under the dominating pulsations of the place. No false note, no discordant gesture was possible.

There were more groups of women than men around the preachers, and as Badji always went to listen to the chanters, I quietly sneaked away and knelt before a preacher's pulpit. A pale man with eyes of liquid flame was speaking, condemning every human being to eternal fire, since his standard for a good Moslem was such that it was quite impracticable to get to heaven. As the natural dwelling-place of Moslem mortals therefore, he described all the quarters of hell—the place where people are burned, the place where they are tortured in all sorts of ways. It seemed to be a case of either endless suffering in this world or the next; that at any rate is the effect which has stayed in my memory as being what he wanted to impress upon us. His arms in their long loose black sleeves had prophetic gestures; his voice had a troubling tone, something so burning, so colored lending itself to the wonderful rhythm and beauty of the verses of the Koran which he read and interpreted. It was really sublime nonsense, rendered in most artistic gestures and tones. I sneaked back to Badji and hid my face in her ample *charshaf*. I was frightened and troubled for the first time with a vague sense of religion.

In the evening the great guns were fired, signaling the time to break the fast, and we gathered about the round low tray on which jams, olives, cheese, spiced meats, eggs, and all sorts of highly flavored pastries were arranged. Milk-father got back his good humor as he ate. In Ramazan the Moslem spoils his stomach as one spoils a beloved child, even the poorest allowing himself variety and plenty.

Our evening prayers received only scant observance that night, for we had to hurry out for the Ramazan prayer, milk-father leading with a lantern in his hand; but turning back he soon lifted me on his shoulders, and swinging the lantern in his other hand, he walked by Badji's side, talking and joking. The streets were lighted by hundreds of these moving lanterns. Men, women, and children flickered forward like a swarm of fireflies, drums were sounding in the distance, and from every minaret the muezzin was calling, "*Allah Ekber, Allah Ekber....*"[15] The grand harmony came nearer

[15] God is great—the beginning of the usual call to prayer.

or grew more distant as we moved on. Then suddenly above the dimly lighted houses, above the mass of moving lights, a circle of light came into view high over our heads in the dark blue air. The tiny balcony of some dim minaret was now traced out as though by magic in a slender illusive ring of light. These light circles multiplied into hundreds, standing out in the bluish heaven, softly lighting up the picturesque masses of the wooden buildings below them, or the melting lines of the domes. And now in the same air, hanging in fact between minaret and minaret, other beautiful lines of light as if by a miracle interlaced and wove themselves into wonderful writing: "Welcome, O Ramazan!" Belshazzar's surprise when he saw the invisible fingers writing on the wall differed from mine only in quality. I was on the shoulders of the tallest man in the crowd. Below me the lights of the lanterns swung in the dark depths of the long winding mysterious streets. Above me light circles and gigantic letterings, also in light, hung in the blue void, while the illusive tracery of the minarets, the soft droop of the domes, appeared dimly or disappeared in the thickness of blue distance as we walked on. And so once more we reached Suleymanié and plunged into the great crowd gathered inside.

The gray space was now a golden haze. Around the hundreds of tremulous oil lights a vast golden atmosphere thickened, and under it thousands of men sat on their knees in orderly rows; not one single space was empty, and this compact mass, this human carpet presented a design made up of all costumes, ages, and ranks. The women prayed in the gallery above.

Nevres Badji left me to watch it all while she found herself a proper place in a regular row. Suddenly came the unique grand call—*"Sal-li-a-la Mohammed!"* [16] and then the rise of the entire human mass. The imam stood in front of the *mihrab,* his back to the people, and opened the prayer. It is wonderful to pray led by an imam. He chants aloud the verses you usually repeat in lonely prayer. You bow, you kneel, your forehead touches the floor. Each movement is a vast and complicated rhythm, the rising and falling controlled by the invisible voices of the several muezzins. There is a beautiful minor chant. The refrain is taken up again and again by the muezzins. There is a continual rhythmic thud and rustle as the thousands fall and rise. The rest belongs to the eternal silence.

It seems as if we should go on rising and falling, rising and falling for the rest of our lives, till all of a sudden people remain longer on their knees than before, and a chorus of, *"Amin, amin,"* sets the pulsing air into an almost frantic rhythm.

Then we leave the mosque.

I have often prayed in most of the mosques of Istamboul, but I have never entered Suleymanié again, although I have walked many times around it and visited the museum which used to be its soup-kitchen in earlier times. I did not want to alter the memory of the divine and esthetic emotion which I had had in the days of

[16] Pray in the name of Mohammed.

WHEN THE STORY BECOMES MINE

my early childhood, and I knew it was not possible to repeat it without destroying the intensity of that first impression.

Whatever my feelings are toward some parts of the Ottoman past, I am grateful to its conception of beauty as expressed by Sinan [17] in that wonderful dome. The gorgeous coloring of the Byzantines, the magic tracery, and the delicate, lace-like ornament of the Arab influenced him in many ways, but he surely brought that flawless beauty of line and that sober majesty in his Turkish heart from its original home in the wild steppes. There is a manliness and lack of self-consciousness here which I have never seen in any other temple, yet the work is far from being primitive or elemental. It combines genius and science, as well as the personal sense of holy beauty which is characteristic of the Ottoman, and it can hold its own with the architectural triumphs of any age.

Before Ramazan was over I went home to granny's. My sister, whom I called Mahmouré Abla,[18] met me at the door with a red and excited face. She was very glad to see me back, evidently, and full of news. First she gave me some pretty shells carefully tied up in her pocket-handkerchief. She had been to the seaside in Scutari and had gathered these for me. In generosity

---

[17] Sinan is the celebrated Turkish architect who lived in the sixteenth and seventeenth centuries and built endless mosques, bridges, *türbahs*, fountains, and kitchens for the poor.

[18] *Abla* is the title given to an elder sister by her younger. Mahmouré is her personal name.

and open-handedness she was unsurpassed. I immediately felt very much disappointed at not having been to the seaside myself. I forgot my own beautiful nights and remembered only the unpleasant time when I had been carried by a porter. I was almost ready to cry, but I was developing a conscious pride which did not allow my old outbursts of temper. And sister never noticed people's moods, while I was like a thermometer for feeling people's inside discomforts.

"We are having great *iftars*" (Ramazan invitations), she said; "grandfather in the selamlik and Granny in the harem. We have got a new man cook and an Armenian woman-servant for Ramazan, and Hava Hanum is all dressed in her grandest things and is receiving the visitors. To-night we are going to have a children's party. Thy Nut-rat is coming. All the girls in the quarter are coming. Auntie [19] Vasfié is bringing that newly circumcised boy of hers, that monkey-faced child who sits at the window in a girl's blue dress and the cap covered with a *nazar takimi*."

This was news indeed, and I began to forget my resentment in my interest in the preparations for the evening. The grown-ups were having their tables laid upstairs in the saloons, and we were to dine in the ordinary dining-room and use Hava Hanum's room afterward as our parlor. Mahmouré Abla feverishly controlled all the table arrangements, counted the tiny *iftar* dishes to

[19] Every older woman was called "auntie" by little children. Boys who had just recently been circumcised wore blue dresses and caps, and dangling down from their caps they had an ornament, *nazar takimi*, made of blue beads and pearls to keep off the evil eye.

see if the same choice of jam, cheese, and other delicacies was being given to us as to the grown-ups. She wrangled with the slave-girl Fikriyar because the green olives were forgotten. She got the syrup-glasses arranged just as she wished on the tray, while I walked at her heels bathed in the glory of her power and importance.

Shayesté's family arrived first—her one-eyed sister looking as cross as ever—and the other invited neighbors one after another, followed with their offspring. Our sitting-room was filled with young visitors all sitting uneasily in a row on the divan and looking at their toes as the grown-ups do, when Auntie Vasfié arrived with the boy in blue and his ornamented cap.

"You must make Riffat play the servant in your games," she said. "He will be a good slave."

The boy Riffat had a dark, sickly face and was evidently perfectly ready to play the slave, so eagerly and meekly did he fall in with all our plans. Up to now I had hated boys and feared them so much that this timid and lowly specimen was a surprise to me. Before long I found out that he was suffering from shyness of the others almost more than myself, although he was older, and I felt obliged to befriend him.

The meal was a failure. I felt out of place and foolishly different from the rest of the little company, just as in later years I have often felt at grown-up dinner-parties. Mahmouré Abla was all eyes, darting fire and reproaches at Fikriyar, who was waiting on us. Fortunately there was Bedrié, a slender and beautiful girl of twelve, the oldest child who in the assembly was already wearing the veil out of doors and got married very soon afterward.

After dinner we all sat together on the same divan and pretended to drink coffee out of dolls' cups. Then we sat down in a circle on the floor and played "The young mouse runs from the holes." [20] Finally Mahmouré Abla said, "This is idiotic; let us play weddings!"

Every one got excited, and every one suggested who should be the bride and bridegroom, while each was hoping to be one or the other of these happy persons. No one thought of the little boy. "Thou shalt be the dowry-slave," [21] they said finally, and he was content.

Binnaz was the bride and Bedrié the bridegroom. She pinned her skirts and made them look like a man's pantaloons. She put some black soot from a candle on her lips to make a mustache, and Mahmouré Abla fetched the man-servant's fez from the selamlik. Binnaz simply covered her face with the white muslin veil which Hava Hanum used to put on her head at her prayers. Now the game of weddings always starts when the pair passes among the assembled visitors arm in arm and every one calls out "Mashallah!" Then they enter the bridal chamber and sit on the sofa.

"What is your name?" asks the groom.

No answer.

"Please open your veil."

---

[20] The Turkish form of "Hunt the slipper."
[21] Well-to-do families give a slave who is called the dowry to the bride before she is married.

This is repeated three times, and no answer is given. But just when we are expecting the bride to comply, as she properly should at this point and open her veil and complete the play she is acting, Binnaz lifts up her voice and wails. The face-seeing present Bedrié offers is a match-box with a "pretend" ring inside. But the match-box is in vain. The wail develops into a regular and very unpleasantly loud howl.

"You are making fun of me; I won't be the bride; I won't be the bride," she cries. None of us at the time could understand the reason of the outburst, but I believe that it was her sensibility as to her blind eye, perhaps even a sudden conviction that this would never happen to her in reality, which had roused her against every one. Our surprise was complete. Mahmouré Abla began shaking her. The others pulled her off the sofa and begged her to stop crying lest the grown-ups should think we were quarreling. It was no use. Hava Hanum came down and scolded her, while Mahmouré Abla rushed out. Her return with Fikriyar carrying a tray full of ruby-colored pomegranate-syrups restored order.

Our evening was not exactly a success, but we had gained a new playmate in Riffat. After this he often joined us with Shayesté in the marble hall. He was as humble as he could be, and queerly enough I tolerated him best after Shayesté. Once indeed I told Hava Hanum that I wanted to play the wedding game with him, and at that stage I had no idea that there was any difference between the game and the reality, both alike being completely unreal. But when Riffat later changed his girl's blue dress for a primary military school uniform, I classified him with the wild species of humanity, viz., boys, and dropped him immediately.

But to return to our famous Ramazan of that year. As Bairam approached, the sewing-machines went on working even more busily, and granny went out every day buying presents. The handkerchiefs, the shirts, and the children's dresses were piling up on granny's divan. Her married slaves came with their children, stayed a few nights, got their presents, and went away again.

The night before Ramazan ends there is such a sleepless feverish sense of waiting and preparation that the day never actually fulfils one's expectations. We began the day by kissing the hands of all the old people in the house. Grandfather was the first person. At Bairam he was especially sad and restless. He had never got over the death of his beautiful grandson Reffet. He wandered round or shut himself up in his room, looking like an old wounded lion in a cage.

But he smiled sweetly at us when we entered and was unusually tender and caressing. He made us sit on his funny corner divan, and roasted bread on the little *mangal* [22] which he always kept in his room for his coffee, and he offered us delicious cheese that had just arrived from Kemah, very salty and creamy. He gave us dried cream and mulberries too, both Kemah products. Then he presented us new handkerchiefs and kissed me

[22] A *mangal* is a brazier.

several times. "Come every day, Halik," he said. "Thou shalt have some more cheese, and I will buy thee red apples." I found out afterward that his calling me Halik was due to the boy Reffet's having always called me by this funny name, a thing of which, however, I had no remembrance.

Auntie Teïzé, as we called the palace lady, was at her best also. She offered us beautiful *loukoum* and gave us silk handkerchiefs. But what makes me remember the day especially was her bringing out picture-books to show us during our visit to her apartments. It was a strange sensation to me, those signs and the pictures out of which a new world suddenly spoke. The book was a collection of African travels, perhaps translated; I do not know. But she actually sat on the floor and read to us the descriptions and explained the pictures. She had not been a teacher in the palace for nothing, for, as granny said, she could make a stone understand things. From that moment I gradually began to find the palace lady very attractive. An uncontrollable desire to learn to read began with the African travels that day.

Mahmouré Abla told me that learning from Djavidé Hanum was not a thing for cowardly little girls who feared Halim Kadin. This was very insulting. Halim Kadin was an imaginary woman whom they had invented to frighten me. She was supposed to live somewhere in the old stables, or in the large wood and charcoal store-places and cisterns round our house which were no longer used. As Hava Hanum believed that each child had to be in awe of something in order to be properly handled, she had created this image for my benefit. Mahmouré Abla sometimes hid in one of the numerous cupboards and produced unearthly sounds which were meant to be Halim Kadin calling, and these sounds always made a creepy feeling down my back.

"I won't be afraid of her any more," I said bravely.

"But thou canst not bear beating, canst thou?"

This made me serious.

"You must be able to bear beating," she went on. "No child can learn without being beaten. Beating has come out of heaven."

This was Djavidé Hanum's pedagogics it seemed, and father's was quite a different system. He only scolded me twice in all my life and took every measure to prevent me from being harshly treated, even when it was a matter of education later on.

Anyhow shortly after this my sister tried to apply Djavidé Hanum's system to me, and I began learning with her in secret. But it did not last for more than two lessons, I believe, for I did not care to learn à la Djavidé Hanum.

But I have wandered again.

Father naturally made a point of arriving at granny's house as early as he could. He had, however, first been obliged to attend the Bairam ceremony at the Dolma Bagtché Palace, and from there he came straight on to pay his respects to his old parents-in-law. He was still wearing his court-dress—a uniform of a long, tight, black coat, buttoned to the throat, embroidered in real gold down the front, a large decoration on his breast, his

THE MAIN ROAD IN ISTAMBOUL

ornamental sword, kid gloves, and shiny shoes. He cannot have been more than twenty-eight at this time, having married my mother very young. To me as I remember him that day, his slender figure, delicate face, with very fair mustache, his wonderful eyes, his well shaped hands, he seemed a very handsome figure. He gave us shining money—all new coins—out of a red silk purse.

After this we children went to kiss the hands of the old ladies in our quarter. Our own house was meantime like a beehive; men came into our selamik for their Bairam visits to grandfather, while all the young were received by granny also, and each would have as a present, after they had kissed her hands, a shirt, a handkerchief, or a tie. Mahmouré Abla did not like these hand-kissing visits. "It is like begging for handkerchiefs," she said.

But we went nevertheless, were given sweets, and received our handkerchiefs, with the same remark everywhere, "You can wipe your mouths with them, dears."

That afternoon father's groom came to fetch me to go with him to Yildiz; and perched on the tall bay horse, sitting in front of the man, I started for the palace. I remember the conversation we had, perhaps on account of the queer coincidence which followed it that very day.

"You give me your hair, little girl," he said facetiously. My unfortunate hair drew out teasing remarks from every one because of the funny way it was done. After some bad illness, probably the one at the Kyria Ellenie school, my hair was cut short; and as it grew very fast and granny hated untidy hair (she herself always wore her hair short), she had my hair done in four plaits, one on the top of my head, one on each temple and one at the back, the four being all tied together on the top of my head with some bright-colored ribbon. The ends escaped and stood out like a squirrel's tail, and the unusual shades of fair and dark gave it a strange appearance. The plaits were so tight that they screwed up my temples and eyebrows, and I had perpetual pains in my head on that account, but I never complained. I was naturally ready to give up my hair to any one. When the man saw that he could not tease me about my hair, he called me a little slave-girl and swore that he had seen me bought from a slave-dealer and actually knew the price that was paid for me, although he kept a mysterious silence on this point.

This was the identical nonsense with which every little girl was teased in Turkey in those days. Yet every little girl minded it terribly, and some stupid ones, like me, almost believed it. So by the time we were climbing the final Royal Road at a gallop up to the palace door I had deep misgivings. Passing through the portals, I saw a man carrying a white cockatoo in his hand. "Happy Bairam," screeched a voice, inhuman and startling, but I had never heard a bird talk before.

The groom whispered: "That bird knows about you too. Shall I ask it?" I was not anxious for more information and I hurried into father's bureau. It was in one of the pavilions on the left of the road with a few steps leading up to it. He was not in. He hardly ever had any holidays. On ceremonial days he was busiest, for all the royal presents and decorations passed through his hands. The head servant told me to wait in father's room; he had been called away as usual by the first chamberlain. But the servant promised to bring me sweets if I would be a good girl.

There in father's room, in front of his writing-table and sitting in his chair, was a eunuch. As these people were familiar sights in the palace, the circumstance was not in itself strange, but this eunuch was different from the stately black men I was accustomed to. His face was a light milk and coffee color; his features were more regular than my own; his eyes were big and of the troubling kind—sad, humorous, and very beautiful. His large handsome head was set on a crippled body with an enormous hunch on the back. I began walking round him in order to get a good view of the hunch, and then I stood and stared at him fascinated. I believe there was the curve of a smile, in fact there were many smile-curves, in the corners of his mouth, but he kept them under control and returned my gaze seriously for a time. Then he sighed and rolled his eyes, his face taking on an extraordinary look of real suffering.

"Ah, I am waiting for my father!"

"Who is thy father?"

"My father?" He looked astonished. "My father is Edib Bey, of course."

"He is *my* father."

"Well, I'm talking of Edib Bey too, but he is *my*

father. At least he was. I was his son, his first-born, till thou, a black foundling from the streets, came and bewitched both of us. I became crippled and black and thou white and took my place, and I was turned into the street."

His face crumpled into lines; his voice sobbed, his eyes became full of tears, yet watched me furtively. I have never been torn between so many different sensations: belief in my wicked witchery, fear lest I might be found out and sent into the streets and become a negress once more, pity for his miserable fate, and hatred toward him for making me feel all this. I have seen many great actors on the stage since, but, it seems to me even now, never one with such sincere and artistic power of rendering emotion. I was trying hard to swallow the painful lump in my throat to hold back the tears that already stood on my lashes. I needed the strength of a dozen buffaloes to keep my mouth from trembling in ever so many directions.

He crawled toward me, gazed at me, and tried to kiss me.

"Thou dear black witch," he said as father entered the room.

"What tricks are you playing on my little girl, Aga?" he said.

"Telling her not to steal the fathers of such poor orphans as I," he answered.

Father laughed and took me on his knees, but did not trouble to explain what seemed a tragic dilemma to me.

WHEN THE STORY BECOMES MINE

I carried a misgiving in my heart about this until its absurdity gradually made itself apparent to me.

That Bairam night I had my first experience of a theater. There was a French troupe in Pera, and father, with the two inseparable friends of his, Sirry and Hakky Beys, had taken a box. I loved Sirry Bey best of all father's friends. Besides his many services to the country and his undeviating honesty, which had stood the test of Hamid's corruption, he was gentle and highly cultivated. He used to translate Shakspere and read his translations aloud. I did not understand the meaning then, but I liked the sound. "The Merchant of Venice" and "A Comedy of Errors" were his two first published translations.

During the play Sirry Bey took the greatest pains to make me understand what was happening, but it was useless. I was wholly fascinated by the lady in blue with wonderful coloring, who sang, her mouth taking impossible shapes and giving out high and unbelievable sounds. I must have gone to sleep watching her mouth, for I found myself in father's bed the next morning. Abla was in her bed, and they were whispering over me. I called my stepmother Abla, for I could not call her mother, as father thought that it would hurt granny.

One night about this time I begged granny to allow me to learn to read. "Thy father does not want thee to learn before thou art seven," she said. "It is stupid of him. *I* started at three, and in my days children of seven knew the Koran by heart." In spite of this I kept bothering her and even speaking to father about it, so that he at last consented, although I was not fully six yet. Thereupon the house began to get ready to celebrate my *bashlanmak,* my entrance into learning.

Little children in Turkey started to school in those days with a pretty ceremony. A little girl was dressed in silk covered with jewels, and a gold-embroidered bag, with an alphabet inside, was hung round her neck with a gold-tasseled cord. She sat in an open carriage, with a damask silk cushion at her feet. All the little pupils of the school walked in procession after the carriage, forming two long tails on either side. The older ones were the hymn-singers, usually singing the very popular hymn, "The rivers of paradise, as they flow, murmur, 'Allah, Allah.' The angels in paradise, as they walk, sing, 'Allah, Allah.'" At the end of each stanza hundreds of little throats shouted, *"Amin, amin!"*

They went through several streets in this way, drawing into the procession the children and waifs from the quarters they passed through until they reached the school. In the school the new pupil knelt on her damask cushion before a square table, facing the teacher. Kissing the hand of the instructor, she repeated the alphabet after her. Some sweet dish would then be served to the children, and each child received a bright new coin given by the parents of the pupil to be. After this sort of consecration, the little one went every day to school, fetched by the *kalfa,* an attendant who went from one house to another collecting the children from the different houses.

WHEN THE STORY BECOMES MINE

The ceremony was as important as a wedding, and fond parents spent large sums in the effort to have a grander ceremony than their neighbors. Each family who could afford a costly *bashlanmak* would arrange for a few poor children of the quarter to share the ceremony and would thenceforward pay their schooling, as well as that of their own child. The old systematic philanthropy of the Ottomans, although fast disappearing, was not entirely dead yet.

The sight of a children's procession with the grand carriage had always caused me certain excitement, mixed, however, with a longing to be the little girl in the carriage and a fear of being the center of attraction in public.

Father had arranged that I was not to begin by going to school, but a hodja was to come and give me lessons at home. The *bashlanmak* too in my case was not to be the usual one. There was to be a big dinner at home for the men, and the ceremony was to take place at home after the night prayers.

Granny had her own way about my dress for once. She could not bear to have me begin my reading of the holy Koran in a blue serge dress. I remember well the champagne-colored silk frock with lovely patterns on it, and the soft silk veil of the same color, that she got for me instead.

A large number of guests arrived, both from our own neighborhood and also from the palace.

Some one held a mirror in front of me after I was dressed, and I looked strange with the veil over my hair and bedecked with the really beautiful jewels of the palace lady. Fikriyar was moved to tears. "Thou shalt wear a bride's dress and I will hold thy train one day," she said. She was wishing me the one possible felicity for a Turkish woman.

Then hand in hand with Mahmouré Abla, who was unusually subdued, I walked to the large hall where every one had assembled for the ceremony. A young boy chanted the Koran while our hodja sat by the low table swaying himself to its rhythm. Mahmouré Abla had already been to school, and so she only knelt, while I had at the same time to kneel and to repeat the first letters of the alphabet, frightened to death at the sound of my own voice. As I rose I forgot to kiss the hand of the hodja, but some tender voice whispered behind me, "Kiss the hodja's hand." All ceremonies in Turkey, even marriages and Bairams, tend to take on a sad and solemn tone; always the women with wet eyes and the men in softened silent mood. What makes other people rejoice makes the Turk sad.

My lessons took place in the same room in the selamlik, before the same table and in the same kneeling attitude as at the *bashlanmak*. My teacher, who was a regular schoolmaster and busy with his own school in the daytime, could only come to our house in the evenings. Two candles therefore were placed on the table and burned under green shades, while I struggled with the Arabic writing of the holy book.[23] Of course it was

[23] All Moslem children used to learn to read from the Arabic Koran, of which not a word would naturally be understood by a Turkish child. In

difficult to go on without understanding the meaning of the words one read, but the musical sound of it all was some compensation.

Our hodja and his wife were recent immigrants from Macedonia and had built a tiny house behind our own. She taught little girls at home, while his school was in one of the poor quarters of Beshiktash.

Mahmouré Abla, who had been under the severe discipline of Djavidé Hanum, soon took advantage of a state of affairs where there was no rod and no ear-pulling. She joined my lessons, but she never studied, she never repeated any lesson unless she wanted to, and when she found out that our teacher's threat, in his funny Macedonian accent, "Mimuré, thou shalt eat it" ("thou shalt eat the rod," or, "I will whip thee"), "Mimuré, I will pull thy ears," were only a form of speech, she went to much greater lengths than idleness and noise. She actually played, and not only with her doll but with a ball as well.

As often as I could now, I went up-stairs to Teïzé's apartment when Fikriyar was dusting her books. I would beg her to take out the book of African travels and open it for me on the floor. It was too large for me to handle, and when she had laid it down I stretched myself on the floor and tried to decipher it. In this position, resting on my elbows, I would struggle on till my eyes ached. It was so different from the Koran, and the words, even when I could make them out, were

the higher classes they would go on applying their alphabetic knowledge to the reading of their own language.

such that I did not understand.²⁴ Meanwhile, Fikriyar was very happy to have some one to talk to. She started each time from the very beginning, telling me about her childhood, Caucasia, the great emigration, the settlement in Adabazar, and how the chief of her clan sold her in Constantinople to an Egyptian palace.

Her adventures I hardly listened to, but she always ended up with the Circassian youth, my father's protégé. "He must buy me when he gets rich and make me his concubine. We are both Circassians."

But what I remember best of all her stories is a particular Circassian peri who controlled the growth of corn in her country. The peri came on moonlight nights. Fikriyar had seen her standing in their fields, measuring the young corn. *"Rakijaki, rakijaki,"* the peri said, measuring some to her elbow which were to be the largest. *"Mejkus, Mejkus,"* she said, measuring with her tiny fingers those which were to be the tiny shriveled ones.

"What did she look like?" I used to ask.

"She had such large breasts that she threw the right one over her left shoulder and the left one over her right."

From the point of view of comparative folk-lore, this surprising trait has interested me since. It is a characteristic of our Turkish women giants; Devkarisé also. But this particular peri had, besides, flowing hair, waving in the wind and catching the rays of the moon. But

---
²⁴ Literary Turkish of those days was a thing apart from the spoken language, and largely unintelligible except to the initiated.

WHEN THE STORY BECOMES MINE

I cannot be sure whether it was Fikriyar who told me this detail or whether I have added it from my childish fancy.

Before I could read the African travels, Mahmouré Abla brought from Teïzé's library a little book in manuscript. I do not know how she obtained it, but I think Teïzé did not think much of it. As it had the Arabic vowel signs inserted in the text, I could read it for myself, and most unfortunately for me I did read it. It was called "The Adventures of Death."

My mind has a habit of making far too realistic pictures of its impressions—sometimes to my delight, but often to my torture. If I had had the talent of a painter to put these on canvas, it would have eased my mind, but there is no clumsier human being with the pencil than I. My mind has also an inner capacity for idealizing, harmonizing, and synthesizing sounds into wonderful musical combinations. If I had had any talent in this direction, the proper kind of throat, I might have given some happy moments to my kind. As it is, both pictures and sounds, as well as the gestures of life, which are still more expressive than the first two, have accumulated in me in a million shapes and forms, as a music which, on account of its compression, has become a thundering harmony inside me. I cannot get rid of it sufficiently to ease my mind and heart. My struggle to give out some of it with my poor pen has neither eased me nor enabled me to externalize all that I have in me. But as my pen is my only outlet, I have to go on with it.

The writer of "The Adventure of Death" must have been a remarkable person although very crude. He had the imagination of Dante without his genius; and his attempt to ease his burdened soul by describing the fantastic pictures which were torturing his imagination had a far greater success over me than Dante's. It began at the very moment when the angel of death, Azrael, takes one's soul away from the body. His manner was gentle with the good, so that death is an ecstasy of becoming one with Allah; but the pain of wrenching away a sinner's soul is agony beyond words.

He tells the tale as if he had been personally through it, so authentic does it sound. On the first night in the grave the examiners of faith arrive. They stand at the head of the grave and ask: "Who is thy creator? Who is thy prophet?" Now although an imam stays close to the grave after the body is buried and every one else has retired and though the imam repeats the proper answers to refresh the memory of the dead person, yet he will infallibly forget them if he is a sinner, no matter how carefully he has committed to memory the articles of the Islamic faith. And when he stammers and fails to answer, the iron knobs of the rods which the angels carry in their hands will fall heavily on his head, beating it relentlessly. Then the author tells the story of bodily decay in forcible and realistic terms, and the dead suffers and feels in his prison in the earth every detail and accompaniment of the gruesome dissolution, the suffocation, the damp earth, the eternal darkness, the scorpions eating into his brain and destroying his beauty of face, the snakes crawling through his skull and the holes of his decaying skeleton. For years I had to fight this image of the grave every night. I would wake up in the middle of my sleep, jump up in my bed, and move my arms wildly around me, feeling for the earth, which I thought was covering me. In every attack of fever that I had I dreamt of snakes coiling all over my body.

When the angels at last blew the bugle, according to the writer, men rose from their graves and marched to the last judgment. This march to the other world was vivid beyond anything; each class of sinners marched under the sign of its particular sin. There was one class to which Mahmouré Abla drew my attention, the tell-tales. They had their tongues sticking out from the napes of their necks. This she told me to secure her smoking from being reported to the grown-up people of the house.

Yet she committed the sin of telling tales herself in those days most treacherously and did not seem troubled by it in the least.

Seeing that "The Adventure of Death" has brought us into the gloomy region of sins, I may as well deal with one of mine here. It would take, of course, more than a book to tell about any person's sins, and I am no exception, but there are two of mine which I am most ashamed of, one committed at six and the other at twenty-five. I shared my first conscious and despicable sin with Shayesté.

One day she told me in secret that she had begun smoking, and she praised its delights to the height of her powers of language. In answer to my question as to how she obtained the tobacco, she told me that she got it from her father's tobacco-pouch when he was not in the room. Pride rather than moral considerations often keeps people from doing things in secret, and I am afraid I was proud to a sinful degree. Nevertheless I went with Shayesté when grandfather was not in his room and took some of his tobacco. It was the nastiest sensation I ever experienced in my childhood, so much so that no amount of persuasion would make me repeat it and go back and fetch the tobacco-paper which we forgot to bring too. I told Shayesté that I would roll the cigarettes with ordinary paper. But we had no time to smoke that day, and we simply hid the stuff among my dolls.

The next morning, Mahmouré Abla called me from our play-room telling me that father was waiting for me in the garden. I found him pacing up and down under the acacias. He motioned Mahmouré Abla back to the house and kept his hands behind his back, ignoring my attempt to kiss them. He looked at me sternly, sadly, and then began to tell me why he had sent for me and why he did not want any one in the world to know what he was going to tell me. I do not remember his exact expressions. They were solemn, they were serious, and I remember rather my state of acute suffering than his words. I neither cried nor answered; I did not try to kiss his hands any more. I walked back to the house in the misery and humiliation which is much the hardest to bear when one has really been guilty of a mean act. I felt sure that it was Mahmouré Abla who had told, but I was too miserable to care. I did not tell any one about her smoking in revenge, but it has left a certain feeling of disillusionment about her, which I know is ridiculous, but which I cannot even now get rid of. It had a good effect on me; I never smoked till I could do it before every one. This feeling of shame although not so violent was still deeper than my fear of "The Adventure of Death."

It was during the summer of the same year when one evening, in our garden, I realized for the first time my charming old great-uncle, Vely Aga.

All of us had assembled in the garden, as we usually did on summer evenings. Grandfather was smoking, walking up and down under the long vine-trellis. Granny and Teïzé were gardening, while Fikriyar, barefooted, was watering, filling her watering cans from the lions' mouths.

Warm, balmy, and sweet was the garden, while in the liquid blue of the twilight sky trembled one single star in a silvery haze. I must have seen the sky many times before, but this was my first impression of a star. As I was looking up through the leaves at the sky Vely Aga slowly came nearer and patted my head softly. He was dressed in those picturesque blue embroidered loose pantaloons and the vest of the Anatolian notable, and over his fez he wore a soft cream-colored silk turban. He had the large eyes of the Eastern Anatolian, the hooked nose and the white beard. His mild air, soft gestures, and the low, quiet voice were as different from grandfather's as the windless summer air is from a storm, yet both had their personal charm for me. He had come from Kemah partly to visit his eldest brother, and partly to buy presents for a son of his who was to be married after the Kurban Bairam. He set me on his knees and looked at my face, saying that I had the eyes and the eyebrows of my Kemah relatives. "So much like Kezban she would be, if she only had pink cheeks," he said to granny. Whoever Kezban was, every one from Kemah told me that I was a city reproduction of her. I asked Uncle Vely about the star. He looked puzzled but could not say what it was. "I don't know what it is," he said. "I know that Allah has created it and the rest of the heavens for us." How incomprehensible it seemed to me! Allah, who created the angels to beat the heads of the dead with iron-knobbed rods, and who kept eternal fire and shut the dead up in earthly prisons, this Allah had also created this most beautiful light. Such a combination of love and torture made me think that Allah had after all as many aspects and attributes as we poor human beings.

Uncle Vely stayed with us a fortnight. He occupied a room in the selamlik. He brought with him a subtle refinement, a balmy atmosphere; and the feeling in the house, which was becoming distraught by the continual ill health of Uncle Kemal, by the fear of the old people that they might lose their last child, and by their money troubles, was soothed into an interval of happy peace. He bought all kinds of beautiful silk vests, blue costumes, printed kerchiefs, and ivory combs, and he

THE YARD OF THE EYOUB MOSQUE WHERE I FED THE PIGEONS AT EVERY YEARLY VISIT

WHEN THE STORY BECOMES MINE

started for Kemah sometime before the Kurban Bairam.[25] I think I missed him most of all, but I was beginning to decipher the book of African travels, which consoled me more or less.

It was about this time that our hodja begged granny to allow us to go to a *bashlanmak* ceremony in his school. Mahmouré Abla was placed with the hymn-chanters and I with those who repeat the *amin*. We walked to the boys' house in two long rows, and he, the son of humble parents and with no hired carriage, merely walked in front of the procession. The little girl near me in the procession had a yellow print dress and a bright headkerchief of the same color. I was so distracted by this color that I was never in time with the general *amin*, and each time I was late the little yellow girl nudged me in the ribs, vigorously reminding me of my duty. When I heard my own ridiculous squeak all alone, I felt hot and cold with shame, all the length of that long, humble Ouzounjova Road with the cool vegetable gardens on one side and the little newly built houses on the other. So the little procession marched on in the dust-cloud it raised, chanting, "The rivers of Paradise, as they flow, murmur, 'Allah, Allah!'"

When the little ones arrived at the school, a watery dish, meant to be sweet, was served with rather greasy wooden spoons. As the children sat happily round it, Mahmouré Abla pulled my sleeve and said I was not to touch it. The pained look of the hodja and my

---

[25] Kurban Bairam is a four days' festival about two months later than the Shekèr Bairam. This one is celebrated with the killing of sheep.

sudden sense of our spiritual separation from the poor children hurt me keenly.

I have a sad feeling about this time in general. My nebulous life was clearing away, and more distinct forms of thought and perception were assailing me, so that I was turning gradually into a tortured interrogation-point.

The day before the Kurban Bairam, granny took me for our annual visit to the *türbeh* of Eyoub.[26] Before my birth, it was very much hoped that I should be a boy, and father had vowed that he would name me, after the saint in Eyoub, Halid. When I disappointed them by turning out to be a girl, they persisted in giving me the feminine form of Halid, which is Halidé; and every year either father or granny took me to the Holy Tomb and sacrificed a sheep for the poor of Eyoub.

As we were driving this year to Eyoub, granny stopped at Hadji Bekir's[27] and bought *loukoum*. "The softest you have," she said. "It is for an old lady of a hundred and ten."

"Who is she?" I asked, as the carriage drove on.

"My teacher," she said. "I have not been to see her

[26] Eyoub, the Turkish form of Job, is a suburb of Constantinople just outside the city walls on the Golden Horn. It is said to have been thus named to commemorate the fact that Eyoub, or Halid (as he was also called), one of the most devoted of Mohammed's followers, made a raid and entered the Byzantine city some hundreds of years before its final fall before the Turkish armies in 1453. The Mosque of Eyoub is one of the most sacred. A *türbeh* is a small building round a tomb, often of great architectural beauty.

[27] The great sweet-shop in Istamboul, specially renowned for its Turkish delight.

for some time, and I need her blessing,[28] especially just now."

So that year we called on the oldest lady in Eyoub, living in the oldest house in the place. Her face was like old white crumpled parchment, her eyes blurred and indefinite in color like those of a new-born baby; and she wore a snow-white muslin veil over her head. As she sat there propped up with pillows, her body looked tiny and dried. Somehow she made me think of Hava Hanum's stock description of the pope of the Christians: ever so many hundreds of years old, wrinkled and parched like yellow wax, and always kept in cotton-wool. Not but that this old lady appeared very energetic in her own way, spoke sweetly, remembered everything, and had none of the ugliness of old age, which I perceived in after years in others. She made one think of a precious candle slowly going out because the oil is all used. She called granny "my child," asked me to come close up to her, and then prayed for the happiness of granny's house, giving us all her blessing in clear tones. A younger old lady who was her daughter-in-law waited on her. The old house, its furniture, and the two old ladies make a regular Rembrandt picture in my mind.

Then we went to the mosque for granny's afternoon prayers and passed on to the Holy Tomb through the wonderful mosque-yard, with its old birches full of

---

[28] A teacher's blessing is especially respected. One of the sayings of Ali is: "If some one teaches me one letter, I am his slave for life."

cooing pigeons, and the blind beggars sitting in a row.

In the green, cool silence of the *türbeh,* the guardian made me go three times through his large black rosary; he gave us sacred water and fragments of the broom with which the *türbeh* was swept. This was to be burned, and I was to inhale it, as it had healing qualities.

At the foot of the tomb, granny knelt, clutching the iron railings. Her lips moved, and a few drops fell from her eyes and slid down her wrinkled white cheeks. I have never seen granny look as lovely as she did that day. As we walked backward keeping our faces reverentially toward the tomb, I asked her in whispers why she had cried.

"I don't want Kemal to die," she said simply.

When Kurban Bairam actually came, the sad and solemn feeling I had had at Eyoub had lost its intensity. That morning I saw eight big sheep, henna-painted, all bleating in the stables. In one corner of the garden some holes had already been dug, and grandfather was still busy with the preparations. He showed me each sheep one after the other. "This is Kemal's. This is thine. This is Reffet's, the child who is in heaven."

I was heartbroken at the idea of killing these beautiful animals and asked whether it was necessary to kill them all.

"How wilt thou cross the bridge Sirrat to heaven?" he asked. "It is finer than a hair and sharper than a sword, but those who have killed their sheep in obedience to the holy commandment pass over it on the back of these sheep, who go up to heaven and wait for us by the bridge."

Then he told me the story from the Koran, identical with the Old Testament account of Abraham's sacrifice of Isaac, except that Isaac is replaced by Ismail in the Islamic tradition. He looked like Abraham himself, his white beard blowing in the wind, his powerful dark arms digging the pits.

There was a little discussion at dinner-time between him and Uncle Kemal. Every male ought to sacrifice his own sheep, but Uncle Kemal, hating the sight of blood, had always refused to do it, and grandfather's Anatolian soul was wrathful at such Constantinopolitan squeamishness.

Early next morning I woke up to hear deep manly bass voices chanting, *"Allah Ekber, Allah Ekber,"* to the incomparable Turkish melody. I sat up in my bed and wondered for a time what was happening; but I soon realized that the sheep were being killed. Once again I felt that slanting cut go through my whole body; and, closing my ears, I lay on my face, my head covered with the quilt. How I hated it, and all the bloody inhuman side of religion, which commands people to shed blood and hurt helpless creatures! I was carried in Fikriyar's arms down-stairs. Every one was in the kitchen, busy cutting up the sheep for the poor. Every one had a blood sign on the forehead from the sheep sacrificed for him, and I was signed with the same sign too.

About this time father took a house in the neighborhood of Beshiktash for his younger family and left the house in Yildiz. He used to ride up to Yildiz on his big bay horse, and in the evenings he usually called in at granny's and took a cup of coffee. I often rode on the horse with the groom and played in the Yildiz garden. The pompous brilliant selamliks [29] of Abdul Hamid I could watch from the Terrace of the Ambassadors just opposite the Yildiz mosque. Abdul Hamid had this mosque built so as not to have to risk his life by taking the longer drive to an Istamboul mosque. Every Friday the place was set out like a grand theatrical stage. Abdul Hamid's Albanian body-guard in bright red, his Tripolitan black guards in green and red, his numberless aides-de-camp in gilt uniforms, the generals, the officers, the royal sergeants (chosen for their good looks) in blue jackets with long hanging sleeves lined with red, the incredibly beautiful horses pawing the ground impatiently, or stepping in time to the lively "March of His Majesty," the grooms in blue and red covered with real gold embroidery, the lovely music, the ambassadors in their grand uniforms, the numerous court officials in their elegant tight long black coats embroidered in front, all elegant men with harmonious and soft gestures and salutations . . . and I, lifted on the shoulders of Ahmet Shevket Bey (an old pasha now, but a royal sergeant and brother-in-law of the sultan then) —we all waited for his Majesty to come out from the great portals in his carriage and make that momentary

[29] The Friday ceremony of the sultan going to prayer.

WHEN THE STORY BECOMES MINE

passage to the mosque, saluting right and left as he flashed by. Opposite him sat Osman Pasha, the old hero of Plevna and of many popular songs too, his hands folded on his lap. The public favorite was thus exhibited in an almost humiliating position, in an enforced attitude of respect and subserviency to the sultan whom every one feared and many hated. I did not realize then that the man with the imposing nose and shifty eyes was the last Turkish emperor at his highest ascendancy. Yet thirty-odd years later I rode through the same door, opened by a half-blind porter, probably a man who had often seen me playing about the place in former days. Everything at Yildiz was and is still in decay, as all vain and wrong exhibitions of power should be. . . . There are indeed lots of these decaying palaces which used to be the scenes of pomp and royal ceremony. They are doomed, yet other human symbols of the same wrong conception of power, though embodied in different forms, rise over the old decay. Sometimes it makes one feel hopeless to watch the dull human intelligence which refuses to learn from the experience of the past.

A baby had been born in my father's house about this time, a beautiful little girl called Neilüfer. She was my sister they said, and she, as well as her *dadi,* who came often to granny's, drew me to my father's house very often now. The *dadi* was a Kurdish woman, a tall slender person dressed in very picturesque native costume. She wore red *shalvars* [30] and a dress over these, which was opened at both sides and in front, these pieces being

---
[30] Loose trousers.

lifted and pinned to her belt. Over her head, she wore a long soft printed material of many colors, which floated in the air as she walked with the particular pretty swing of Kurdish girls. Her dark eyes squinted when she sang, and she often sang the following lullaby, rocking the baby on her knees.

"The pears shake on the branch and get sweeter as they shake. If the boy is a vizir, he has to beg the girl . . . *nanni, nanni* . . ." She was the original of the Kurdish heroine in my novel, "Kalb Arisé" (heartache), and her popularity with the public I believe is due to the pleasure I had in putting her into a book.

I got my second and last scolding from my father about this time, and I am glad to be able to say that on this occasion if I was guilty it was unconscious guilt.

Swearing attracted me very much as a child. Every one around me talked in a more or less refined manner, and, as it seemed to me, with a stupidly tame and dull politeness. Even grandfather, who had a touch of the common people, did not swear at all as the men and boy porters and the cabmen in the streets do. I used to stop and repeat to myself whatever I heard them say, quite unaware of the meaning. These phrases had a kind of flavor that was excluded from my own home. So one evening while dining at my father's house I repeated to him a whole series of these violent oaths. Knowing their meaning, I cannot repeat them now. Father's face was crimson, and lifting his knife he shook it at me angrily. In a moment I felt wronged and hurt, and pushing my plate away I began to cry silently. At first he waited for my tears to cease, but they did not. They went on falling, falling quietly. I felt a nasty scar somewhere inside me which hurt so that it made my tears flow on. Father, finally, must have suffered even more than I, for he began to caress me and give me bright coins. He tried to play with me, but in vain. It was the greatest childish humiliation I remember. Years later I saw a parallel case of suffering in my dog, and I am tempted to tell the story.

The dog before it belonged to me was with the revolutionary band of the Circassian Edhem, and had been evidently trained to catch sheep from the flocks and bring them to the band. The dog was the manliest and noblest creature I have ever known, and certainly did not realize the moral wrong of this clever feat.

I had only had him for a few days, but we were learning to love each other. In my long lonely rides he always ran after my horse and used to make signs of delight at the sight of every flock of sheep. One day, my orderly came in and told me that Yoldash had dragged a sheep out of a flock and brought it to him. I hastily ran out. There he was, sitting and wagging his tail, laughing his broadest and jolliest dog laugh. I walked up to him and whipped him hard.

The surprised pain of the dog and the suffering expressed in his barks at my incomprehensible cruelty reminded me of my own state of mind when I saw my father's knife held up and I knew that he was ashamed of me, though I could not understand the reason. Yoldash will never know why masters or mistresses he loves are so different in their conceptions of wrong, as I have learned in later years.

This is the way the great sorrow began which ended forever our life in granny's wisteria-covered house. Granny was making syrup for us in the dining-room, and the day was very hot. Uncle Kemal came back from his office and joined us, asking for some of the cool drink. Things seemed perfectly normal to me, when all of a sudden granny hastened out and fetched a bowl of cold water. Dipping a handkerchief into it, she put it on Uncle Kemal's head, and then she, with Hava Hanum, helped him to walk up to his room.

A silent house, people moving about on tiptoe, Mahmouré Abla continually getting scolded for making a noise, which only produced worse or more frequent outbursts of anger from her.

How long this oppressive silence lasted I cannot tell. Granny was always up-stairs. Teïzé seldom appeared below. She was nursing Uncle Kemal. (Granny's sons were destined to be nursed by palace ladies on their death-beds.) Grandfather grumbled and wandered aimlessly about, and we were forgotten, left to ourselves. I used to sit down-stairs and feel the heavy air laden with mysterious warnings. Something in the air had grown as hard as the darkness in Nevres Badji's room, and it seemed to be actually pressing upon me and hurting me physically by its weight. A silent child by nature, and no longer with Shayesté to talk to, even occasionally, I was forgetting the sound of my own voice in ordinary talk. I remember the surprise with which I heard myself repeating the Koran aloud to the hodja, and I can even tell the very *surés* [31] I was learning at the time.

One morning we woke and found granny's bed empty and unused. Fikriyar came into the room and began to dress me hurriedly. Father was standing at the door, which quieted Mahmouré Abla. He was the only one in the house whom she loved and respected.

We went straight to father's house. No explanation was given us, and the same heavy air and the same painful expectation seemed to follow us there. But I found a new comfort. Once more I took refuge in the sweet friendship of a dog. Her name was Flora, and she belonged to a valuable breed, so they said. She had extremely delicate paws, and a short-haired coat, brown, shiny, and soft as velvet; with light brown eyes, very large and reddish rays of vivid light shooting from their depths at times. She was miserable in that house, although for very different reasons from mine. No one wanted her except father and me. Gülly Hanum would not let her into her room, because she prayed five times a day, like a good Moslem, and she did not believe that angels came to places frequented by dogs. Abla did not want her in her room, for she tore the bedcovers and quilts. Rosa, the Armenian woman-servant, with a bosom larger than me and Flora put together and a regular black mustache, did not want Flora anywhere in the house. The only places where she was allowed to go were the small marble hall and the terrace. But

[31] *Surés* are verses of the Koran.

even there she was often scolded. The poor creature whined and cried at this cruel treatment so sadly that each time she was hit by Rosa I felt that same old slanting pain through my body. As it was a cold autumn I was forbidden to go out to her, but I escaped all the same and played with her and kissed her enough, as I hoped, to make up for Rosa's hard treatment.

In the mornings father used to have us all in his room. Mahmouré Abla was allowed to hold the baby on her lap, while Flora and I sat on father's knee. Flora was caressed as much as I, and he used to say, "They have the same eyes, Flora and Halidé." I believe we had. Both had the same sadness and the same wonder at what we found in this world, where we felt lonely and homesick, though for what precisely I don't know—probably for a kindlier state of things altogether. Flora must be dead and happy in a dog's paradise by now, but I have had to go on from one stage to another, seeing the same tame and apparently harmless human specimens of my childhood act in such a way that I have felt not only the sadness and wonder of a dog but a dog's rage as well.

The foreboding atmosphere came to a climax one evening. I slept in Gülly Hanum's room, and that particular night I woke up with a nameless anxiety and fear. I could sleep no longer. Gülly Hanum tried in vain to soothe me. I mention this particularly, for since that occasion, which was perhaps my first telepathic experience, I have felt telepathically every real sorrow which has affected any one I loved.

WHEN THE STORY BECOMES MINE

Early the next morning there was an unusual commotion in the house. Father came down dressed, and whispered distinctly to Gülly Hanum that we were not to leave the house that day, and I was not to go to the rooms which opened on the main road.

I stayed in the room with Gülly Hanum, daring the angels to keep Flora with me. Flora seemed as much oppressed as I was and whined continually. I heard everybody trying to keep Mahmouré Abla from going out. "I saw the caldron and the *teneshir*,"[32] she screamed. "They are for *him*." Finally I heard the door slam and knew she had escaped, and I asked no questions.

Two days later father took me up to granny's house. We went through the selamlik door and walked up the selamlik stairs. In the middle of the guest-room there was a floor-bed,[33] and grandfather was sitting up in it, leaning against Suleiman Aga, a new servant and a distant relative of his from Kemah, whom I now saw for the first time. He was breathing heavily, and his eyes looked intently at me. A depth of sorrow and the sudden realization of the mystery of the hereafter seemed to be in them. They were bloodshot, wide open, impressive. He motioned father to bring me to his bed. I leaned over toward him, and he patted me on the head

---

[32] Each Moslem quarter has a caldron and a *teneshir* (stretcher,) which are used respectively to heat the water for washing, and to lay the dead out. Men and women are specially hired to do the washing of the dead. Those who follow this profession keep it a secret, for it is looked upon as something very degrading.

[33] The usual old-fashioned Turkish bed was merely a mattress laid on the floor.

for a while, then motioned again to father to take me out. I returned immediately to father's home.

A few days later Mahmouré Abla and I came back to granny's house. There was neither Uncle Kemal nor grandfather. The old man had followed his last child to the grave in three days.

Granny sat in her usual corner. Her face looked stupid, expressionless, and empty. But as the human body reacts against disease, so does the human soul against sorrow. Granny's empty face, dry eyes, and the listless hands, which I had seen without work only during this short interval, were getting a fresh purpose. She was going to leave the scene of her sorrow and take a new house on the other side of the Bosphorus, in Scutari. As soon as she had found the place she wanted, the old wisteria-covered house began to be broken up, most of the furniture was sold, and the things we were to take were collected together and packed.

The morning of our departure and the night before it are marked by two childish memories. Playing with granny's canary in Hava Hanum's room, Mahmouré Abla dropped a box of blocks with which we used to make pictures, and killed the bird. "We will pretend that we found it dead. Do thou go and tell granny and cry a little." I, who was too timid to express the most natural desire of my own, could not possibly bring myself to do such a thing as this, needing as it did a boldness which I totally lacked. I must have refused her, for she said, "Wet thy eyes from thy mouth then and come with me." She ran up-stairs dragging me by the hand. She darted into granny's peaceful room with a showy grief.

Granny, reading a Turkish translation of one of the Dumas types of novel so charming and so distinctive a product of French genius, was sitting on her bed. Her lamp was on a low table, and she was reading aloud to herself as was her habit. She looked over her glasses at us, and I think that her face had got back some expression into it, for she smiled, as she said: "Come here, Halidé. Tell me if it is true." But I must have looked pitifully distressed, for she changed the subject suddenly. "It is time for you to go to bed. We have to start early to-morrow," she said. As Fikriyar undressed me, I listened to the story granny was reading. It was about a kidnapped girl and two brothers, one blue-eyed, standing for goodness, and the other black-eyed, standing for wickedness. Since then I have read ever so many novels of this kind, hoping to find the rest of the story, but I have never succeeded. As for granny, though I asked her, she had forgotten its name, and so my curiosity as to the fate of the poor girl has never been satisfied.

The next morning I got up with a sore feeling against Mahmouré Abla. I had a dim idea that granny knew about the canary and that we had made ourselves very ridiculous to the grown-ups. I hid a few earthworms in my hands and walked up to Mahmouré Abla, who was packing the dolls' beds. "Shut thy eyes and open thy mouth," I said, and she did as I told her, hoping for the usual sweet which we offered each other in this manner.

Throwing the wriggling creatures into her mouth I ran away. I cannot to this day think or explain how I planned such a disagreeable revenge.

Thus closed the first period of my life, in the wisteria-covered house, at Beshiktash.

ENTRANCE TO EYOUB MOSQUE

CHAPTER III

OUR VARIOUS HOMES IN SCUTARI

THE new house was in Selimié, an old Turkish quarter looking over to the Marmora across the inky cypress line of the Karadja Ahmed Cemetery on one side, while on the other hand the misty Istamboul Point with its hundreds of minarets rose softly into the blue dome of sky beyond the Bosphorus. The house belonged to an old minister of war, and one half was still occupied by the owners. But our side was even as large as our old house in Beshiktash, while a wild garden, especially full of rose-bushes, stretched toward the cemeteries, giving us an ample sense of space and freedom. The whole quarter had a number of immense wooden houses purpled with age and on the brink of decay, each belonging to some grand vizir of half a century ago. Granny, repelled by the raw ugliness of new things, unerringly chose these beautiful old places in spite of their being half tumbled down. The house itself and a great part of the whole quarter is now burned, but I have several times since wandered among its ashes in my visits to the old haunts. Besides the rose-bushes, the garden had a very big walnut-tree, up which Mahmouré Abla used to climb daily. Its height made me dizzy even to look up at it.

The imam of Selimié was engaged after our arrival to come and teach us every evening. Before long father came to live with us too, bringing Abla and his whole household. There was a new baby girl now, Nighiar, who took Neilüfer's place as the most despotic and spoiled creature in the household. My life slowly drifted from the harem to the selamlik, which was, however, now no longer as important a place as it had been in grandfather's lifetime. The men-servants interested me more than Abla's Anatolian maids and Fikriyar. There were no more evening talks in Hava Hanum's room, for she had taken charge of Neilüfer, and the child was put to bed in her room early in the evening.

Suleiman Aga stayed only for a short time, for on account of being a distant relation he took on such airs that he displeased granny. To me he was distinctly attractive, for he was full of fairy-stories of Eastern Anatolia, and also of personal adventures, which I thought even more wonderful. Mahmouré Abla teased him incessantly, because she found out that he had three wives in Kemah. He explained the reason for his polygamy in words which I cannot forget, and which I think made me feel that he was justified. He classed his wives according to their capacity to cook *pilaf*.[1] "My first wife," he would say, "cooked it badly. It was much too dry, so I married the second, hoping for something better; but she, not knowing my taste in *pilaf,* and thinking to please me by her economy, cooked it drier

[1] Known to the English as "pilau"—the national dish made of rice which appeared at the end of almost every Turkish meal.

still. So I married a third before the second had been with me forty days. Lo! a *pilaf* appeared delicious and buttery, so much so that the butter dripped down from my mustache and beard. Then I felt that I had found the woman I wanted, and I have never married again since."

After Suleiman Aga appeared Ahmed Aga, a short small man from Eghin, dark, sly, and intelligent; a man who could read and write and handle, or rather rule, his masters with psychological insight. From him I got a great deal of my early education. The fact that it was not given in lesson form made it all the more effective and appealed to the more artistic part of my nature. It was by a mere chance that I fell under the influence of a man of his type, but it was this chance that opened to me the folk-lore, the popular Turkish literature, which none of the rest of my generation of writers have enjoyed.

As some one had discovered a musical talent in me, which I never possessed, I began to take piano-lessons about this time. It must have been a funny proceeding, for I had to be lifted on the chair, and my hands, though naturally big, were not yet big enough to strike the notes properly. Still I worked on at it earnestly, as I did with the rest of my lessons, but I lived only when Ahmed Aga was reading stories or when we were wandering together in the cemeteries or over the meadows stretching toward Haidar Pasha.

The reading of Ahmed Aga covers a period of nearly three years; that is, from the time when he first came until I had been at the American College for my first year. The first story I had from him was "Battal Gazi." I found Ahmed Aga reading a big black book one day and asked him to tell me the story. He read something which charmed me so intensely that I got hold of the book and struggled on by myself, reading aloud and asking him a thousand questions about things I did not understand. So this crude story, which was the great military epic of the janizaries and had fired their imagination in their martial feats, was my first plunge into the heroic fiction of olden times.

Battal Gazi,[2] a man from Malatia, really lived and fought against the Byzantines. His tomb is in Seid Gazi, a place near Eskishehir, the scene of hard battles between the Greeks and the Turkish Nationalists in 1921.

It was not so much the meager historical facts in the book but its Oriental imagination which took hold of me. It was as long as the African travels, so that despite hard reading it took me more than six months to get through. The book is a series of battles; and the color, the force, and the sound of fighting are there. Battal's war-cry sends twenty infidels to hell, their eternal abode as he calls it. He is so big, such a symbol of force and fear, that the Greek women sent their naughty children to sleep by frightening them with his name. There is another mighty man with him, three hundred years old, once a companion of the Holy Prophet, who has, how-

[2] *Gazi* is an old Moslem title given to those who fight for the Faith and who are thereby entitled to a place in paradise.

ever, left him behind on earth so that he may help the Gazi in this world.

Battal kidnaps one Greek princess after another, and the Byzantine Cæsar builds the Leander Tower in the middle of the Bosphorus to hide the most beautiful one from the great Gazi. But of course he finds and marries her all the same. The struggle goes on for a generation, but the name of the Byzantine Cæsar is always Heraclius; his army each time is exactly three hundred thousand men, while the Gazi's army numbers only a few thousand. It is, however, not the men of the Turkish army but the Gazi and the Old Man who caused the Greek routs and killed more by their very war-cries than the Greeks could by real fighting. So said the book, with its tremendous din of battle, the high dust-clouds rising under the tramp of armies, the danger, the clever escapes, and the great victories. The book could not have charmed the early janizary ancestors of ours more than it did me and Ahmed Aga.

The next book of Ahmed Aga's was on the same kind of funny yellow paper and in the same bad Persian print as the first. It was in verse, and told all about Abamouslin Horassani. This was the Persian hero who took the part of the fallen house of Abbassides against the Ommiads. The struggle was long, bloody, and cruel beyond human endurance. It almost provides a parallel to the Inquisition in Spain. I confess that the book gave me cold shudders, and I liked it distinctly less than Battal's frank and picturesque story, but through it I got an insight into the subtle and complicated Asiatic soul, with its inheritance from how many forgotten civilizations permeating the chivalrous Islamic Arabic world and introducing there its germs of decay, which completely destroyed its political unity and independence.

The wonderful Islamic democracy, based on the people's choice of great and idealist leaders, full of humanity and common sense, became an Asiatic despotism of dynasties, based on personal ambition, distrust, and mutual hatred, leading to the unscrupulous and diabolic destruction of each other and of hordes of innocent people supposed to be on one or the other side.

The book seemed to squeeze my heart in an iron band, tightening with the ugly passions and demonstrations of power of the famous heroes. I wondered all the time what the simple little children were doing when all this bloody and cruel struggle was going on in a country, whether they dared to go into the streets and play, and what sort of nights they had and what dreams they dreamed. Years after when in Syria I was walking in the Beirut streets with Colonel Fuad Bey, the chief of staff, and the little Arab children saluted him, as they usually do salute uniforms, he suddenly turned to me and said: "The saluting of children shows that there is something wrong in our rule. They should not be aware of us." Whenever I see or read of a great military hero performing his deeds, and of history or literature recording them, I wonder in the same way, not about the children only, but about the simple grown-up people as well. If only history would refuse to record martial glories, and literature and art to immortalize them, there might be some semblance of peace and relative human happiness in the world.

Neither Battal Gazi nor Abamouslin Horassani were my personal heroes. It was rather the grandiose scenario of their lives, and the ensemble of the dramatic events in which they took part, which riveted my imagination. But I found my hero at last in Ali, the fourth caliph, the Lion of Allah and the son-in-law of the Prophet.

The stories of Ali were also war-tales, but I never wondered about the fate of children and the simple crowd under his sway. On the contrary I felt confident that they had a greater peace of mind and felt safer simply because Ali lived among them. Ali mostly killed dragons who ate people up. He destroyed the personified fear of the primitive mind against which the others of his time had not the strength to stand. There is a strange similarity in the popular heroes of all peoples. The fighters of great battles, the slayers of men, even when these are the enemies of their countries, are admired, but feared at the same time; and their fame rises or falls according to the outlook of the times. Napoleon or Alexander have not kept their position; but the heroes of the popular mind, the killers of dragons, are eternally beloved, whether it is the northern Siegfried, the Russian St. George, or the Arabic Ali. Man always has a tender spot for such in his heart. In some way they express the fight against darkness and fear, the hero who does not stand in the historical arena for personal success but for the peace of his fellow-men's minds and their moral security.

From the material and the political point of view, Ali is the least successful Islamic hero. Every adversary of his takes advantage of his nobility of heart. In the Battle of Saffein his enemies, unable to conquer him in fair fight, put Korans on the ends of their spears and appeal to his veneration for the sacred word. Ayesha, the great woman warrior and orator, the widow of Mohammed, merciless when she wins, is forever taking advantage of his chivalrous respect for women and of his admiration of the Prophet. He finally dies unsuccessful but undaunted, always morally clean, manly and humane to his enemies, tender and good to the weak. No wonder there are so many religious sects that worship him, not only as a great hero but even as the incarnation of Allah. The Western mind's conception of Christ's achievement of success in the highest spiritual domain, obtained at the cost of suffering, shame, and a humiliating death, has its counterpart in the mind of the Moslem in the personality of Ali.

During our own early republican struggles at Angora, Mustafa Kemal Pasha was studying the epoch-making struggles of the Islamic Republic in the seventh century A. D. I was interested to observe his contempt for what he considered Ali's weakness. "Ali was a fool," he used to say.

Mahmouré Abla was eleven years old now and wore the veil when she was outside; but nothing would persuade her to do so in the garden, although it was exposed to the view of the passers-by, having only a low railing instead of a wall. She ran out and played there like any tomboy, usually perched on a high branch. A queer scene took place under the walnut-tree one afternoon. She was up in the tree picking walnuts and throwing them down to me, when Fikriyar came running out and told us the *geurüjü* [3] had come for Mahmouré, and she must come in instantly to get ready to see them. This Mahmouré Abla obstinately refused to do, and she did not move till the whole household had gathered under the tree, including granny, who begged her for some time most ineffectively. Although granny did not think of marrying her off so young, still the *geurüjü* could not be refused lest they should never come again.

Finally she descended and went in. They dressed her, I remember, in some of our stepmother's clothes—her own grand grown-up dresses not being, I suppose, yet fully prepared for her—and she followed Fikriyar, who went in before her carrying the coffee. The best chair in the house was put in the middle of the room for her. She made the proper graceful salutation to the company and then sat down, while the ladies slowly sipped their coffee, inspected her carefully, smiled their formal smiles, and made formal remarks about the

---

[3] Literally, the seers. When a girl is known to be of marriageable age, ladies from neighboring families will call to look at her and report on her appearance to a would-be bridegroom. If a girl does not show herself on such occasions, the word will probably go round that it is useless to seek her hand.

weather and the social position of the bridegroom. When the first lady put her cup on the tray this was the signal for the departure of the would-be bride. She saluted and retired. The time taken by the *geurüjü* in drinking their coffee was the clue to their opinion of the girl. One often heard it asked with painful excitement after a *geurüjü* visit whether they had handed back their coffee-cups too soon or not. Although the first time was exciting enough, the business was in reality a dull and unbearable ceremony. But it was the key to the entrance to life for the Turkish girls of that time.

One afternoon granny sent us to the theater in Haidar Pasha with Hava Hanum. We were to see Abdurazzak, the famous Turkish comedian of that time. When Turkish art is properly studied he will have an acknowledged place as the Nassireddin Hodja of the Turkish stage.

The Turkish theater had two origins. The first was the national one, *orta oyoun*,[4] which corresponds in some ways with the first European open-air plays. These representations consisted mostly of reviews, skits on the peculiarities of all the different nationalities and classes in the country, satires on social vices, or veiled criticism of the political evils of the day. It was mostly improvised by the actors on the stage, although of course based on some sort of plan or story agreed on beforehand.

The second origin was entirely French. This was introduced by Namik Kemal, Noury, and Ahmed Midhat

[4] Open-air plays.

Beys. They founded the Guedik Pasha Theater about 1867 and translated or adapted plays from the French for performance there. Gülly Agop, an Armenian, a talented actor, with his troupe, really started the romantic style of acting in Turkey. He and his whole company were trained in Turkish pronunciation by Namik Kemal. Ahmed Vefik Pasha's adaptation of Molière and the translations of Dumas *fils* furnished the Turkish stage with comedy and romantic drama to begin with; and Kemal himself wrote some patriotic plays which became very popular. This Europeanized school continues to the present time and has formed the origin and the basis of the Turkish stage of to-day. We have now good Turkish actors, although the influence of the French stage is still very marked.

At the same time the open-air national theater, the *orta oyoun,* was affected by this change. It migrated from the open air to fragile wooden stages with closed roofs. These were most affected by Molière's humor in their comic plays, but they continued to give old Turkish love-legends such as "Leila Mejnoun" and "Asli Kerem" for their romantic dramas, queerly dramatized by the actors themselves. This still goes on in the second-rate theaters to which the poorer classes go.

My first impression of the Turkish theater was the crowded condition of the place. It was crammed. The women's part, divided off by lattices, smelled of every imaginable thing. Every one was eating all kinds of fruit and sweets, throwing the bits on the floor, drinking syrups, calling for more; and through all this eager business the play went on as an exciting accompaniment.

The entry of Abdi aroused a perfect thunder of applause. He was a fine middle-aged man, with a round brown beard and eyes such as only great comedians have. They seemed to me to have points in them; they were smiling, mocking, and at the same time very, very sad. Their liquid mobility of expression was wonderful as they passed from one mood to another. The continual roar of laughter, the fond and loving gaiety his presence aroused, could be only explained by the subtle immaterial quality of a real artist. The recital of any of his scenes may not mean much to a European reader now, but every one who went to see him was infected with his humor, which was as much that of the masses as Nassireddin Hodja's and the Karageuz's.

Abdul Hamid feared the popularity of two men, Osman Pasha and Abdurazzak. He kept Osman Pasha away from the public by attaching him to his royal person, and he followed the same tactics with Abdi. The famous comedian was taken into the royal Music and Amusement Department and was forbidden to play in public. A despot is not a real despot if he is not jealous of every popular talent not exclusively used for his royal pleasure, and permitted to the public only through him. It is not perhaps political supremacy that has the greatest influence on the people. Art has a still greater power, and once it has gained sway, it cannot be dethroned from the public heart. Nero's theatrical caprice was only a despot's natural desire for lasting power. Abdi's life in the palace created a series of legends, and he was restored to the public after the Constitutional Revolution of 1908. But the interval of his absence corresponded with such a poor and imitative period in our theatrical life that the public taste was utterly perverted. I saw him in 1914, and it was really a pitiful spectacle. He had had to act in some vile films in order to regain the notice of the public, and when he appeared between the acts with his famous broom, in the dress of the stupid servant, there were only a dozen small children and six grown-ups present. I shall never forget him as he came on the stage. We clapped with all the sincerity of his old audiences, and he stood leaning on his broom and smiling at us in a friendly and intimate way. The sadness and the conscious deception of that artistic smile actually hurt one.

About this time father took us to a circus, and the young girl in the jockey's costume who made the horses jump took my breath away with such admiration that for a long time afterward I had the greatest ambition to be a circus girl.

At this time in my wanderings in the cemeteries of Karadja Ahmed with Ahmed Aga I often saw an old man with white beard and untidy clothes walking aimlessly among the graves. One day I met him with granny, and to my great surprise she walked up to him and asked him how he was. Later she told us his story, which impressed me strangely. He was a man hardly forty years old, but he had lost his wife about fifteen years ago, and his mind had wandered after her so that for a whole year he had raved, trying to open her grave and see her once more. Finally, after consulting religious opinion, they had the grave opened. The sight of the half-decayed body of his wife brought his senses back, but he still haunted the tomb. In that cemetery of forgotten and half-destroyed graves his wife's always had flowers and a nightly lantern burning over it.

After moving to several houses of the same type as the one I have already described, we took one at Ayazma by the sea-shore, on the Scutari side of the Bosphorus. This also was spacious and had a lovely back garden with a rich cluster of plum-trees. In front of the house men used to come to wash in the sea the pretty printed muslins which are made by the hundreds in Turkey. Hung on strings between sticks stuck in the sand, they fluttered their colors above the bright beach, of which at times each pebble would seem to catch the evening sun, all together glistening in a thousand hues, while the sea-waves with their frothy crests washed them in a slow harmony. Leander's Tower was only about a hundred meters away in the sea, in front of the house. I bothered Ahmed Aga so much about this that he hired a caique one day and took me to see the inside of it. It was only a prosaic lighthouse after all, kept by guards, who, however, happened to be from his country. I wanted to know from exactly which chamber the Greek princess had been stolen, but no one in the place was able to gratify my curiosity.

Not long after we had taken this house a letter addressed to father arrived from Mahmouré Abla's father, Ali Shamil, who was then in exile. It was now that I learned the dramatic episode of father's friendship with his wife's first husband. Putting together Hava Hanum's tales and my father's version of the meeting in Mecca, I was able later to piece together the story of my mother's two marriages and the friendship of her two husbands afterward.

Bedirhan Pasha, the famous Kurdish chieftain, was brought to Istamboul after a rebellion in Kurdistan. The government, wanting to keep some sort of hold over him on account of his prestige in his own country, gave him a big *konak* [5] for himself, his forty children, and his ten wives, and allotted salaries to each member of the family in exchange for their vast property in Kurdistan, which had been requisitioned.

One of the younger, and perhaps the handsomest of these numerous children, Ali Shamil, at the time a young lieutenant, married my mother, then a girl of fifteen. In my mother's case it was arranged that her husband should make his home with his parents-in-law. This is called *ichérriyé almak* (literally, to take inside; i. e., the bridegroom). In the opposite arrangement, when the bride goes to her parents-in-law, it is called *dishariya-vermek* (literally, to give outside; i. e., the bride). In some cases, however, the young couple started in a separate house of their own. Love was not lacking between the youthful couple, and Ali Shamil with his countless brothers, who were constantly visiting him, introduced a gay but very wild tone into the sober quiet house,

---

[5] An old-fashioned Turkish town house, belonging to a person of considerable standing.

completely disturbing its traditional routine. Very often there was music, dancing, drinking, singing, and sometimes shooting for the mere fun of it in the garden. Ali Shamil, however, went further than shooting outside and one day fired through the ceiling of the room where he was roistering, the bullet going through the legs of poor Trigül Hanum, who happened to be in bed just above. The hole was still in the ceiling when I was a child, and granny used always to tell about it in the same excited tones of horror. After three or four years of this sort of thing the quiet Anatolian Turk in grandfather could bear it no longer, and he obtained my mother's divorce. I can imagine her, with those sweet eyes of hers, quietly obeying her parents' wishes. Mahmouré Abla was a baby of two when she married again, after some discreet flirtations through the windows. This time it was a young palace secretary who had come to live in their quarter. Father must have been very much in love with her, and he was very fond too of the little girl. To this day indeed he is perhaps more attached to her than even to some of his own children.

Before many months had passed after their marriage Abdul Hamid decided to send an extraordinary commission of inquiry to Mecca with orders to set up Abdillah Pasha, whom they took with them, as the sherif of Mecca, and to depose the sherif Abdullah, who had been the cause of some political agitation. Father went as the secretary of the commission under Lebib Effendi, one of our greatest judges and a man of high moral

A SELAMLIK IN ABDUL HAMID'S TIME

standing. It happened that Ali Shamil was appointed as aide-de-camp of the new sherif. Their adventures in crossing the Mediterranean might have been the model for Harry Dwight's "Leopard of the Sea." As a matter of fact, all government commissions and voyages in official boats in those days were the same. Abdul Hamid, afraid of his own navy, kept all his war-ships shut up in the Golden Horn. When a special commission was to go anywhere, one of these old hulks was brought out and despatched in an absolutely unseaworthy condition. The obedience due to the sultan forced his envoys to accept all risks without demur, but each of them took farewell of his family knowing well that it might very probably be his last, and many made their wills before starting.

Their journey through the desert was quite as extraordinary—no railways, only camels to ride, and naked Arab bandits buried in the yellow sand, lying in wait and rising at the approach of the caravans. Finally, however, they arrived in Mecca and read the firman[6] to the thousands of pilgrims assembled on Arafat.

The usual cholera in Mecca was a little worse that year, and the commission tried hard to avoid contagion. But the young Kurdish aide-de-camp was obstinately neglectful of all hygienic measures and caught the epidemic. No one cared to go near him, but the young secretary, for whom Ali Shamil had already shown a

---

[6] A firman is an edict. Abdul Hamid as caliph had authority over the whole Moslem world.

decided inclination, stayed by him and nursed him. This episode of manly affection between the two men must have been full of dramatic effect, for Ali Shamil did not know who father was, while father all the time knew him to have been the first husband of his own wife. In one agonizing moment when Ali Shamil felt that he was dying, he spoke about a young wife, the daughter of Ali Effendi, whom he had been forced to divorce, and the baby girl he had left with her. He begged his new friend to take them his watch and his few belongings and his last blessings when he died. Then father told him that he was the man who had married Ali Effendi's daughter and that he loved the little girl as his own child, so that her father could die in peace. He covered Ali Shamil with his fur coat, which he kept as a souvenir for years. But the young soldier did not die. He had still further to fulfil his eventful destiny, sometimes very brilliant, but sad and ugly in the end. Ali Shamil gave me his version of the story many years later.

On his return from Mecca he had brought on himself Abdul Hamid's anger by attacking in a savage brawl the court astrologer, Ebül Hüda. He and some of his brothers were exiled to Damascus, but when later he was restored to favor he used to come often to see us all. For me he had a specially tender feeling. A very handsome man, with burning beautiful eyes and an eagle nose, mighty shoulders, and a brilliant uniform, he is still vivid in my memory. He was a pasha then and one of the most influential men around Abdul Hamid. I was about twelve years old, but he treated me with a chivalrous and rather funny respect such as is generally only given to older women. With me he never even hinted at the risqué stories which he was very apt to tell to others. "She has her mother in her," he used to say.

One particular morning, I remember, he had come early to our house in Sultan Tepé, and I met him in the garden. To be able to run comfortably, I had twisted my plait round my head, and I smiled joyfully at the vision of strength and vitality which his very presence created. As I kissed his hand I saw his face take on a sad expression. "You have her look this morning, Halidé," he said, "that funny trick of the single dimple, and that hair-coil. I did love her so!"

Then he drifted simply into the story of their life. Many years had passed since he had divorced mother, and he had married nine women one after another since. Strangely indeed not one of his wives lived long except the last two. He told me that none had stirred his heart as my quiet and homely mother had. "I am glad she spent her last years with a better man than I," he said generously, and then went on to tell me the story of Mecca—how he had loved father and how grateful he was to him, but how he wanted to kill him when he learned that he was now *her* husband. Yet in his exile he was happy to feel that his daughter, after losing her mother, was still in loving and fatherly hands.

I am glad that father outgrew the bitterness of the finding of the portrait at mother's death, and seemed sincerely fond of Ali Pasha. The letter, whose arrival

I mentioned at the beginning, was to ask for a photograph of Mahmouré. This father had taken and sent it to him in Damascus.

From these stories of heroism and adventure I must pass on to the simple, tedious, but charming love-legends with Ahmed Aga. They were also on yellow paper, and in very poor print with the queerest of pictures. We often sat by the sea-shore, I eating my breakfast of bread and cheese and melons, and he reading aloud.

A Turkish Wagner or Tennyson would have made wonderful music and poems out of them, for they are fully as beautiful as the medieval legends of Europe. As it is, only Leila and Mejnoun have passed into immortality in the poems of Fuzully; the rest are still in their yellow paper and crude print, and I don't believe any Turkish child reads them now. They are not the up-to-date love stories which everybody demands. There is, however, one among them, "Kerem and Asli," a very beautiful poem which an Azerbaijan musician has set to music and has called it an opera. The story is this:

The shah of Ispahan had a beautiful son, Prince Kerem, who fell in love with the daughter of an Armenian priest. The priest, being a fanatical Christian, did not want his daughter to marry a Moslem prince. Too much afraid of the shah, however, to refuse, he gave his consent and named the marriage day on which the royal procession was to come and fetch the bride from his house.

On the appointed day a grand procession started with Prince Kerem at its head. As they approached the house the prince stopped the procession and went on alone. The doors were open and the house empty! The family had fled. Then Kerem all of a sudden became a poet, like all the lovers of his type, and he began to sing to the belongings of his beloved—her embroidery-frame, the divan she sat on. . . . And all the furniture began to answer him in song.

Then Prince Kerem, changing his dress, took the simple garb of a bard and, with his lute, wandered away in search of Aslihan. He sang, asking news of his beloved from the clouds, the mountains, the fountains, the maidens washing clothes by the rivers, and the flying cranes. And each answered back in song.

In one city he almost succeeded in his quest. Aslihan's mother had become a dentist. The prince discovered this, and pretending to have toothache, he went to her and asked her to pull out his tooth. She placed his head on Aslihan's knee so as to extract the tooth. So enraptured was he in this position that he begged to have all his teeth pulled out. In the middle of the process, however, he was recognized. This made the family fly once more. After endless further adventures and suffering he found them again in an Anatolian town. Here he charmed the governor by his singing, and the notables of the city took his part, forcing the priest to give his daughter to Kerem.

The priest, however, was well versed in witchcraft and proceeded to make a magic dress for Aslihan, which buttoned from the neck right down to the hem of the skirt in such magical sort that no one could unbutton it.

On the nuptial night, when the girl tried to divest herself of it, all her efforts were vain. Kerem had recourse to the help of his enchanted lute and his own potent singing. Sure enough these availed. The buttons opened one after another down to the bottom, but no sooner were they undone than they buttoned themselves up all over again. This exasperating scene lasted till morning, when the first light of dawn filtered through the windows. Kerem was in the last stages of torture. The fever in his heart was turning into real flames. With one last sigh a fire broke from his mouth, and his whole body was consumed and turned to ashes.

Along with my attachment to Ahmed Aga, which filled the outdoor side of my life, was a growing affection for Teïzé, which was as it were the indoor complement of the other. I had become her child. Every morning I went into her room, where she bestowed excellent care upon me, including such personal attention as brushing, combing, and washing me. Then she kept me occupied according to the daily plan which she had prepared. I had a feeling of really belonging to her. This sense of being some one else's property did not worry me in the least as it would have done later. It was a mild repetition of the Kyria Ellenie affair. Mahmouré Abla, who was on rather bad terms with Teïzé, used to snub me and say, "She has designs on father." As a matter of fact, I believe it was more a case of father's having designs on her.

OUR VARIOUS HOMES IN SCUTARI

Several times that year on Ramazan nights I was allowed to go to "Karageuz" with Ahmed Aga. The entertainment took place in a large coffee-house in the Scutari market. The streets were lighted—a sign of festival in those days—and we passed through a mixed crowd of both sexes and children.

Little wooden stools were placed in rows; and in a corner hung a small, white cloth,[7] behind which burned brilliant torches. A queer colored picture of a dragon or a flower, cut in card, was showing from behind the cloth when we entered, and a mysterious buzzing sound, presumably emitted by this creature itself, kept the little crowd happy and expectant till the real play began.[8] Meantime the children made a tremendous noise, tapping their feet impatiently in a common rhythm and calling out all together: "Wilt thou begin? When shall we begin?"

The tambourines rattled, and the really pretty entrance song began to be sung behind the curtain. This of course quieted the little audience. But when Karageuz's sly and feignedly stupid profile appeared

---

[7] This cloth or screen, as in the shadow-plays one sometimes sees in Europe, or as in the old-fashioned magic-lantern shows, was the stage on which the whole performance was enacted. The performers—marionettes of a peculiar kind—were figures cut in camel-leather or some similar substance, their faces, clothes, limbs, etc., being partly distinguished by coloring, partly by slits, cut something after the fashion of an elaborate Japanese stencil-card. The leather was rendered translucent and both shape and color were clearly visible when the torches threw them as mellow-tinted shadows on the screen.

[8] This was the *geuster melik*—the advance sample (to translate very freely) of what was to come—and it vanished from the screen, giving place to the full excitement, when the proper moment arrived.

near the top of the screen on one side and he began the dialogue with Haji Eivad, peeping out from the other, the general laughter started. At the leap of Karageuz to begin the traditional mutual beating between him and Haji Eivad, the small audience expressed its delight with uncontrollable roars.

I was charmed beyond description. The music, the color, the humor, the absolutely original tone, the unpretentious artistry, and the extraordinary ensemble have kept Turkish children, as well as the grown-up public, in thrall for centuries. It is one of the heartbreaking facts of to-day that our new taste, or rather lack of taste, has killed this wonderful and simple art. Its origin as known commonly among the Turks is this:

Among the builders engaged upon the mosque of Murad I there were two men: one, Haji Eivad, a sententious, pompous, and pedantic person with a solemn conceit in regard to his own merits; and Karageuz, his friend. The latter was a simple fellow, full of the most exaggerated common sense and a humor incorrigibly every-day. Although every incident of their story began with a hearty fight, this merely served to clear the air comfortably, and one appreciates that a real and inextinguishable attachment united them. Their funny conversations delighted the other builders, and it was a gay band that worked at that mosque. Whether it is really true that the work did not progress as a result of their presence, or whether their sallies were of the kind which make the powerful uneasy, we cannot now ascertain; but anyhow their conduct was unfavorably reported to the sultan, and he ordered their heads cut off. It is not indeed their actual words that since those days have constantly attacked the great in veiled and humorous language; it is something of their spirit that has lived on and has continued to attack, not only social weaknesses, but political deficiencies, in the same irrepressible manner. Karageuz, after his death, became something like a popular saint, and people light candles at his grave to this day in Broussa. As in the *orta oyoun,* a review of the different nationalities and their peculiarities, as well as a caricature of all social types, appears, though in coarser and cruder language, in "Karageuz." Karageuz and Haji Eivad are deeply symbolic characters to me. Haji Eivad is a caricature of the Turkish intellectual class, while Karageuz is delightfully typical of the simple Turk, always badly treated, beaten, his apparent stupidity mocked at and taken advantage of, forever in such desperate situations that one is sure he will be done for, yet extricating himself somehow, or beginning all over again. I have often cried as a child when I have seen him beaten by the cruel eunuch, the drunkard, or the Albanian, sentenced to death by torture, and yet, lo and behold! by some subtle means there he always was in the end intact, safe —and his enemies, the cruel rulers, in ridiculous positions.

Even the Jew, who is always represented as in perpetual fear of everybody else, becomes a pefect bully toward Karageuz. There is a Bairam scene, in which Karageuz has erected a swing for children, and a Jew comes along and asks to be swung. "Now swing me," he says. But as soon as Karageuz begins to swing him he screams and beats Karageuz for his stupidity. Then he calls out again, "Don't swing me," and Karageuz obediently stops the swing. Again he is beaten by the Jew for his stupidity. After a long scene of beating and quarreling, the Jew explains, "When I say, 'Swing,' don't swing; and when I say, 'Don't swing,' swing." The sentence has become proverbial of the Jews, and is used for any one else who has the characteristic of liking to give trouble to people.

His wife and his son are the only persons who beat Karageuz on his own ground. The little street boy who comes in as his son makes the children wild with delight. He always catches Karageuz in his mischievous escapades. There is a favorite scene when Karageuz has climbed up on the dome of a bath to steal the towels hung round it. The son appears at the critical moment and takes away the ladder. A brilliant conversation follows, until the son manages to get whatever he wants from his father, usually a few piasters to buy walnuts.

As a stage performance "Karageuz" is now in a decadent state. The simple but famous artists who used these two characters in ever new and yet ever characteristic scenes are all dead. Yet Karageuz's spirit lives. The humorous paper published in 1908 under his name continues to have a great circulation all over the country, especially in Anatolia. It is really the Turkish "Punch."

Another childish amusement was the Punch and Judy

show, which we called the Dolls. A man went around the streets and, putting up the simple stage, made the dolls act the unique piece. It must be of Byzantine origin I believe, for it is acted both in Greek and Turkish, but always there is a Greek priest and a Greek funeral.

In contrast with the foregoing, which may be classed as traditional or folk literature, there is very little humor in the early written literature of the Turks. It is usually of the nature of rather heavy satire (sometimes of an obscene kind) and contains a great deal of very bitter irony. One feels in reading it a contraction of mind, a perpetual tone of hatred, combined with, or perhaps indeed rising out of, a sense of helplessness in the spirits of the old writers themselves. The more exaggerated and bitter, even foul-mouthed, they are in writing of their enemies, the happier they appear to feel. It is this glaring difference between the satiric wit of the literary men and the innate humor of the people which makes me see humor as an internal expansion and a healthy, sometimes even a tender, thing; while satires of really important writers seem more like a nervous paralysis, which ultimately cripples the mind and the sympathies. But we cannot be surprised, even though we may condemn this morbid tendency toward bitterness, for every person who gave signs of the slightest power of criticism or originality was exposed to unscrupulous extermination, or at best to continual oppression. Every great poet had to have some great protector, and it was hard to please the great without incurring danger from some opposite quarter. A satire was wanted for a rival, but who could tell how soon those rivals might not be holding the lives of the writers in their hands? As an instance of this insecurity, I may refer to Nefi. He was one of the four greatest of our early poets and belongs to the seventeenth century. He was protected by Murad IV, the cruelest but the most powerful of all our sultans. One can imagine Nefi, of all men, feeling pretty safe. He was the writer of the most famous *kassidé* [9] in Turkish, praising all the greatest men of his time, while describing his sovereign's wars in glowing colors in other poems. With an arrogant pride in his art, however, he allowed himself to praise equally his own talents and artistic achievements, ranking himself as incomparably superior to every other human being. His satiric vein led him on to attack Bairam Pasha, the powerful vizir. The sultan evidently encouraged him to the extent of hearing him read these satires, but nevertheless advised him not to indulge in any more of them. Sometime later, at a moment when he was high in favor, Bairam Pasha procured from the sultan a sentence of death on his critic. Nefi was imprisoned in the wood-houses of the Sublime Porte, strangled, and his body thrown into the sea in a sack. Not even a grave notes the memory of the man who created so many beautiful things. Another story is told illustrating his disdainful temper. When he was lying in the Sublime Porte the head eunuch saw and pitied him. Calling him in, he inquired into Nefi's circum-

[9] A poetic eulogy of a sultan or other great man.

stances, and himself wrote a petition to the sultan asking for pardon. Nefi's satiric vein got the better of him as he saw the good negro writing and dropping his ink clumsily on the paper. "The *aga* is feeling hot," he said. "I see the drops falling on the paper from his forehead." The insult doubtless made the eunuch regret his intervention, and he left Nefi to his fate.

One may not condone Nefi, but one can see that this sort of treatment of poets did not encourage humor among the intellectuals. But the people, further away from the court, passed their delicious stories from mouth to mouth, unnoticed and safe.

At this period of my life it seems to me I was hardly aware of the activities of the grown-ups at home. My life was centered in my story books, the outside world, my lessons, and Ahmed Aga, when a sudden event startled me and made me feel intensely my family circumstances.

One incident might have suggested to me the possibility of the event, if I had been a few years older. Teïzé read me a letter in her room one morning. It was a polite and formal demand of marriage. As I was accustomed to seeing girls marry before they were twenty and had been fed up on stories of child marriages, I never connected Teïzé with this very youthful phase of life—as I always regarded it. I was a little stupefied and did not make out the reason of her reading it. In some dim way I felt that she was expecting something of me, but I sat and stared stupidly till she said, "If I marry I go away of course." Then I realized that it was my personal calamity she was announcing, and all of a sudden I began to cry quietly and helplessly. Granny suddenly appeared and scolded Teïzé, so far as it was in her to scold any one, for reading such a letter to me. The incident evidently affected me more than it was in me to express, for Granny told me much later that afterward I developed a habit of walking and talking in my sleep which made her very anxious, and we paid a visit to Arzié Hanum. She had a regular consultation with the peris, breathed some prayers over my head, burned some pungent things in her silver bowl, and made me inhale some smoke.

She said I was troubled in the spirit and probably had the evil eye, and that I must not be pressed with much study. Every evening before I slept granny sat by my bed and made me say the two *surés* of the Koran, and in addition I repeated after her: "I lie on my right and turn to my left. Let angels witness my faith. There is no God but Allah, and Mohammed is his Prophet." I must confess that these simple words soothed me to a curious degree.

One day soon after, Abla went to spend a week with some old lady friends in Beshiktash, and in her absence father married Teïzé. I cannot say that the event either pleased or comforted me, although there was no longer the danger of her leaving me.

The event was received coldly by the household, and with the marriage ceremony there settled upon the hitherto serene atmosphere of the house an oppressive feeling, a feeling of uneasiness and wonder at the possibility of unpleasant consequences, which never left it again. Sympathy and pity, as well as conjectures as to how Abla would receive the news, filled all our minds, and I fancy a rather violent scene was expected.

If there is an ecstasy and excitement in times of success, there is a deeper feeling of being singled out for importance when a great and recognized misfortune overtakes one. When a woman suffers because of her husband's secret love-affairs, the pain may be keen, but its quality is different. When a second wife enters her home and usurps half her power, she is a public martyr and feels herself an object of curiosity and pity. However humiliating this may be, the position gives a woman in this case an unquestioned prominence and isolation. So must Abla have felt now. The entire household was excited at her return. As she walked up-stairs and entered the sitting-room, she found only Teïzé standing in the middle of it. But the rest must have been somewhere in the corridors, for every one witnessed the simple scene of their encounter. Teïzé was the more miserable of the two. She was crying. Abla, who had somehow learned what awaited her home-coming while she was still away, walked up to her and kissed her, saying, "Never mind; it was Kismet." Then she walked away to her own room while her servant Jemilé wept aloud in the hall. Hava Hanum, whose heart was with Abla, probably because of her own past experience, scolded Jemilé: "Is it thy husband or thy lady's who was married? What is it to thee?"

Although this dramatic introduction to polygamy may seem to promise the sugared life of harems pictured in the "Haremlik" [10] of Mrs. Kenneth Brown, it was not so in the least. I have heard polygamy discussed as a future possibility in Europe in recent years by sincere and intellectual people of both sexes. "As there is informal polygamy and man is polygamous by nature, why not have the sanction of the law?" they say.

Whatever theories people may hold as to what should or should not be the ideal tendencies as regards the family constitution, there remains one irrefutable fact about the human heart, to whichever sex it may belong. It is almost organic in us to suffer when we have to share the object of our love, whether that love be sexual or otherwise. I believe indeed that there are as many degrees and forms of jealousy as there are degrees and forms of human affection. But even supposing that time and education are able to tone down this very elemental feeling, the family problem will still not be solved; for the family is the primary unit of human society, and it is the integrity of this smallest division which is, as a matter of fact, in question. The nature and consequences of the suffering of a wife, who in the

[10] The word haremlik does not exist in Turkish. It is an invented form, no doubt due to a mistaken idea that "selamlik" (literally, the place for salutations or greeting, i. e., the reception-room, and therefore, among Moslems, the men's apartments) could have a corresponding feminine form, which would be "haremlik." The word is, however, a verbal monstrosity. "Harem" is an Arabic word with the original sense of a shrine, a secluded place (cf. Harem sherif, the Holy of Holies in the Kaaba at Mecca). Hence it came to be identified with the seclusion of women, either by means of the veil or by confinement in separate apartments; and hence again it came to be used for those apartments themselves.

SULTAN TEPÉ

same house shares a husband lawfully with a second and equal partner, differs both in kind and in degree from that of the woman who shares him with a temporary mistress. In the former case, it must also be borne in mind, the suffering extends to two very often considerable groups of people—children, servants, and relations —two whole groups whose interests are from the very nature of the case more or less antagonistic, and who are living in a destructive atmosphere of mutual distrust and a struggle for supremacy.

On my own childhood, polygamy and its results produced a very ugly and distressing impression. The constant tension in our home made every simple family ceremony seem like a physical pain, and the consciousness of it hardly ever left me.

The rooms of the wives were opposite each other, and my father visited them by turns. When it was Teïzé's turn every one in the house showed a tender sympathy to Abla, while when it was her turn no one heeded the obvious grief of Teïze. It was she indeed who could conceal her suffering least. She would leave the table with eyes full of tears, and one could be sure of finding her in her room either crying or fainting. Very soon I noticed that father left her alone with her grief.

And father too was suffering in more than one way. As a man of liberal and modern ideas, his marriage was very unfavorably regarded by his friends, especially by Hakky Bey, to whose opinion he attached the greatest importance.

He suffered again from the consciousness of having deceived Abla. He had married her when she was a mere girl, and it now looked as if he had taken advantage of her youth and inexperience. One saw as time went on how patiently and penitently he was trying to make up to her for what he had done.

Among the household too he felt that he had fallen in general esteem, and he cast about for some justification of his conduct which would reinstate him. "It was for Halidé that I married her," he used to say. "If Teïzé had married another man Halidé would have died." And, "It is for the child's sake I have married her father," Teïzé used to say. "She would have died if I had married any one else." Granny took the sensible view. "They wanted to marry each other. What has a little girl to do with their marriage?"

The unhappiness even manifested itself in the relation between granny and Hava Hanum. The latter criticized granny severely for not having put a stop to it before things had gone too far, and granny felt indignant to have the blame thrown upon her by a dependent for an affair she so intensely disliked.

Teïzé, with her superior show of learning and her intellectual character, must have dominated father at first, but with closer contact, the pedantic turn of her mind, which gave her talk a constant didactic tone, must have wearied him. For in the intimate companionship of every-day life nothing bores one more than a pretentious style of talk involving constant intellectual effort. Poor Teïzé's erudition and intelligence were her outstanding qualities, and she used and abused them to a maddening degree. When, after her dull and lonely life, she gave herself, heart and soul, to a man, the disillusionment of finding herself once more uncared for rendered her very bitter; and she either talked continually of her personal pain or else of some high topic, too difficult to be understood by the person she was talking to. Somehow her efforts to dethrone her rival from the heart of her husband lacked the instinctive capacity of the younger woman's, and it was only granny and poor me that sympathized and suffered with her in a grief which did not interest any one else.

The wives never quarreled, and they were always externally polite, but one felt a deep and mutual hatred accumulating in their hearts, to which they gave vent only when each was alone with father. He wore the look of a man who was getting more than his just punishment now. Finally he took to having a separate room, where he usually sat alone. But he could not escape the gathering storm in his new life. Hava Hanum not inaptly likened his marriage to that of Nassireddin Hodja. She told it to us as if she was glad to see father unhappy. The hodja also wanted to taste the blessed state of polygamy, and took to himself a young second wife. Before many months were out his friends found the hodja completely bald, and asked him the reason. "My old wife pulls out all my black hairs so that I may look as old as she; my young wife pulls out my white hairs so that I may look as young as she. Between them I am bald."

The final storm, kept in check for some time by the good-mannered self-control of the ladies, broke out in the servants' quarter. Fikriyar and Jemilé were always running down each other's mistresses. Fikriyar called Abla common and ignorant, and Jemilé called Teïzé old and ugly. "Besides, she is a thief of other women's husbands," she added. One day the quarrel grew so distracting that the ladies had to interfere, and for the first time they exchanged bitter words. That evening father went up to Abla's room first, and he did not come down to dinner. The next morning it was announced that father was going with Abla and her little girls to Beshiktash to the wisteria-covered house, and we, the rest of the composite family, were to take a house near the college,[11] and my education was to begin seriously.

It was in 1893 or 1894 that I went to the college for the first time. I was perhaps the youngest student, and my age had to be considerably padded in order to get me in; and no amount of persuasion was available to have me taken as a boarder, so that father's plan to remove me from the influence of "that woman" as he now called Teïzé had to be postponed.

My impressions of the college at this time are rather vague. I learned English fast enough, but my pleasure in the new language only began when I could read in

---

[11] The American College for Girls as it was then called; an institution founded by American missionaries for educating girls in the Orient. It is now represented by the Constantinople College for Girls, but it is no longer connected with any missionary societies. It was at first housed in an old picturesque Armenian house in Scutari.

the original the childish stories chosen for me by Woods Pasha, a fine English gentleman in the service of the Turkish navy, and a very good friend of father's.

I made no friends, but a big and beautiful Turkish girl called Gul Faris used to speak to me sometimes. Miss Fensham became a little interested in me also, and, knowing Turkish, she used to take me up to her room and help me in my translations. Miss Dodd was another good friend. She generously offered to teach me at home when a year later I had to leave the college in obedience to an imperial iradé.[12]

Ahmed Aga and Teïzé objected to certain points of my English education, and this caused me some trouble. Ahmed Aga regularly took out the eyes from all the pictures in my reading book. He said it was sinful to make pictures of man, who is created in the image of Allah. When I asked him why he did not mind the pictures in the Turkish story-books he said: "Those are not like men. But look at these; they are as good as created, and if they did not lack tongues they would speak to one."

Teïzé was horrified at the sight of the Bible. "Thou wilt become a Christian before thou art aware of it," she said. I could have been made into neither a Christian nor anything else by the verses from the Psalms I had to learn by heart. I did not understand their meaning in the least, and the Old Testament stories the teacher told us about David and his time sounded to me

---

[12] An iradé was an order made by the sultan having the force of law. It could be made, as in this case, to have reference to a single individual.

so like Battal Gazi stories that I did not associate them with anything religious. It was not therefore on the score of orthodoxy that I was troubled, but by something quite different. I soon found that every new Bible disappeared mysteriously as soon as I brought it home; and I despaired. Without a Bible I could not learn my verses by heart, although I managed to remember the longer stories told by the teacher. I was too timid to ask any of the girls to lend me her Bible, and I had no special friend, as all the girls were considerably older than myself. I bought three Bibles from the college book-room with my own money, but had I bought a Bible daily it would have disappeared. I hated being scolded at school, and this continual struggle at home about the Bible embittered my life during my first year at the college, although I did not speak of it to any one. Mahmouré Abla teased me mercilessly about the Bible too. "Thou art a Christian and thou wilt burn in hell," she would say. Hava Hanum consoled me: "All children are Moslem-born, and till they are nine years old they go straight to heaven if they die, whatever they are," she said. But the old horrors of "The Adventure of Death" were awakened in me in addition to the trouble of not being able to get a Bible, which sounds funny perhaps now but was very tragic then.

A big and very stupid Jewish girl was in the same class with me. She had been in the college for some years but had not yet learned enough to talk English. Her stupidity was proverbial. Her eyes opened with fear and wonder at any one who addressed her. She seemed always to be expecting a blow or some sort of assault and appeared as if she were wondering when it would be delivered. I believe it was the unconscious mark of a persecuted race. Strangely enough, when the great persecution and break-up of Turkey began after the Armistice of 1918, I remembered that look and wondered in horror whether the Turkish race would come to have it too and how many years it would take to give the proud face of the Turk that piteous aspect.

One day the teacher asked me to help this girl to learn her verses by heart. This gave me a sudden hope. I would learn from *her* Bible. But to my dismay I found that she was in the same position as I and had the self-same domestic troubles. "I know I shall go to hell, and that makes me very miserable; and the people at home who take my Bible away make it worse," she said. But she was slightly better off than I was. The teacher, taking her stupidity as an excuse for the loss of her Bibles, wrote out on a paper the sentences that she was to learn.

About this time Teïzé had a little daughter and left me in peace about the Bible for a while. The baby had convulsions, which brought into relief the real divergence of opinion about treatment of diseases between granny and father. Convulsions were caused by peris, according to Arzié Hanum. Father insisted on a doctor. Arzié Hanum's intelligent attitude toward doctors saved the situation. She strongly recommended the ladies to have a doctor in addition to her own remedies.

We had a jolly winter. The Christian quarter, where

we lived, had a gay carnival, very bourgeois but very hearty. If I had not had bad dreams like Hamlet, if I had not seen Teïzé getting more and more miserable because of the increasing supremacy of her rival, if I had not had the beginning of chaotic doubts about religion, I should have been happy. For the reading of the Turkish stories was still going on, and we had besides the Turkish theater opposite our house. It was Hassan who was the chief actor then, a successor to Abdi and almost equally popular. I gave my daily money to Ahmed Aga to save for Sundays, when we went off together to the theater. Hassan was a tall slender man and had very brilliant eyes, black and smiling, with a strange oblique look in the corners. He played and danced and did the part of the stupid servant. His very walk, as well as his speeches, brought the house down. It was a series of roars. He was indeed the last famous comedian of the old Turkish theater. They used to play the stories I read in the old yellow Persian-printed books. The lady star, Perouse Hanum, an Armenian who was said to be sixty years old at that time, was especially admired for her dancing. Her popularity was almost equal to Hassan's, and I believe her imitation of a drunken man and her duets with Hassan were sometimes quite realistic.

I used to see a dried-up old man at the door of the theater. He wore blue beads on his fez against the evil eye, and there was an expression of beatitude on his face. Perouse Hanum bought him *simids* (rolls) and gave him money as she left the theater and entered her carriage in state. Ahmed Aga's explanation of this proceeding was that she had eaten his money and burned his heart and thus reduced him to this state. "He was not her only victim," he would add, "thanks to her lovely eyes." Her eyes after this made me very uneasy. I imagined her literally burning people's hearts with fire which she held with tongs, and eating, even chewing, their gold with her white teeth.

Father came to see us once a week, but sometimes he could not come, and then he sent his groom to take me over to Beshiktash, where I spent the night. These visits made me miserable. Teïzé did not like me to go, fearing the influence of the other woman; and I felt an atmosphere, if not cold, at least unwelcoming. At my return home I was exposed to a cross-examination, and it cost me a great deal to sit and keep my mouth shut. Anything belonging to Beshiktash, such as a handkerchief of father's, made Teïzé swoon with hysteria. She declared it to be bewitched; she imagined Abla and her mother going from one hodja to another to get charms for father and charms to destroy herself. The same sort of belief prevailed at Abla's house. She would also become hysterical at the sight of a handkerchief or a shirt given to father by Teïzé and would tear it to pieces at once.

I was now obliged to leave the college. Abdul Hamid did not want Turks to send their children to foreign schools. He feared that somehow liberal ideas might be learned later. "They can have governesses," he used to say. So as there was no more reason to stay near the college, this time we began to look for a house in a Turkish quarter. Granny soon found one in the Grande Rue of Scutari—one of those old-fashioned houses with the same sort of space and garden that she always chose—and we moved on there.

The invisible struggle between granny, Teïzé, and father ended now in father's complete triumph. One day granny told me that I was to go and live with father in Beshiktash. I said nothing, but the idea of their giving me up so easily to the other house broke something in my heart. My only consolation was that Ahmed Aga was leaving us to go back to his own country.

Granny had made me a red *charshaf* which I used already to wear sometimes; but I used often to take it off in the middle of the street and give it to Ahmed Aga to carry. Dressed in this and with a valise containing my little wardrobe, I started with granny to the steamer for Beshiktash. We walked up from the landing-station together, but granny never entered the wisteria-covered house, both on account of her own past sorrow and the presence there of Abla. Just before we reached it she left me with an old neighbor, and as she walked away with intense sadness on her big white face I felt lonely and abandoned beyond expression. Kept from tears only by a pride that would not give way, I went into the wisteria-covered house, with the old lady and her servant carrying my belongings.

CHAPTER IV

THE WISTERIA-COVERED HOUSE AGAIN

THE large hall and the double stairs no longer had the same charming light of the old days. The house looked entirely different. Granny's room no longer had that pleasant white-covered divan; it was Abla's room and had European furniture.

The whole thing brought back my first visit to Abla when she had just married father. Most of her family were there, and I had the feeling of being a stranger whose face and manners are being closely watched. I did not particularly belong to anybody in the house; no one was interested in what I did, and no one would give me that individual attention which Teïzé had lavished upon me. In a dim way I felt that the house would be suspicious of me and I should be left alone as little as possible with my father. The house would suspect me of influencing father in Teïzé's favor.

Father himself was as joyful as a boy when he saw me; and he ran up-stairs with me to show the rooms he had had specially prepared for me. Teïzé's old room was turned into a study-room, with a large writing-table, nice English arm-chairs, and a rocking-chair which charmed me most of all; while Uncle Kemal's room was to be my bedroom. I remember the brown bed-curtains which I used to draw and sit inside of whenever I felt out of sorts. There I felt as secluded from the outside world as a nun in a nunnery. Father had given much thought and personal care to the furnishing of the rooms. And I felt comforted and assured that after all he was a familiar and loving figure in this strange atmosphere; so I hugged him fast and tried hard to gulp down the foolish tears which threatened me so often in coming back to the old place.

I slept alone in a room for the first time in my life that night, and gazing at the night-light which always reminded me somehow of Queen Victoria's profile, I wondered about the kind of life I was going to have in this house. I was to begin Arabic lessons the next day. A well known clerical official called Shukri Effendi had invented a new system for teaching Arabic grammar, and he was going to try his system on me. I should soon understand the meaning of the Koran, I said to myself, and I should be able to pray in the right way. I thought of granny's caution: "That woman does not pray at all; no one is religious in the proper way among those people. Do not forget to say thy *surés* at night before thou goest to sleep." The *surés* were from Al Falaq, and as my Arabic lessons went on I began to realize the beauty of the words, which till now had been nothing but soothing sounds:

Say: I seek refuge in the Lord of Dawn,
From the evil of the utterly dark night when it comes,
And from the evil of those who cast wicked suggestions on
    firm resolutions. . . .

THE WISTERIA-COVERED HOUSE AGAIN

I remember falling asleep at last while imagining the letters I meant to write to Teïzé.

The next morning I missed Teïzé very much. There was no one to help me dress, no one to comb my hair. I was at that rather ugly stage of a child's development when the features seem exaggerated into sharp edges; and as I looked into the glass, I felt the full weight of this disadvantage. The beauty of the blue-eyed people down-stairs, who had criticized my looks so cruelly years ago, frightened and humiliated me as if it had all happened only yesterday. My sense of ugliness overwhelmed me. I was so clumsy with my hair, which was much thicker than I liked, that I remember cutting pieces off to try to improve matters. The memory of my helplessness at that time impressed itself upon me enough to make me insist on my own boys' doing their dressing for themselves when they were hardly more than babies.

Abla's niece Feizié, a large blonde girl, gradually grew into something like a playmate, and I took to playing dolls with her whenever I got the time from books and lessons. I avoided appearing before Abla's visitors as much as I could, my timidity being doubled by the sense of my personal plainness, which soon amounted almost to torture.

My Arabic teacher was an elderly gentleman with an enormous white turban and a gray beard. His system proved excellent, and I soon got to understand my Koran. But this had an unpleasant side to it. He often asked strange gentlemen, Arabic scholars, to come and listen to our lessons. He wanted to prove the efficiency of his system. Fortunately I was not very self-conscious with men; they did not notice one's looks as women did. Shukri Effendi approved of my pious spirit, and after each lesson he gave me a talk on the holiness and beauty of Islamism. Islamism taught by an orthodox person is very clear and full of common sense, but like everything very orthodox it lacked a certain mystic emotion, and this led me to long as I grew older for the mystic tendencies of the dissenting spirit of the *tekkés*.[1] I learned enough from my teacher, however, to make me fairly correct in my daily ablutions and daily prayers. Every Thursday and Monday afternoon I used to sit in my room and chant Yasin[2] for the souls of the dead. The large hall, with the five rooms opening off it where my own rooms happened to be, was entirely deserted except for myself, and my voice had a way of resounding to its furthest corners, like a strange and searching call for the years that were gone.

Abla and her family had a close and intimate home life of their own which was like a door closed in my face; and I felt keenly the fact of being excluded and alone. This threw me more than ever to my own internal resources and thoughts, which at that time had a deeply religious side to them. The need of some internal sup-

---

[1] *Tekkés* are Moslem institutions, something of the character of Christian monasteries. The dervishes who are the members of them are distinguished not only for great religious fervor but also for non-orthodox mystical tendencies.

[2] Yasin is the name of the chapter in the Koran which is chanted for the souls of the dead.

port and sympathy, as well as the development of my intellect and reason, groping as they were for the meaning of things which seemed so far enigmatic, awakened in me an intense soul life. I did a great deal of rather precocious thinking at this period. Hamdi Effendi, of whom I will speak later, intensified this feeling by his constant philosophical and mystical conversations. I knew no other way of thinking out the puzzling significance of life which was thus dawning on me, except by calling to my aid the religious dogmas which I was being taught. I performed my obligatory Arabic prayers very carefully at the set times, but after each one I had a Turkish prayer, almost a talk, with Allah. I asked him mostly questions about the reasons which control men's cruel acts and thoughts, and about the position of the non-Moslems, which seemed to me the primary injustice of my religion. Why not the same measure of goodness and holiness for every one? I have found to my dismay, after a rather complete experience, that no doctrine, religious or otherwise, includes humanity in the sense my childish faith and longing required.

It was perhaps my objection to the exclusiveness of orthodox Islamism which made me love the simple and beautiful birth poem of Mohammed by an early sixteenth-century poet of the mystic order of the Mevlevi-Suleiman Dédé. He too must have suffered from the narrowness which shuts the doors of heaven on some people, to attribute to the baby Mohammed the sublime pity and universality of love. He makes Eminé, the mother of Mohammed, describe the child, when only a few minutes old, as having its little face turned to the wall, its eyes full of tears, mourning and praying for the low and sinful who were destined to eternal fire.

The old lady's house, where granny had left me on the day of my arrival at the wisteria-covered house, became a refuge for me whenever I wanted to escape both from the unnatural tension of my inner self and from the uncongenial atmosphere of my home. Peyker Hanum herself was from the palace like Teïzé and had been the chief acrobat in Sultan Aziz's Music and Theater Department. A strong healthy dark woman with a heart and tongue of incredible frankness, she was almost adored by her friends. Her acrobatic feats in the palace were legends of marvel. She must have had great musical talent as well, for she played on the piano very beautifully, turning without pause from one opera to another, mostly Verdi and Bellini. Her best performance I thought was "Carmen." I cannot say whether it was my extreme impressionability at the time, but it still seems to me that I have never heard "Carmen" played by any one else with the same go and rhythmical charm. All this was by ear, for she could not read a note.

Besides these attractive qualities she dared to be herself among the chains of conventions and the social tyranny of the time, keeping a just measure and avoiding too much gossip. She received her husband's men friends with him, and could talk on all subjects with intuitive and intelligent understanding. In fact she

Alexandre Pankoff

ISTAMBOUL

had something of the man in her, although she was a very capable housekeeper. Her youth, which had been passed in lifting tremendous weights, had given her, with her great physical strength, something of the frank charm of one of the powerful things of nature.

Her husband Hamdi Effendi, whom I have already mentioned, was one of the many old men friends of my childhood. He had a mystical mind and called himself a pantheist. He loved music when his wife played, and he talked of pantheism to me, interpreting all human and natural phenomena by it. His talk soothed and somewhat interested me for a long time, but the moment came when I used to lose all sense of who is who and what is what, and I saw Allah, the familiar objects, chairs and tables, trees and water, the universe, and all the rest of us in a hopeless jumble.

Hamdi Bey and Peyker Hanum's house had a clean comfortable Turkish air, and rather clever people frequented it. Hamdi Effendi had been the personal friend of some of the early martyrs of liberty and spoke from personal knowledge of their lives in prison and under torture. I got my early notions of liberty in his humble salon and learned that the powerful sultan in Yildiz was a hated despot, destroying all who try to give happiness and freedom to the Turkish people.

The old couple had a stalwart son in the military school, and the house on Fridays was full of young men in uniform. As young men appeared to me to be very much of a repetition of the hateful little boys, I kept out of the house on those days.

A certain Saffet Effendi, an Albanian student, lived in their house in the vacations. He was considered very clever, and I believe he helped a great many young students with their work. I think of him now especially, for Saffet Effendi was executed by the Revolutionary Tribunal.

My little sister Neilüfer was working her way slowly into my heart. After her pretty and short babyhood she was in a way put aside with the arrival of the other little sister Nighiar. Her mother was entirely taken up with the younger child and left Neilüfer in the hands of the servants or of the great-grandmother. Neilüfer began to look like a neglected stepdaughter and was developing very unpleasant habits. I remember her biting people if she got into a rage, and tearing her own hair from over her temples, which made her look very strange. Her white face, with deep gray eyes under dark and straight eyebrows, carried the menace of a perpetual storm. I found her gradually coming to my room and leaning against my table, watching me keenly at my work, till unconsciously she became an inmate of my room. I cannot trace the proceedings which brought her little bed beside my own, but till I went for the second time to college in 1899 we slept together, and she became a second Nut-rat, but infinitely more loved and cherished.

My first visit to Scutari was a great event. The whole household there had made great preparation to receive me with joy and festivities. There was an astonishing quantity of sweet dishes, and every one examined me carefully as if I had come from a long voyage. Teïzé said that my hair was badly combed and that I looked thin, which was true, but the poor thing herself seemed more miserable than when I left.

It was during this visit that the great earthquake of 1895 took place in Constantinople. I was in Teïzé's room, absorbed in some talk of hers, when the mirrors and lamps began to shake. Knowing nothing about earthquakes I did not understand at first what it was, but I saw her crouch down in terror and her lips move in prayer. A tremendous underground sound and a sudden stampeding noise in the street made me run to the window. There on the Grande Rue of Scutari people were flying panic-stricken in a cloud of dust. I saw shopkeepers joining the crowd, as well as half-naked men with bath-towels around their loins and wooden clogs on their feet, coming from the street opposite, where there was a big public bath. Their clogs gave a certain character to the noise of the stampeding crowd, while a muffled groan rose at times: "Allah, Allah."

"Come down quick," called granny, and I ran after her into the garden. As I jumped the last two steps to the ground a big wall crumbled down close by, covering us with dust.

Not understanding the extent of the danger we were in, I was rather interested in what was happening. I remember going to a swing which I had made for myself in the garden and quietly swinging there till an unearthly sound of a pipe playing a tune in most discordant notes made my hair stand on end with terror. For all of a sudden a passage in "The Adventure of Death" came into my mind: "On the last days of the earth, Tejjal will rise and play on his pipe. The dead will leave their graves and follow him to the Judgment day." This therefore was Tejjal, and the earthquake was the sign of the last day, for it was said of the Judgment day in the Koran, "When the earth is shaken with shaking, the earth will cast off her burdens."

Mahmouré Abla, who was the most terror-stricken in the house, had got the same idea, and running about in panic had discovered Hussein, our new Anatolian man-servant, playing on a crude pipe which he himself had made from a willow branch. "It is Hussein," she shouted to me. "Don't be afraid, Halidé."

The next morning granny read a vivid description of the great catastrophe in the papers. A part of the great bazaar, many mosques, baths, and ever so many houses had fallen, crushing a tremendous number of people. People mostly slept out of doors for the next few days, but we lived in the house except Mahmouré Abla, who wandered in and out still imagining another shock whenever the boards creaked or some one walked down the corridor. Her case appeared serious to father, and I remember his bringing Dr. Mulich to examine her. Her face was drawn and gray. She took to praying more than her five times a day; and indeed there was a general air of repentance and extra praying in every household. I also became affected and hardly left my prayer-rug, vowing to be good and specially never to wear silk or grand dresses again. This penitential mood did not last long, for a few months later Mahmouré Abla got married, and the whole household had silk costumes to celebrate the event.

During the marriage preparations I stayed mostly in Scutari. The event seemed to come at a good time, for it took our thoughts away from the earthquake, which seemed to haunt us continually. Father also came oftener now and spent more evenings in Scutari. As a matter of fact he was as much interested in the trousseau as granny and talked everything over with Mahmouré Abla in connection with her clothes and the furnishing of her rooms. The bridegroom was to come to our house as had been done in mother's case.

The night before the marriage we had a little music for a few intimate friends who were invited to come in. The Gipsy Hava, who must have been the one who had performed for granny in her happier days, brought a few other Gipsy girls to play and sing. There were a violin, a banjo, and a tambourine. They sang, with the peculiar charm of Gipsy voices, the beautiful Turkish song of "My Kerchief":

My red kerchief, my purple kerchief, wave it from garden to garden, but pass not from the door, O beloved: my heart is so sore.

While this rather sad strain was sung by the solo voice an emphatic and lively refrain was given by the rest, the tambourine marking the rhythm tempo with its pretty rattle.

She costs five thousand gold; it is dear. It won't be dear. Oh, take her and come; if she comes not beg her and come.

Mahmouré Abla was fifteen, and in her genuinely Turkish bridal dress the next day she looked uncommonly sweet. On her forehead, cheeks, and chin shone four diamond stars, very cleverly stuck on. On her head she had a diadem of brilliants; long silver threads were mixed in her dark wavy hair, falling on both sides down to her knees. Her silver-embroidered veil hung down her back. She seemed unusually subdued as she kissed father's hand in public and he put round her waist the traditional belt.

At my return to Beshiktash I heard of a rather exciting event. Two Abyssinian girls, one bought for Abla and the other for me, were shortly to arrive from Yemen. And in two days arrive they did.

Abla's was not an interesting creature, but Reshé, the one bought for me, was as pretty as an Abyssinian girl could be. As a rule I believe colored people have sad dispositions, but when they arrive in a foreign country as slaves, hardly speaking a word of its language, they must feel sad indeed. Granny used to say that Turkish chickens and Abyssinian children are the most delicate creatures in the world, and I thought of it as I saw Reshé blinking at us and looking around with what seemed more like fear than curiosity.

I remember very clearly the first night of her arrival. As no room had been assigned to her yet, she was put to sleep on a floor-bed in my room. When I went upstairs to my room, Neilüfer was already in bed, and the two little girls, one coffee-colored and the other fair, were staring at each other, their heads queerly raised up from their pillows.

"What is it, Nelly?" I said.

"I am afraid to be left alone with her, Halidé Abla," she answered. "Art thou sure she is not a cannibal?"

We were told a great many stories of cannibals, and their characteristics according to our information were two canine teeth sharper than other people's and a tail. I did not believe in these stories, but all the same I leaned over Reshé's bed and looked at her. Under the colored night-light she laughed nervously at my face. It was a strange grimace rather than a smile, and her white teeth shone brilliantly. She looked more like a black kitten showing its teeth when it is frightened and at bay than a child. Politeness forbade my making further examination, but I told Neilüfer that I had examined her teeth and she was not a cannibal. My next recollection of Reshé is when I found her one day in my room executing a most extraordinary Abyssinian dance. Her hair, which she had evidently loosened for the performance, stood up on her head like bright wool; her eyes and teeth glistened, while she herself squatted on the floor, and jumped or rather hopped like a grasshopper from one place to another. This quick and continual hopping without changing the position of the body was wonderful, while she sang something loudly, something like a constantly repeated *"Chouchoumbi,*

chouchoumbi," as she jumped. I immediately tried to do this wonderful feat too, but it was evidently designed only for Abyssinian knees, for I could do nothing like it. This happened in her joyful moods, but she had often melancholy moods too, when she would sit perfectly still, her eyes turned to the ceiling, singing in a very soft tone, *"Fidafanke fidafanke tashaashourourourou."* I never learned what this wonderful song meant, for by the time she learned Turkish she had forgotten her own Abyssinian. But it had indefinite pathos and longing. From it I caught a glimpse of the misery of her past days before she was able to tell me about the way she had been stolen with her little brother from a wonderful Abyssinian forest and made to walk for months under the lash of the slave-dealers. There was that in her song, especially in the way she sang it, which made one guess the dreary suffering through the meaningless words. Whenever the oppression and weariness of life settled on my heart too heavily, I used to ask her to come to my room and sing me that song. As I closed my eyes to listen, that endless *"Rourourou"* stretched into some infinite distance, whether of the desert, of the sea, or of the heart I cannot tell.

When Reshé learned enough Turkish to talk, it was most amusing to hear her impressions of the first night in my room. They were identical with Neilüfer's. Some one had told her in Yemen that white people, especially those of Constantinople, were in the habit of eating Abyssinians. She was accordingly waiting to be killed and eaten any moment. Each time she had seen Neilüfer's frightened face eagerly watching her, she had said to herself: "She is watching me to see when I go to sleep. If I close my eyes she will go and tell the others, and they will all come and eat me up."

It was now that she told me her heart's desire, which appeared simple enough to gratify. She wanted to dress exactly as I did. So I promised her that when I was grown up and married and had a house of my own, I would see that she should have the same dresses as I did, as well as a servant and a nice room to herself. At the same time I wrote a "liberating paper," worded exactly as granny told me she had written the liberating papers for her slaves, so that Reshé no longer technically belonged to me. I gave her this paper and told her to keep it in order to insure her freedom in case I died and any one else tried to sell her as if she were still a slave.

She soon grew into the atmosphere of the house and joined us in all our childish games, enjoying them as much as the rest of us.

One evening Feizié, the Anatolian servants, and I decided to do a horrible thing. We had been told by our elders that if one said a certain prayer entreating the aid of the cypress-tree spirits and then drew up forty buckets of water from a well, treasure would come up in the fortieth bucket. We tried it one Thursday evening,[3] but we did not go further than drawing up a very few bucketfuls. The echo of the bucket as it

[3] Thursdays and Mondays are both holy days and especially propitious for exceptional undertakings.

touched the stones in the bottom of the well was so strange and deep that we almost imagined all the cypresses with their enormous green turbans in the neighboring cemetery marching toward the house. We ran up-stairs as fast as we could, and Feizié and Reshé as well were so terror-stricken that they passed the night in my room.

Wells had their own peculiar and rather weird characteristics in those days. Each had its own secret and treasure. The haunted well of a certain stone *konak* in Nishantash had a story which both frightened and charmed me, and in the first days of my story-writing I wrote "The Enchanted Well" on the lines of the old story. I altered and added a great deal to the original, but I think that now I prefer the crude folk-story, which I will repeat here.

"A peri man with a beautiful face dwelt in the well of the stone *konak*"; so began the story. One of the young Circassian girls in the harem of the house, while drawing water from the well after midnight, saw the beautiful creature. She fell in love with it of course. After this she constantly wandered round the well and very often tried to throw herself into it. Her behavior appeared so much like a case of fairy enchantment to the other inmates of the house that they took her to a famous hodja, who was an expert in ailments of this kind. The hodja taught the slave-girl to repeat a certain charm the next time the peri appeared to her. Late in the night, when every one was asleep, she went to the well again and looked in. The peri appeared as usual. But as she repeated the words of the charm which the hodja had taught her, the peri turned his back. What she saw was so disgusting that the girl was immediately cured of her love, for the male peris have their backs open and all their insides exposed. This is why they always take care only to show their faces to mortals whom they want to attract. But if one can once get them to turn their backs their charm is gone forever.

There used to be wishing-wells, wells in which one saw one's future or any other desired thing. The most famous of these is the Eyoub Sultan Well. To this day simple people take their unmarried daughters and make them look into the well, where their future husbands may be seen. They look in this well, too, to find out about lost things. They are supposed to appear in the hands of the thief. I have heard quite sensible people tell queer experiences about having seen certain things in this well, but whether it is to be explained by the play of light and shadow made by the green leaves over it, or by autosuggestion, I cannot tell.

The talk about father's buying a house in Sultan Tepé [4] coincided with a general epidemic of influenza which attacked every one in Beshiktash. It was only after Mahmouré Abla's marriage that we learned about the place through Youssuf Bey, her husband. It belonged to some relations of his, and they wanted to sell it very badly.

[4] A summer resort on a hill near Scutari.

The house was almost going to pieces, and the garden was so big and wild that no one cared to buy it. These considerations made the owners offer it at a very low price. It looked indeed as if the outlay for repairs would be considerably greater than the purchase-price.

Father saw in its purchase the possibility, as he hoped, of bringing about a happier state of things for every member of his incompatible family. Here in this very spacious place there would be room to divide the house into two practically separate establishments on opposite sides. One of these was to be taken by each of the wives, and each could have a very large garden entirely to herself.

Father hoped too that the beauty of the place would promote the happy development of all his children; and having them near him, he would be able personally to see to their health and education. He actually lost his worried look for a time, and he talked of nothing but of the different plans for the alteration and repair of the house. This naturally made him visit Scutari oftener in order to make his plans for Sultan Tepé on the spot. It was during one of these Scutari visits of father's that I was drawn for a short time very near to Abla. All of us, including the servants, had caught the influenza about the same time. As there was no such thing as a nurse in those days in Turkey, father, as the only one who was able to be on his feet, did virtually all the nursing.

I was moved into father's room, and he gave me his own bed opposite Abla's and nursed us both together there, going to bed very late himself and then only on a sofa in another room, where he hardly got any proper rest.

It was during this time, but when Abla had lost her fever and felt much better, that he went on one of his expeditions to Scutari one evening. Teïzé had just borne him a son, which might have been looked upon as a great event by a man who had so far had four daughters.

But I don't think it was in father to love a child more because it happened to be a boy. He loved all of his children intensely and seemed only to be fondest of them when they were of an age when they needed most his care and protection. Up to now he had been only paying day visits to Scutari, and this evening visit aroused Abla's jealousy, more especially because she herself had longed passionately for a son. She poured out her woes to me, and for hours I listened until I felt that I could really sympathize with her position. Then I realized that she had worked herself up into a perfect frenzy of jealousy. As a matter of fact I was very ill and rather feverish that night, but I understood as I had never done before that something which may mean immense pleasure to one person may cause great pain to another.

Already weak and restless, Abla now seemed getting quite beside herself with helpless misery and she called me near her and began to talk almost deliriously, although I know that she had no fever. I was so touched by her appeal to me that in childish sympathy I gave my heart to her that night with eager desire to comfort and to love her. I remember very clearly my feeling of intense bitterness against polygamy. I saw it as a curse, as a poison which our unhappy household could never throw out of its system.

I had been so full until now of Teïzé's suffering and was so constantly haunted by her face, almost fierce and distorted even when she was kneeling on her prayer-rug, and by her pale thin cheeks inundated by tears, that this vision had hitherto been like a barrier between me and Abla. Yet the one emotion of sudden pity now for Abla was as natural to my heart as the other.

In her morbid condition she easily passed from jealousy to the fear of death. As she sat up in her bed, the black shadows around her small blue eyes appeared enormous, and her cheeks were thin and hollow already from her illness. All this added to my pity. "Halidé," she screamed, "I want a doctor, and I want thy father."

I crawled to her bed and sat on it, and she clutched my hands nervously. The old Turkish streets were in pitch-darkness and deadly still. Only the dogs barked now and then in some deserted corner. We had no man-servant, and no one could go out in the dark, but I promised her that I would go to Auntie Payker's with the first light of the morning. The pity I felt for her made me forget the splitting in my own head, and I held her hand for hours till she asked me to read to her a bit from the Koran. "Surely I am dying," she kept on saying. I took the Koran that always hung in its embroidered bag on my bed and slowly chanted the Yassin in very low tones. The convulsive agitation of her face ceased, and with the slow rhythmic chant she closed her eyes. I remember now how the sight of her closed eyelids comforted me. I crept back, dressed noiselessly, and walked to Auntie Payker's with the first dawn, leaning against the walls for support as I went. I had to wake them up, and auntie scolded me for coming out in the state I was in. Leaving the situation in her capable hands I went back, feeling puzzled and muddled about all the confusion in human destiny and life.

When we eventually moved to the house in Sultan Tepé I regretted two things chiefly in Beshiktash: auntie and her husband, and Noury Bey.

Noury Bey was a great friend of mine in childhood and in my early youth. Our friendship began when I was seven and he something like sixty.

He was one of those who had started the Young Turkish movement with Namik Kemal, whom I have mentioned before as the greatest Turkish patriot and one of her best poets. They had passed their early life together, mostly in Paris. For some reason or other Abdul Hamid, after crushing Namik Kemal, had overlooked Noury Bey and some other less prominent leaders of the movement.

His absorbing interest at this period was in art, and he maintained an intellectual and musical salon. He was in addition to this translating books on political economy, which seemed a subject strangely unlike his poetic nature. Young writers and musicians usually made their début in his salon, and each could count on his protection and loving encouragement. He wrote very sweet Turkish songs himself, with a personal and gentle touch and charm in them all his own. Some of these songs are very well known, especially the one called "The Peasant Girl," which has been set to at least three tunes. Of the attempts to deal with a simple Turkish subject it is the one which has succeeded best, I believe. All the amateur lute players, violinists, and pianists who were then esteemed in Turkey were there, and the talk was on a high intellectual plane; but politics was carefully excluded. It would not have been safe to do otherwise; Abdul Hamid's spies were everywhere.

He loved me dearly, and with his charming simplicity which knew no distinction of age he had crept into my head and heart. He was one of the few souls with whom I could talk freely. The first time I accompanied his violinist friends, he himself lifted me upon the stool and stood turning my pages. Years later he wanted me to sing his own songs to him, and sitting on a low stool near the piano, with his thin spiritual face and his sensitive blue eyes, he listened in rapt thought. Among the gray-bearded men and the grown-ups I was the only small inmate of his salon. However full it was I always had my place near him, and we enjoyed each other's conversation with mutual eagerness. It was in his salon some years later that I met Riza Tewfik and finally had him as one of my numerous teachers.

THE HILL OPPOSITE OUR HOUSE IN SULTAN TEPÉ

THE WISTERIA-COVERED HOUSE AGAIN

The house in Sultan Tepé had not been repaired when we moved in, and it was an exquisite old place. Each room had eight windows and plenty of space in the good old style. It stood on a hill overlooking the winding beauty of the Bosphorus and the serpentine green hills with lovely towers above. The garden was a pine-grove and the grounds a wild daisy field. It had no end of fig-trees, old wells, elaborate ruins of ponds and cascades, now covered with a thick growth of ivy which denoted a time of past opulence.

But the curse of polygamy followed us here also. I felt personally very uncomfortable, now that granny and Teïzé occupied the opposite side of the house I was living in. I naturally felt bound to visit them daily. Accordingly Abla and her servants made all sorts of difficulties for me, while the fact of my living at Abla's side adversely influenced granny's and Teïzé's attitude toward me. The period was nothing but a series of troubles and illnesses to me. The uncomfortable stage of growth that I was in, with the many lessons I had to do, besides my unhappy home conditions, made me pass most of my time shut up in my room, moping and sullen, alone with my books and piano.

Before the year was out Teïzé was divorced, and she moved away with granny and her children to another house. I was in bed with the mumps and did not see them go, but the crying of the babies in the garden as they left the house gave me unbearable pain, and I made up my mind never to marry. I was ignorant yet of the force of circumstances which makes us like fragile leaves blown away from the trees where they looked so green and happy only a moment before. I had now a series of resident English governesses and an Italian music teacher, an old lady with a wonderful voice who had been a singer on the stage; and my plunge into Italian music with an Italian gave me a period of intense dramatic enthusiasm.

My Arabic lessons continued with Shukri Effendi. It was after a lesson one day that he took up a solemn attitude and made me a surprising harangue. "Give my compliments to your mother, Halidé, and repeat to her clearly what I am going to say now. You know that our holy religion allows us to marry four times." (I wished it did not, but I listened respectfully.) "But no man is allowed to remarry without substantial reasons." (They always invented one, I thought.) And he went on recounting all the reasons. "But the foremost reason is when the wife is a cripple and cannot serve her husband. Now I have a crippled wife, and I am obliged to remarry. So I want a real lady to choose me another lady. I beg your mother to find me a wife. Tell her my message and bring me the answer."

I began to understand why the old man was constantly peeping out of windows, staring at the door when it was half opened to catch a glimpse of the female figures in the corridors. Probably he had asked father and had been advised with the bitter experience of wisdom. I told Abla of Shukri Effendi's message, and she was horrified at the idea of such a holy man's doing such a thing. Yet the crippled condition of the wife gave him some justification, she thought. To my childish heart, the fact that she was a cripple made her something more to be loved and not hurt; suffering makes such a strong claim on simple hearts. Abla refused to have anything to do with the matter, but she was afraid to hurt the holy man, so she would not say anything definite and left me to manage him myself as well as I could. As I am more than stupid in such ambiguous positions the situation took away all my enjoyment of the Arabic lessons, for he would constantly question me as to Abla's views before he would let me begin to recite.

One day a tall lady called on Abla with her little daughter and introduced herself as Shukri Effendi's wife. "I have come in person both to make your acquaintance and to show you that I am not a cripple," she said. "My husband is in the habit of telling all his friends that I am a cripple in order to get their help in marrying a second wife."

Shukri Effendi never mentioned the subject of marriage again. My poor old teacher, to whom I owe so much, is dead, but his wife is still alive,[5] and we are very friendly at our rare meetings; besides her refined character I always feel a personal gratitude to her for appearing as she did and putting an end to my agitated situation.

We had an interesting English lady as a governess. She was recommended by Woods Pasha and had been the wife of a well-to-do tea-planter in India. It was she who first aroused my interest in India, and she told

[5] She died in the summer of 1925.

me all sorts of interesting personal adventures. Although she had not the teaching capacity of Miss Ashover, a charming English teacher I had for some time, she had a more personal and grown-up style of conversation. It flattered me a good deal to have her talk to me of her personal life and troubles. She used to teach my sisters English nursery rimes and tell childish stories in a way that delighted me. In my lessons she took a different tone and set me to reading more serious literature, especially Shakspere and George Eliot, and awakened my first ambition to become a writer sometime. Her educational methods were in some ways very much like those of the French sisters. She kept a red tongue with "liar" written on it, to put in the mouth of the child who told a story, which made our little world rather uneasy. Excepting for this and her fixed idea that the Turks were some sort of natives, inferior to the English, which view I greatly resented, she was a good woman and very kind at heart.

Our lessons together were more reading then anything else. She used to make me translate from a queer little English book, "The Mother"; and Mahmoud Essad Effendi, very well known as writer and teacher of Islamic law, used to correct my Turkish and compare it with the original. His corrections almost amounted to rewriting, for he put it all in high and difficult Turkish, while what I had written was in very simple language. Mahmoud Essad Effendi liked the result so much that he asked father to have it published with my name and with an introduction by himself. This was done, and the whole edition was given to the exhibition opened in Yildiz for the families of the soldiers killed in the Greco-Turkish War of 1897. As every one who gave a present of a certain value was decorated, I also got a decoration from the presiding commissioners. But the whole thing left an unpleasant feeling in my mind. In the first place the book was really by Mahmoud Essad Effendi, and in the second, a decoration from the sultan was now in my eyes a moral degradation.

When I returned to the college in 1899 as a student once more I was at great pains not to speak of the decoration incident; but to my great surprise and sorrow it got into the college calendar, and I cannot suppress the disagreeable fact.

The departure of this English teacher was something of an exciting incident. One day her little daughter, who also lived with us and was a great favorite, said that the under gardener had called her a *halaic*. She asked me what this meant, and I told her laughingly that it means a slave. And before I could explain to her that it was a teasing word which is used for every little girl in Turkey, she ran out and broke her parasol in two pieces over the garden boy's back.

A week later the mother was frightened by some Kurdish boys in a back street, and she left for London. She had a brother in India who had married a half-caste girl. The girl had soon died, leaving him very unhappy. His sister, thinking that his broken heart might be mended with a Turkish girl, asked me whether

I would marry her brother. As I have no class feeling I did not mind being thought of as pretty much the same as a half-caste; besides my governess often told me about the docility and the mild sweetness of their character. But behind the outwardly quiet little person whom she thought she knew something about, she did not see the stormy forces which made it quite impossible that the little Turkish girl should have the mild and sweet disposition of the Indians, even despite the fact that she was supposed to have something like them in her eyes. So my first marriage offer came from an Englishman, who did not know anything about either it or me.

After the departure of my last English governess Riza Tewfik began to give me lessons in French and Turkish literature. He was then a man of perhaps forty and at the height of his artistic and intellectual power. He was interested in philosophy and was a very enthusiastic admirer of Herbert Spencer. He always carried in a bag the pictures of the great philosophers as well as the books he loved best. With his long hair and fine head and his books, he was simply called the philosopher by every one. Besides being of a very studious turn of mind, he had great imitative capacity and could imitate perfectly the dialects in the country and the peculiarities of all sorts of people, which made him a general favorite with his friends. His Herbert Spencer talk did not interest me so much as his knowledge of Oriental mystic philosophy and of Oriental art and poetry. He was a good Arabic scholar and had a perfect mastery of Persian. He opened to me an unparalleled world of beauty and thought. The philosophical and mystical beauty of Persian literature with its exquisite delicacy of form made me feel that there is a spirituality and significance in form when it attains to the heights which it undoubtedly has in Persian literature. But its very perfection is a danger to any other literature and art which fall under its sway. It acts upon them very powerfully and always in the direction of destroying originality. The admirers and imitators of the Persian culture were entirely enslaved and chained by its form as well as by its spirit, and any slavery to form creates rigid and conventional artists. Once caught in such a formal school, any new and freer personal expression of beauty is stifled and killed. And this was what happened to the old Turkish literature. In spite therefore of the grandeur and perfection of form in our older poets, I felt a stranger to them, while the simple and original expression of the people in their songs, stories, music, and mystical literature of the religious kind charmed me and made me feel akin to them. Their familiar, simple, and laconic way of telling about spiritual ideas as well as about human weaknesses, their humorous outlook on life, their familiar chidings of Allah for the apparent muddle of human destiny, their mystical adoration of the perfect order of the universe, were the expression of a child's simplicity and humor.

Riza Tewfik must have felt this too, though perhaps almost unconsciously, for in spite of his continuous talk about the higher and more sophisticated expressions of Oriental art and Arabic philosophy, he had a very rich collection of popular songs, poems, and stories.

He was a great talker and never tired, so that his listener would fall exhausted, losing all power of attention and receptivity, long before he had done. He often spent nights with us at Sultan Tepé, and I remember father's falling asleep every now and then. But to me at that time he was a new world; and I was taking in, sucking down to the very roots, all that his memory and mind had to give me as the dry earth takes and sucks in both rain and sunshine.

He was interested in the free, profane, and at the same time mystic and religious quality of my mind. I used to write little things which he read enthusiastically and encouraged generously.

The outward and final break of the Turkish language away from the Persian conventions and Arabic phraseology was already in the air, although so far it was only Mehmed Emin who had dared to publish a few short poems in simple Turkish language and in the simple Turkish metrical form used in the people's songs and ballads. At first there seemed a certain clumsiness of form by comparison with the more musical and complicated harmony of the Arabic meters used until this time, and the old Ottoman poets have not become reconciled to them even to this day. But Riza Tewfik applauded them as an attempt to free Turkish poetry from its chains. He himself wrote in the same popular meters some ballads and songs which are perhaps the only

Turkish masterpieces in this style. I think his success was due to his great command of our language and to his dexterity and ease in handling it. Although he could not publish at this period, because of the restrictive nature of the press censorship, this was his best and most prolific period; for it was then that he wrote the large number of poems and studies which he only published much later.

In the popularization of philosophy, in giving ideal form to Turkish meters and in describing truthfully the very beautiful landscapes of Anatolia as he did in some of his poems, he is a great pioneer. Further than this I do not think he had gone. He had great enthusiasm in expressing his ideas to young disciples, and for some months he often shone as a great light. Then a period of repetition would begin, but by that time he would have communicated some illuminating point of view. I cannot express how much I owe to him in my first embryonic efforts to attain to a new form and style which would give free expression to myself and to my ideas. If he had adopted a hard and doctrinaire attitude in questions of form he would have hindered me in my thought life and in all my future literary activities; and in accomplishing my intellectual destiny I should have had to spend far greater energy and effort. With my maturer appreciation of the accumulated artistic beauty in the world, I count myself as naught among its exponents, but it is a certain satisfaction to have dared to be myself in every line of life. In thought and art, Riza Tewfik unquestionably opened the way to me, where many others would probably have closed it.

In later years, in spite of his bitter opposition to the Unionist government, I retained the same feeling of admiration for him, although I no longer shared all his opinions; but we became completely separated when he passed over to the side of the enemies of my country with Ferid Pasha in 1918. I do not regret his government's condemning me to death so much as the unhappy fate which made him the instrument to sign the intended death-warrant of Turkey, the Treaty of Sèvres. But I believe confidently that a day will come when his political acts and opinions will be subordinated to the fact that he was a link in the cultural development of the Turkish people.

Sister's father, Ali Shamil Pasha, appeared on the scene all of a sudden. He had got back into palace favor, and in two months he was made a pasha and governor of Scutari. He lived in Kadikeuy in a very large house with his family. He had an Abyssinian wife and a very fair and young Syrian one. The story of his marriage with the colored lady was peculiar. On one occasion during his exile he had felt himself very ill, and indeed dying all alone, with no one but an Abyssinian woman who had been the slave of his wife who had just died. Pitying her forlorn and unprotected condition he married her so that she might have a pension after his death. But he did not die, and what was more important still he wanted a white wife so badly that he married a young Syrian lady. He fell entirely under the influence of the fair one and ignored the colored lady in her presence, but he had such warm affection for the colored wife that he could not conceal it the moment the fair one left the room. He had six children besides Mahmouré Abla, three white and three colored, and he showed the same affection for them all. In fact his eldest boy, who was quite black, was the most like himself and the most charming among them all. I sometimes went to visit them and found the house always full of visitors and servants who changed very often. The Syrian lady managed everything very diplomatically and with womanly capacity. She seemed indifferent to the presence of the Abyssinian and affected a proud manner toward Ali Shamil Pasha, which almost reduced him to a state of slavery to her. He had built three houses opposite his *konak* for three of his daughters, and Mahmouré Abla now occupied one of them with her family. She already had three children.

Ali Shamil Pasha was especially gay in the evenings and joked and talked all the time on the occasion of my visits. He would dress his boys in Kurdish costumes, both the white and the colored ones; and with Mahmouré Abla playing a Kurdish air we would start a Kurdish dance all together, Ali Shamil Pasha leading, waving a red handkerchief, whistling and holding my hand; while I held on to the others behind in a row, we turned rhythmically swinging and singing and feeling very excited and very happy, while the chandeliers rattled and the old hall creaked, and the whole household crowded in in the most familiar way to watch the scene.

The Abyssinian lady sat on a floor-cushion and the fair one in an arm-chair; but when she went out Ali Shamil Pasha would run to the colored lady and caress her cheeks like a naughty child, saying: "This is my lady, with the real and unfading color. Try her cheeks, Halidé; no color comes off." This made the colored lady scold him, but it made her extremely happy all the same.

His brothers, who were divided into factions one against the other politically and personally, spent their lives in perpetual warfare; but several that I have known had chivalrous and noble manners and have been patriotic and loyal to the country, while some unfortunately embraced foreign causes in Turkey.

With Teïzé's divorce the uncomfortable and oppressive conditions in our family did not entirely cease, although we now had intervals of peace at home. My visits to granny and Teïzé's house filled me with the old painful sympathy, while the visits of Teïzé's babies to us always aroused domestic tempests. Abla had an Anatolian servant who was a perfect genius in creating trouble, and on the visit of the babies she would invent some story or other about witchcraft exercised by Teïzé through the servant who brought the children. Sometimes it would be that she had rubbed lard on Abla's door so that there might be a "pig chill" [6] between father and her; or she had left dog's and cat's hair mixed under their bed so that there might be quarrels between them. And the babies, already upset by the unhappy atmosphere of their own home, felt the cold reception and the hostile feeling of Sultan Tepé unconsciously and had a sad look all the time, which wrung my heart.

In 1899 I went again to the college with Neilüfer, I as a boarder and she only as a day-scholar, so that our lives were separate for a time.

[6] Pigs, being unclean animals in the Moslem world, naturally symbolized disagreeable things. A coldness involving especially unpleasant features is designated as a coldness of the pig, or a pig chill.

CHAPTER V

COLLEGE FOR THE SECOND TIME

THE influence of the college on my life was so strong that I must give a brief analysis of its general and particular effects upon me.

After the first period of my life in the wisteria-covered house I was no longer a child in mind and was very far from living the natural and normal life of a child of my age. I was permeated and colored by the pains and the daily troubles of my environment. These took so much space in my heart and thoughts that my already timid and somewhat dumb nature recoiled into itself to an abnormal degree, and the free development of personality, which demands a certain amount of selfishness and an uninterrupted view of one's own soul in calm intervals, was in danger of being seriously thwarted.

As a whole, college had a liberating effect upon me, giving me a much greater balance and opening up to me the possibility of a personal life with enjoyments of a much more varied kind. Some of the already strong tendencies of my thought also now found new vistas into wider paths.

I was most concerned with matters of religion, and I was in a questioning and critical mood in that respect.

The reverent and emotional tendency of my soul, and its absolute need of a spiritual reality higher than the human realities I had so far touched, was foremost. I had been hitherto a faithful Moslem in heart and practice, but I was not orthodox in mind. Somehow the Sunni [1] teaching did not satisfy me; and I believed, like Gazali, that the door of *ijtihad* [2] could not be closed against any one and that the mind could not rightly be required to accept any barriers in its continual search for higher truths, which should properly strengthen rather than weaken its faith. I had an infinite longing for the infinite, in religious thought as in every other thought activity, and I was ready to refuse a salvation and felicity in which all mankind could not share. I would plunge into any kind of knowledge the pursuit of which was recommended by the extraordinarily free and tolerant spirit of Islam, which I felt to be struggling against the conventions and the secularization of the Sunni church. The simple saying of Mohammed, "Search knowledge though it be in China" (the most improbable and remote region to an Arab's

[1] The orthodox division of Moslems, to which most Turks belong.

[2] The accepted ways of verifying the divine truths according to Islam were: the writings of the Koran; the interpretation of the imams, that is, the four great fathers of the Moslem churches; the sayings of the Prophet; the logical and free interpretation of the human mind based on the given data, which is called *ijtihad*. This last was not accepted by the church fathers, who claimed to have said the last word on divine truths. Gazali, the great Arab philosopher and religious teacher, contended that the doors of *ijtihad* cannot be closed, that the logical and free interpretation of the human mind cannot be forbidden, and that no interpretation is absolute. The persecution and the excommunication of the Gazali school, which is called the Mutezile, led the teaching of Islam to a narrower and more fanatical path.

mind), I always regarded with reverence. I plunged into a passionate study of religious creeds, and strangely enough I felt charmed and soothed by my reading of Buddha. This seemed to me to be the creed which came nearest to promising a universal happiness. In a later stage of mental suffering, when the greatest ill seemed to me the continuance of consciousness, I should have been cured if I had still been in my Buddhist phase. To cease to be appeared to me as the highest felicity. Yet it is strange to me to recall at this earlier period the action and reaction of my soul and of my thought as distinctly dual personalities. While I was free from all material and past influences in moments of unrepressed thinking, some other part in me, a strange and distinct part, claimed to be an outcome of Islamic culture, a product of mosques, candles, cemeteries, and set prayers. With strange insistence I held on to the outward aspect of Islamism, and in some mysterious way I struggled to fit all the new outlook of life, acquired through my education in the college, into Islamic experience and belief.

My contact with Christianity gave me a sense of its hard intolerance as a directing influence in the lives of its devotees, while the historical developments through which it has passed seemed to me almost contrary to the teaching conveyed by the life of Christ himself. Individuals excepted, Christianity set up barriers which shut out non-Christians from a possibility of ultimate bliss more than did any other religion.

It was Miss Fensham, one of the ablest teachers in

the college, who, although she was by no means exempt from this exclusiveness, represented for me the highest type of Christianity, especially in its intellectual aspects. She gave us Bible lessons, and her intellectual and somewhat imaginative presentation of the Bible intensified its artistic qualities and helped me to appreciate fully the tendencies in European literature and art which cannot be explained by classical influence.

The college at this time had two distinct tendencies, separately embodied in two distinct personalities, Miss Fensham and Dr. Patrick. Miss Fensham, with her marvelous power of speaking and her firm Christianity, stood for the purely Christian side, while Dr. Patrick seemed more universal in spirit; she had wide sympathies and represented altogether a freer line of education based on a human international understanding. Had Miss Fensham prevailed, the college would have been a missionary institution, intense, but particular and limited in its appeal. Dr. Patrick struggled to give a larger scope and significance to all its works.

Of the great qualities of Miss Fensham as a speaker I have a very vivid recollection connected with a Christmas night. Strangely enough, perhaps the hardest way to get a spiritual message to people is through speaking. It is much easier to convey thought and sentiment by writing, acting, music, even by dancing. Artistic powers, intellectual and physical equipment, all combined fail sometimes to make a good speaker for the purposes of spiritual teaching, while an intangible capacity of presenting oneself in naked sincerity to a public makes one supreme over the souls and minds of audiences. Miss Fensham had this power. She merely told the story of Christ's birth and his mission in the simplest possible language, just as she felt it herself, and it was like a marvelous spiritual flame which passed from her into one's heart, purifying and warming and arousing intense emotion. Down my back I felt a series of strange tremors; on my cheeks my tears fell as long as she spoke. My highest religious emotions hitherto had come to me from the Song of the Birth of Mohammed. The poem, to which I have already referred, is by a simple Turkish poet, and I know nothing more beautiful in literature than that unpretentious and unconscious revelation of a great soul in the throes of pain for suffering humanity. Miss Fensham by giving a parallel picture of Christ aroused the same emotion in me, sincere Moslem though I was; and I believe this to be the true form of emotional teaching, which arouses the best and the highest in every one according to his own lights.

I had reëntered the college as a sophomore. Although I was ahead in literary subjects I was very far behind in mathematics. This was a good moral discipline for me. I had a disagreeable sense of superiority to the girls of my age, and even to grown-ups, which is an ugly thing in youth. I represented to my inner scrutiny a very complicated portrait of an unevenly taught and strangely brought-up girl. My absorption in the problems of my home life in a way developed my heart so that it had an understanding of older people, but it did not prevent me from having a considerable quantity of intellectual conceit. The absence of any companions of my own age and the habit of living intensely within myself had left me ignorant of the joy of simple and every-day contact with other girls. Before I went to college I was almost unaware of having physical powers, nor did I dream that the free development and movement of a young body is one of the important elements of happiness. College, with its healthy young people, its sober and tasteful environment, immediately acted on me. My simpler self, the self that had been smothered after the first years of my childhood, reawakened. I experienced as it were a leveling both up and down of my under-developed and over-developed faculties respectively. I was astonished to find myself playing and enjoying play like a child of eight. This part of me, which had hitherto been dormant, now had full scope, and I passed my playtime among the little ones of the preparatory department with complete satisfaction. I was feeling like a numbed limb which has recovered its normal movement in life.

Beyond the little ones in play I mostly looked to the teachers for my friends. There was a rhetoric teacher who treated me like a grown-up, and we spent many delightful times together in the old haunts of Scutari.

Granny and Nevres Badji came often to see me in the college, bringing delightful Haji-Bekir *loukoums* with them. But the entrance, on one of these occasions, of the groom, the old Natcho, who came into the reception-room to speak to a teacher, and the unveiled condition of my head at the time, disgusted my poor milk-mother so much that she never came to see me at college again. Her sense of propriety was hopelessly shocked to think of my appearing openly before a man and a Christian. "Let my eyes not see thee again in that sinful way," she said.

I was so much absorbed in my many personal interests that at my first monthly holiday I realized with surprise to how great an extent I had already escaped from the oppression of other people's lives and troubles. My first interest was in an Armenian girl considerably older than myself, a brave dark Anatolian who struggled with English heroically. The mocking attitude of the other girls at her bad accent made me take to her in the first instance. She was a fervent Protestant, evidently new in the faith. She was very much concerned about my soul and did her best to convert me. More than what she said, however, her old Anatolian Turkish, twisting itself into quaint phrases to convey her theological thoughts, amused me and attracted me.

Among all the different nationalities those natures which exercised the most vital influence over me were the Bulgarians. My most passionate liking was for one of them whose name was Pesha Kalcheff. She was the only girl senior in my class and took many of her lessons, especially the electives, with me. After two years of camaraderie we all of a sudden developed a short but very strange and warm attachment for each other.

I have often wondered why my liking for her was so exceptionally strong, and I find it very difficult to account for. It is true that she had the characteristic

Slavic physique, which always attracted me. She had those deep-set eyes, the high cheek-bones, and the dominating expression of strength of character. She had a clear and penetrating mind as well as an intensity in her likes and dislikes, and all of these had their share in drawing me to her. She had a dramatic way of expressing herself too, which was all the more forcible because it was so unconscious and simple. Somehow this attachment, which I cannot class with any other I have had, I think of with reverence. I cannot say that it was due to admiration of any kind and still less to a foolish sentimentality. And yet there was something peculiarly perfect about it which seemed to arise out of her power of satisfying my soul's claims at the time.

We made a great many plans together for the future; she was to be a doctor and I a violinist, and we would study in Paris. I am sure that she knew as well as I that all this was foolish and impossible; but we enjoyed the illusion of lengthening our friendship into years. It was one of the quiet bays of contentment, an escape and a refuge from my somewhat tiresomely stormy nature; and all my attachments of this kind have given me a similar sense of sudden rest.

I got to know Philip Brown in my last year, meeting him in one of the social gatherings of the college. He took a great interest in the Turks and in Turkish life, as well as in Oriental poetry, which drew us together for a time. This charming friendship unfortunately lasted only for a few months, as he was only a passing visitor in the place. He was one of the very few who showed a friendship and interest for my country and people when the entire world treated us as outlaws. I think of the occasion almost tenderly. He first drew my attention to Fitzgerald's translation of Omar Khayyam, and it was a source of delight to me for years.

College had not only taken me away from home and family worries; its free atmosphere, with normal and intellectual people around me, had put out of my thoughts the suspicious, smothering, and over-oppressive machinery of absolutism to which my home life was constantly exposed. So when Miss Prime proposed to take me with her to visit some people on an American yacht that was anchored in the Bosphorus I went with her as naturally as an American girl.

The yacht belonged to an American gentleman named Armour, and he had a Mrs. Mott and her family as his guests. We took tea with them and were returning with our *caiqueji* about sunset, but before we had gone far some one from another caique shouted authoritatively to us to stop in the name of the law.

In a flash I felt rather than judged the situation. The other caique had been sent, on the information of spies, to prevent a Turkish girl from going aboard a foreign ship. I saw us taken by the police, passing the night in some horrible hole, with no end of diabolical questioning, and above all the shame and humiliation of having to go through this before Miss Prime, an American. We must escape and get to the college at any price. Then I felt for the first time that complete mastery of will and nerve, that power of making an instant decision and acting upon it, which at similar moments since in later life has taken possession of me like some strange being, so different is it from the timid, clumsy, and undecided personality of my every-day existence. I leaned forward and explained to the rower that if he reached Scutari ahead of the police and landed us before we could be caught, I would find some means to justify his conduct and to save him and us. He was a single rower, while the police-boat had two, but the moment he took in the situation he passed into action. Our man was middle-aged but wiry and thin, and the muscles of his neck and shoulders stood out like those of a figure in the Laocoon group. Drops fell regularly from his face, which became purple all over, but he rowed on calmly though with gigantic effort. The police were following us. It was an interesting chase as I think of it now; but then I was conscious of every second as if it were an interminable and indefinite race against time. I remember noting the wonderful ruby blaze filtering into the purple dusk of the evening which bathed the minarets in its glow, but I was also vividly aware of the changing size of the flag on the police caique, growing big now as it drew nearer to us and mercifully smaller as we gained in distance. We reached Scutari and jumped into a carriage before my pursuers could land.

In twenty-four hours a distorted version of the affair went round Istamboul asserting that Edib Bey's daughter had fled to Europe on an American yacht. It was a hard job to save the *caiqueji,* who was arrested the same night. Finally some good friends of father's explained to his Majesty that I was hardly sixteen and had only been paying a visit and had no intention whatever of attempting to run away from Turkey.

In the year 1900 I remember only one single event of interest in our home life. A lady whom we called the sheik's wife arrived from Macedonia and stayed with us in Sultan Tepé as father's respected and much loved guest. She had adopted father when he was a very small orphan boy and had brought him up. She and her husband Sheik Mahmoud were very well known persons in Saloniki. Father had come to Constantinople with Mehemed Bey, a high official from Saloniki, and after some more schooling he had entered the palace as a secretary with the younger brother of Mehemed Bey. The sheik's wife, whom we saw only once, and Mahinour Hanum, an old Circassian woman who always came to the house, were the only persons we have ever known from father's past.

I saw her for the first time, as I came home for a monthly vacation, sitting in the pine-groves with father, taking coffee and talking about father's gentleness and goodness as a little boy. She had come all the way from Macedonia to visit him in his family. The things I remember well about her were her round, old, but healthy face shining with constant washing and her black eyes, which looked out with that decisive strength peculiar to Macedonians. I did not see her as much as I wanted to,

Alexandre Pankoff

A TOUCH OF THE PAST

for when I came back home a month later for the vacation she was gone and father was extremely sad.

The visits of two interesting and famous speakers to the college and the coming of Salih Zeki Bey into my life as my professor of mathematics blur the home and college events of 1900 for me entirely.

The first was the coming of Père Hyacinthe and his stay as a guest in the college. He was a famous French priest who had started a universal religion which could unite the followers of every other creed, a Christian parallel of Bahaism. His sincerity, intellect, and brilliance of speaking had gained him a considerable number of followers. The Vatican was furious and watched him suspiciously. It was through the representative of the pope that an imperial iradé was issued forbidding his speaking publicly in Turkey.

He spoke only to the students of the college, and it was a privilege to hear him. Strange to say, I, who in those days could hardly speak freely before even a few persons, already took an immense interest in public speakers and the psychology of their performance. Père Hyacinthe was a short stout person with a round jovial face, small benevolent eyes, and curly white hair, whom one could hardly imagine as an imposing figure in the pulpit. Yet the power of his soul, the sincerity of his thought, the artistic triumph of his language made him a living figure in my memory. Perhaps his mouth too is "stopped with dust" now like those of so many other great speakers, but the echo of his voice will be with me to my grave.

Swami Vivicananda, a celebrated Brahmanist, also visited the college and gave one of his famous speeches, which had the reputation of hypnotizing his audience. The dark slender man was clad in a loose robe, the thin hands moving with a life which seemed distinct from the rest of his body; the expressiveness of his graceful physique, and the mystic charm of Asia's voice, these were evident in him.

I was captivated by his artistic manner, but even at that age I could feel that he had a certain quality of make-up and that he appealed to one's senses rather than to one's head and heart—the opposite of all that was so evident in Père Hyacinthe's addresses.

At the end of the year I had to think of making up for my backwardness in mathematics if I meant to graduate, and I had to do this as quickly as I could. So it was decided that I should have a special mathematical tutor.

When I received father's note at college saying that Salih Zeki Bey had undertaken to coach me for my mathematical course I was surprised, curious, and afraid. As children we had been brought up to respect his fame as that of a great intellectual light. At this time he was director of the observatory (a meteorological one) and professor in two of the highest schools in Turkey.

He was about my father's age, but his face still gave evidence of an intense intellectual life and a keenness far above the ordinary. The two set of expressions which characterized respectively the lower and upper parts of his face gave it a striking aspect. His mouth and long thick chin had hard, mocking, almost sneering curves which made people uneasy in his presence, while the upper part of his face had a personality and force rarely seen. He had two long, thick, straight eyebrows rising slightly at their meeting-point, half questioningly, half thoughtfully over the sober and calm eyes which betrayed a dominating intelligence. If the human face is ever a symbol of the inner man the upper part of Salih Zeki's symbolized the deep mental effort which he constantly made, and which he embodies in a large number of books on science and philosophy.

At college hitherto I had never worked for approbation or marks. I had been left perfectly free to read, think, and work on the subjects that I loved, and I had been allowed simply to scrape through in the subjects for which I did not care. But my new teacher made me feel that I wanted to do more than well in a subject which was not my strong point; the mocking challenge of his face irritated me. I worked myself into bad headaches, but before the end of the month the sneer around his mouth relapsed and he began to show the interest a teacher feels for a promising pupil.

In the vacation I had four lessons a week, and each of us tried hard to help and please the other. Salih Zeki Bey was an intellectual aristocrat. For him the only real world was that of the savants who opened the way for what was otherwise a savage existence. For the ideals of the physical world he maintained a sneering and cynical attitude, and he kept the two sides of life completely apart, letting himself live both, however, to their full. In this way he overdid or over-lived life so much that his great natural bodily and mental health gave way under the strain, and he died in an asylum, a very sad and ruined man, before he was sixty.

He opened entirely a new life for me. It was a positive world, a world where no half lights and shades were allowed. He was a great admirer of Auguste Comte and published a great deal about him in Turkish. I had belonged to a world of mystical and spiritual absorption. This new phase was therefore of great educative value to me and acted as a counterpoise to my natural bent. He had an absolute mastery over the abstruse subjects he treated, and he illumined them with a sharp and blinding clarity when he explained them to the pupils who gathered round him in the manner of disciples. This blinding clarity and simplicity are usually characteristic of the real mastery of a subject, but such a treatment was so different from my own somewhat dreamy mental temperament that I fell completely under its sway. Though it gave my mind a new direction and helped it in its development, it also blurred for me for a time the value of spiritual things, and I became in a mental sense enslaved to another mind. I always indeed retained the humble attitude of a child and a student toward him, and his evident interest in me induced me to make an extra effort to appreciate scientific values. So now once again I put away from me the outburst of simple childishness which college life had awakened, and I consciously imitated the attitude of an older person. I remember with sad amusement that before he would come to give me my lessons I used to run out into the garden beforehand so as to have a little fun before going in and taking on the serious work which his teaching entailed. Life never again offered me the chance of being free and young. My own personal experiences, which have involved me in all sorts of intimate tragedies and crises, and my public career in the midst of suffering peoples have carried me on their overwhelming torrent.

For years I had to suppress the youth which wanted its life. If the passion of my poor art has appealed strongly to the Turkish public it is I believe because it was a virgin force, and its only outlet was the pages in which I have given it vent. The struggle to keep these human outbursts within myself, or within the limits of imaginative writing, has maintained in my heart a childhood and youth still emotionally intense and sincere. The self-imposed facts of a passionate nature have doubtless their effect in after-life, and in my own case I think they have kept me younger than my years.

After a time of successful mathematical study I went back to college, but the following year developed my knowledge of Salih Zeki Bey through the correspondence we carried on. He wrote long and serious letters on philosophical subjects. In spite of the abstract character of the matter, he had a simple and effective style, full of original charm. I keep his letters of the period for his sons, who may sometime write his biography; for I feel I can never write it, although I once promised to do so. Too near a perspective gives as wrong an impression as a too distant one.

I graduated in June, 1901, and I married him at the end of the same year. We had a delightful apartment with a lovely view in Sultan Tepé. We furnished and prepared it together. No little Circassian slave bought from the slave-market at the lowest price could have entered upon our common life in such an obedient spirit as I did.

CHAPTER VI

MARRIED LIFE AND THE WORLD

MY life was confined within the walls of my apartment. I led the life of the old-fashioned Turkish woman. For the first few years I even cēased to see father's old friends whom I had known as a child. I belonged to the new house and its master, and gave the best I had, to create a happy home and to help him in his great work. He had begun at this time his colossal work in Turkish—the "Mathematical Dictionary"—and I prepared for him from different English authorities the lives of the great English mathematicians and philosophers.

It was at this time that the Sherlock Holmes series appeared in English. I cannot describe with what childish interest both my father and Salih Zeki Bey listened as I read these stories out in Turkish. Father used to tell us that the interpreters in Yildiz were translating them as fast as they could, for Abdul Hamid had an extraordinary liking for criminal and police stories, especially for those of Conan Doyle; the chief of the royal wardrobe, Ismet Bey, read them all night behind a screen. Although I also found the stories curious and interesting, there were a yellow face and a man with a wooden leg in the stories which frightened me constantly in my dreams.

For my own satisfaction I took to reading French literature and that with deep interest. At first I did this with a view to perfecting my French, but its mere form, so inimitably beautiful, impressed me as something almost spiritual. Yet I did not linger long with the stylists. It was the French soul in its fastidious insistence upon beauty, and still more upon truth, which held me in subjection. Good old Daudet with his warm, loving, and tender soul I always adored, but Zola I did not appreciate at first when I was wading through his gigantic productions one after another. After having digested his more difficult material, got over his blinding, lurid, and often chaotic coloring, overcome my disgust at his too often ugly sexual and degrading descriptions I became gradually aware of Zola himself. Although he was without a refined sensibility I could not deny his mastery of words, his powerful if clumsy application of light and color in human descriptions. I do not say this of his portraiture of individuals, for these he rarely created. But he lighted up portions of the human soul with his fastidious and very French idealism; he chastised men by making grotesque statues and pictures of their vileness. All this, however, ultimately effaced itself from my mind, while Zola has remained as perhaps the most powerful educator of my soul. To me he represented that rare idealist fight for truth in which he persisted, just as an ordinary man fights for breath if his mouth is closed by force. Zola's soul sensed an invisible oppression created by the lower powers which dominate man and make him eager to suppress truth.

There is no other writer I know who stands up for truth with such temperamental passion. He wanted the whole of it; his meticulous idealism would not allow him to temper it. The higher the standard he set before himself for man the harder he struck at his weaknesses. He attacked man's vices, exaggerating into absolute folly the sexual ones. I do not know why he was so much haunted by man's sexual weaknesses; there are plenty of other shortcomings. But Zola seems to have been aware of them also, though only in his later works, as "Les Quatres Evangiles." Zola evidently thought that the sexual perversions were fundamental ones in man's character and that unless he were made sane and normal in that respect he could not reach higher levels.

I always identify Zola with a picture of Christ chasing the money-lenders from the Temple. I do not remember whose the picture is, but in it Christ has the unrelenting eyes of a destroyer, full of a holy horror, such horror as Pasteur would have had in his eyes if he had seen a tube of microbes of some terrible sort getting loose in a human dwelling. Zola has that same horror at the sight of vice let loose among human beings, and he attacks it with the relentlessness of a force of nature. He does not stop to see if there is anything to be said on the other side. His impetuous honesty to destroy not only the vices and ugliness of the human heart but man's self-created illusions and shams nearly killed my mystical comfort from the Divine and the Unseen. If Zola had lived and seen the destitution and misery of to-day he would surely have encouraged men to hold fast to the elevating and purifying influence of the spiritual world in every sense.

He made me put these questions to myself: Was it the eternal desire for inward support and comfort which kept me tied to the Unseen? Or was it the fear that I could not keep the needed strength of soul in my struggles for the highest? Could I stand and face the ugly truth of human realities without spiritual aid and still have the strength to serve my kind?

The extraordinary greatness and inward power of Zola was this: seeing men, as he did see them, cut off from every spiritual belief, he still fought for their betterment in his own way. Zola's test is the hardest test for sincere and piously inclined souls, but if they can come out of it whole nothing afterward can change their belief in the existence of a Divine Power.

I had already been shocked by my first contact with the reality of life, and when I came to feel that one's own eternally isolated and very ephemeral soul has to stand alone and struggle and bear as well as serve mankind (a mankind as presented in Zola's coloring), it almost destroyed my mental equilibrium; and in the mental disturbance which followed I was much under his influence.

In the autumn of the year 1902 I had a nervous breakdown. Such illnesses and mental affections are worth studying in oneself as well as in others, for if they are the source of degeneration and discord, even of anarchy in the masses, they are also in some instances landmarks in individual souls.

My trouble seemed like simple insomnia at first. I ceased to sleep. Something in my head and in my inner conscience had awakened, and I had the feeling that I should never sleep again.

Some light in my head was constantly burning. I could look and see the inside me clearly with a light that was never dimmed, never lessened. When I closed my eyes in sheer exhaustion, still that intense consciousness glared on in me.

At first the idea that I should never sleep again frightened me, but when the conviction became settled, I ceased to fear. My consciousness of the time seemed really to solidify; minutes, hours, nights were eternal. Even after nights through which I passed, sitting by the light of a succession of candles which burned up one after another, I had the feeling that time was there; it was not moving, and it had never moved. Then I felt that immortality, an unceasing consciousness in a light which will never be extinguished and which will never liberate a mortal, is horrible.

I was at last slowly and ironically settling down to bear my new condition patiently. Every warm color in me had somehow faded into a somber gray. Every desire in life had left me. There was no sense of values, no sense of possible physical satisfaction. That wonderful garden and the coiling Bosphorus, that marvelous night of purple blue in which sharpest forms take fluid outlines and the stars glisten like drops of water, gave me no more emotion. All nature was gray to me, and gray all the time.

I believed I was quietly fading away, and I waited for the end. I covered the looking-glasses in my room at night, for my face in its sharp lines and my eyes in their strange stare frighened me.

Some other self of mine seemed to watch this queer stranger. I suddenly felt that I had fallen into a world among people who were strangers, and that I had nothing in common even with the most familiar and the dearest. Surely this girl I watched in the mirror was related to these people around, and she was an inhabitant of this senseless place, but the inside me had no relations or interests. And the inside me was after all the real me. I saw the values of life in glaring lucidity, as I have never seen them since.

My life before this strange experience and my life after it are separated into two stages with this lucid but gray interval between them.

Of course I had all the nerve experts, and they did everything to make me sleep and eat. They naturally thought I was a foolish young girl, and a stubborn one too, who had hypnotized herself into this stage. There was one of them who talked interminably and made me swallow eggs, trying hard to overcome the silent inward resistance of his disagreeable patient, till I heard his exasperated voice one day say, "Why are you crying?" Only then did I realize that the cheeks and the hands of this very foolish girl, which was my physical self, were wet with tears.

In the end it was Mahmouré Abla who called me back to life from this gray mental monotony. She came often from Kadikeuy; she kissed me and scolded me and handled me as if I were one of her many babies. It was after one of the numerous Turkish baths she gave me that I suddenly had my old sense of life. As I lay in my towels I had a physical feeling of comfort, and that flicker which awakened with her motherly touch repeated itself with the baths from that time onward.

With sleep and the ordinary human feelings came a very serious illness. And that illness was a complete cure, for with it came also a new creation. I was to create a being. How mysterious and how unutterably divine is the act of creation! The greatest genius creating the greatest human masterpiece is not the equal of a simple woman in whom a new soul is called to life with all its infinite complications of the vital mechanism. There is indeed an infinity of hard labor in all the creative processes of nature, and if nature itself is conscious, what infinite and inexplicable divine pain there must be too! But for me now this mental disturbance which had seized me withered like a great natural catastrophe which comes and leaves behind only some peaceful landscape.

These years are dream years for me, but in the middle of the interminable night sufferings of the time I had a symbolic dream. Some one said to me, "Here are the souls of men; which will you choose?"

"I choose Ayetullah," I said, and so loud that I woke up with my own voice. Ayetullah means the sign of Allah, but I do not know whether it was the meaning or the sound of it that made my say it in my dream. In the morning when I told my dream they told me that this was a sign that my baby would be a boy and that I must call him Ayetullah.

I saw him in Mahmouré Abla's lap, in a towel—the most astonishing piece of creation, as every baby is—and he was called Ali Ayetullah, the first name after my grandfather. He was a big fine creature with a face and head that looked three months old. The face was my own face repeated in a darker shade, the head covered with very black hair, and eyes that had none of the bleared, miserable, sorry old looks of most babies when they realize that they have stepped into man's den. Then came to me the strange bliss that never comes to any one except at this particular moment, every atom of one's physical being, the farthest confines of one's tormenting inner self bathing and expanding in light and ecstasy.

Everything was done in the old Turkish way. Nevres Badji was there to make the red [1] sherbet for seven days, and an elderly Greek nurse with Mahmouré Abla took care of me and the child. Everything belonging to him was pink, as simple and as sentimental as it could be. Above me, two onions tied in white muslin with pretty red bows were hung on the wall. The Greek nurse with that precious human bundle in her arms, its soft long pink shawl trailing on the floor, walked up and down on the thick carpet, singing in the softest and lowest murmurs, *"Tolililicamou. . . ."* It

[1] Red in order to ward off the peris.

meant nothing, but the simple melody also seemed to trail like the ends of the shawl, and my heart trailed and crawled after it in this first and highest realization of love. How often have I put my arms round that fat Greek woman's neck and kissed her, and how often has she hugged me and called me foolish names and sung me to sleep as she did the pink bundle! Her attachment, which began at this supreme moment, lasted for years after.

The old sheik of the Euzbeks, a dear and holy neighbor of ours, gave the baby its name. He sat by my bed and chanted the call to prayers in his grave tones into its ears, and three times he called, "Ali Ayetullah, Ali Ayetullah, Ali Ayetullah!"

When the gray cloud of my mental misery was completely lifted by this event I began to agree with the doctor who thought I was a foolish little girl self-hypnotized into neurasthenia; and after this I felt that nothing could shake the equilibrium of my soul, no matter how hard the things might be which I might have to undergo. Ali Ayetullah undid the complicated knot of life's dilemma; he cured me from my over-intellectual suffering and made me realize the beauty of the simple and common affections, which I shared with all the other women of my kind.

For three months I lived on wrapped in Ali Ayetullah, though sharing him with his devoted nurse. Then I had a psychical experience in connection with him which is perhaps worth recording.

It occurred in this way. Father did not come home

as usual one evening. Salih Zeki Bey told me that he was going to have an operation in the German Hospital the next day, and he had not wanted Abla and me to know of it before it was over.

I had a bad night; my conscience smote me, for since Ali's birth all my heart had gone out to him, and I seemed hardly aware of the existence of any one else. This lack of affection on my part toward my father during the recent months now troubled me very much, and early the next morning I went to the hospital and decided to stay a few nights at an English friend's to be near my father in the hospital during the days of his convalescence.

The first night I had a dream. In the large grounds of Sultan Tepé there is a raised mound with thick clustering fig-trees, looking over the sea. There among the trees a tall and half-naked woman in white drapery, her black hair streaming and a torch in her hand, walked up and down. I woke with a strange anguish and feeling that something had happened to Ali Ayetullah. There was no reason why I should connect this dream with the ill omens of the old childish stories told by the servants, but my depression and anxiety could not be put aside by any amount of reasoning or will-power.

I tried to be natural and cheerful with father, but before I left his room the man-servant appeared with a strange look on his face, telling me that Salih Zeki Bey asked me to go home that evening. He was not really ill, he said, but he was not feeling quite well. I arranged to go home at once. All the way there I could not bring myself to believe that the call was really for my husband.

As soon as I reached our house, I ran straight up to my room, and before the door stood Salih Zeki Bey, leaning against it almost as though to prevent my going in.

In the middle of the room Mahmouré Abla was leaning over something laid on a floor-cushion. "The fit is over, Halidé," she said, as I went in.

The baby was in a towel; the little face was still in the hard and painful purple stare of a convulsion; the little mouth was still pulled into the diabolical travesty of itself that convulsions give to babies. But he opened his eyes and gave me that melancholy smile which was peculiar to the heavy eyelids and the greenish depths of the eyes hidden under their long fringes.

"I don't want him to die, Mahmouré Abla."

There followed a long period of fighting against the convulsions. For months I sat up night after night with that bit of human flesh, which seemed so essential to my life. Very often the doctors gave him up, but we went on struggling, and I could not believe that he could die while I was still a dweller on the earth. Each time before a fresh fit I dreamed of the same woman. She usually appeared on the sea-shore, and sometimes she would be swimming. She was always half naked, but the color of her eyes, although often the color of dead seaweed, was at other times black and she stared at me hard. After each dream-meeting with her, I was sure that Ali Ayetullah would have fresh convulsions, and he always did. The torture and tyranny of the dream are inexplicable. Salih Zeki Bey tried hard to influence me against believing in it, but to no effect. Once there was an interval of twenty days when I did not have the dream nor he the fit. Then I saw her again. But the baby looked well and I wanted to make myself believe that it was nervous imagination which I must overcome. So defying my superstitious fears I went out to shop, for the first time for months. But before I entered the boat from Scutari the man-servant came running breathlessly after me. The baby was in a bad fit.

It was the worst he had, and I was seriously alarmed. But he lived, and that was the last dream I had of her and the last of his fits.

The dream woman appeared once more, when Ali Ayetullah was ten; that is, ten years later. He had had a long attack of pleurisy, and although weak he seemed out of danger, and so I had taken him to my cottage on the little island of Antigone. This time she was dressed when she appeared and sat by me with a mocking smile in her eyes, the color of dead seaweed again.

"You are some one I know; tell me your name," I said.

She sat and smiled on. As I woke and felt the anguish of the old days I jumped out of bed with sudden mental recognition, crying, "It is she." Three days later Ali developed typhoid fever, an extraordinarily severe case, from which he was saved almost by a miracle. And that was the last of the fateful dream woman.

In 1905, before Ali Ayetullah could walk, the great Japanese war came, and Hassan Hikmetullah Togo, named after the great Japanese naval hero, appeared with red tufts of feathery hair, bleared baby eyes, and a continual screech. At first he did not seem to be of much account, but in two months he shot out into the loveliest of small creatures, with a perfect golden complexion, golden curls, and golden eyes that had a lively language of their own. Ali Ayetullah had expressed the slow melancholy of my inner self, but when Hassan arrived he came with a temperament, life, and energy all his own. At eleven months I had quite an uncanny feeling as I saw the tiny being running about and talking Greek and Turkish to the conversation point.

In 1905 we left Sultan Tepé and went to live in the upper apartments of the observatory on the Grande Rue of Pera. Hassan was fifty days old at the time.

The life in the Grande Rue of Pera was strange to me. I was already living a secluded life, but the noise, the vulgar amusement, and the bustle of the whole place threw me further into my inner shell. Fortunately there were rooms at the back of the house, and I preferred to look out at the dull dirty courtyards full of rubbish-heaps, and at the tall ugly apartments, over the smudgy lines of which the Golden Horn stretched out in a thin blue line amid the curve of its purple hills.

I had a tiny study with my books and piano, and I spent all my leisure hours there alone. After Zola I had gone back to Shakspere.

Some of Shakspere had already been translated by

Sirry Bey and Abdullah Djevdet Bey, but it was done in over-literary Turkish. There is a wild harmony in the Anglo-Saxon diction of Shakspere the parallel of which I thought I could find in the simple but forcible Turkish of popular usage, the words and expressions of which belong more to Turkish than to Arabic or Persian sources. This was at the time an unheard-of and shocking thing, but as I had no intention of publishing I was not hindered by any considerations of what the public or press might say. Shakspere with his amazing genius had created much of his own English, expressing psychological and philosophical complications of the subtlest order with words never before so employed. The popular Turkish genius in its language was a thing rather apart, although it had greater resemblance to the forcible Anglo-Saxon than the refined Persianized Turkish could be made to have. Still I had to do a great deal of twisting, especially as I had begun with "Hamlet," which is so full of abstract thought. But the task gave me great intellectual amusement. Salih Zeki Bey also became interested, and as he was not able to enjoy the masculine grandeur of Shakspere's art as revealed in its original English it was the intellectual side of the work which interested him. He had read "Hamlet" in the French rendering, which is an extremely poor one, and he was shocked at my vulgarizing Shakspere by the use of such simple Turkish as I had chosen; so he used to go over my version scratching out with a red pencil here and putting in Arabic words and the usual orthodox terms of high literary Turkish there.

As he always maintained an air of professional authority I was scolded a great deal, but I went on doing the work in my own way, he scratching out and writing in his own version. When I began the sonnets, however, even his mathematical accuracy and correctness in expression felt that there was some intangible lyrical vein which one could not always convey in strictest orthodox phraseology.

I have often returned to Shakspere since that time, and later on I translated a great many of his works, but I believe that my fullest realization of him was in this same year 1906. Shakspere, although more impersonal than any other human genius that I know, revealed the dominant personality of his mind to me then. He made me feel clearly that there is such a thing as a difference between man and woman in art, in religion, and in all forms of culture. I cannot say that one is higher than the other, but they are distinctly different. The highest art and the highest beauty may be revealed by persons of either sex indifferently. Genius is a divine gift which either a woman or a man may have; and sometimes indeed it is a woman who may express the man's note in art while a man may express the woman's. It does not depend on their sex; it depends on the quality of their souls.

For me, both our poet Suleiman Dedé and Jesus Christ in their sublime note of love strike the supreme note of women in religion and art; while Mohammed and Shakspere sound the highest note of man, or rather the male note in the same realms. It is strange to admit that what Mohammed gave me in religion, Shakspere gave me in art. There is no Christian feeling in Shakspere. He is a man, clearly chanting the creative manliness of his barbaric ancestors, toning them down to harmony, indeed bringing into formal beauty the chaotic ideals of their dreams and struggles, and painting them in terms with which every human being in every decade of history may become familiar.

Mohammed, though the last Semitic prophet, is not influenced in his soul to any great extent by the series of prophetic predecessors who left behind them their tradition and their prophetic art. Though somewhat impressed by the organizing power and the manly capacity of Moses, he is otherwise but little touched by the Jewish art in the Old Testament, which not infrequently reaches a strident note of complaint, sometimes very beautiful but usually very hysterical. The sublime but womanly gestures of Christ did not touch Mohammed either. In his love, in his pity, in his social organization and his whole conception of life both here and hereafter, Mohammed is essentially a man. The mystic and somewhat sickly tendencies of his own people had to find satisfaction by infiltrations from other sources into his clear and well balanced creed; while the manly tone with which Christianity was tempered by means of its iron organization of later years all came from church organizers and personalities of somewhat Roman tendencies rather than from Christ's own teachings.

MARRIED LIFE AND THE WORLD

In the spring we went back to Sultan Tepé and spent the summer there. This year my sister Neilüfer married a young sheik in Broussa. She was only fifteen years old.

The second important event of this year was poor Mahmouré Abla's trouble. She was the first victim of the old régime in our family

It happened in this way. Ali Shamil Pasha with his new and constantly increasing power was brought into conflict with other influential men around Abdul Hamid. His nephew Abdurazzak, a young and impetuous Kurdish aristocrat, had begun a quarrel with Ridvan Pasha, the prefect of Constantinople, a great personage in the immediate entourage of the sultan. The quarrel arose about the mending of a piece of road in front of Abdurazzak's house. Ridvan Pasha had near him a man called Ahmed Aga who had some unofficial but very influential post in the road-mending department. Ahmed Aga refused to give orders for the mending of the road before Abdurazzak's house. Abdurazzak, having heard of this, kidnapped Ahmed Aga, imprisoned him in his house, and handled him in Kurdish fashion, threatening to keep him in his house as a hostage till the bit of road was repaired. Ridvan Pasha, with whom Ahmed Aga was a favorite, took the matter up and complained to his Majesty. I believe an iradé of the usual kiss-and-be-friends kind was issued, but Abdurazzak was in his fiercest Kurdish temper and by no means in a kissing mood. Ridvan Pasha sent the road repairers under his command to release Ahmed

Aga, and they bore down upon Abdurazzak's house with their spades and other road-making implements. A fight took place, and men were wounded on both sides. Another iradé removed Ahmed Aga from the scene, and an apparent calm was established; but it was the unnatural calm that precedes a worse storm.

One afternoon father came home earlier than usual looking distressed and pained. Serious events had taken place the night before. Ridvan Pasha, going to his summer residence in Erenkeuy, had been murdered in his carriage by four Kurds who attacked him on the bridge near Ali Pasha's house in Haidar Pasha. They were arrested and brought to Ali Shamil Pasha as the governor of Scutari. He imprisoned them for a few hours but released them the next morning, evidently at the instance of his nephew. This aroused the fears of the sultan, and that very night all the Bederhani family, of which Ali Shamil Pasha was the head, were arrested, packed into a boat, and sent off to Tripoli in chains. Ali Shamil Pasha's house and the little houses opposite where my sister lived were under the strictest guard, and no contact with outsiders was allowed. My poor brother-in-law, who had done nothing all his life but humbly and conscientiously mix and prepare drugs as a chemist, was huddled into the boat with the others and put in chains also. Even boys of twelve were taken from school and exiled. No male Bederhani was to be left in Constantinople; consequently a great number of Bederhanis who knew nothing whatever about the quarrel of Abdurazzak suffered with the rest. Poor

JENI-JEMI MOSQUE, AND THE DRESS OF THE TURKISH WOMAN OF NINETEEN HUNDRED

Ali Shamil Pasha was the victim of his family pride, for he had not approved of the quarrel, but his nephew's influence had made him release the hired murderers of Ridvan Pasha.

It was impossible for any of us to get at Mahmouré Abla. But the railway ran below the street where she lived, and so we used to take the train and casually appear at the window of the car as it passed her house, trying to see if she were ever at the window or on the balcony. As Ali Shamil Pasha used to come to our house a good deal we expected father to be arrested also; for the sultan did not like father on account of his well known liberal ideas. At such times of course the paid spy army were endlessly active, trying to deserve their salaries or to get new honors by new discoveries and reports, while a new set of men who were ambitious of joining the easy profession of the spy were even more active. To get into the favored set the worst passions and ambitions were aroused. God preserve any people from such a system; for apart from the great misfortune of the individual suffering, the more dangerous and deep the corruption becomes, the wider does the low habit of spying spread, men finding an easy way to success by merely reporting their neighbors. When such a class is once formed in a country it is like a hidden moral poison, and every succeeding era is poisoned by it.

Mahmouré Abla had four children, the eldest at this time nine and the youngest eleven months; and another was to arrive in five months. In my futile train rides I never got a glimpse of any one on her little balcony.

Once only I saw her white veil, which she used at her prayers, hung up to dry, and so great was my pain that even this upset and excited me to a night of fever. Father went more frequently and mourned for her like a lost soul. He saw her once on the balcony, and their eye or rather soul contact was described to me by her after her release. "When I saw him pass, forgetting the police guard under the window, I waved my hands; he was searching the house with his eyes. The moment he caught sight of me he sat down in the carriage and covered his face with his hands." He was sobbing aloud, and that in a public train. After he came home that day he sat by a table and cried as he used to do after mother's death. Meanwhile granny and Teïzé had taken a house in Sultan Tepé not far from ours, and during all these days of anxiety I went often to see granny and talk about Mahmouré Abla. She also cried bitterly and continually. After two months of this helpless suffering, she told me one day that she was going to try and get to Mahmouré Abla. Father went on trying hard in the palace through influential friends of his to get some relief for my brother-in-law. Humanity, although so cowardly at times, is not entirely extinguishable even in the worst régime, so that he had some hopes.

Granny said a significant good-bye to me one day, and taking a humble one-horse carriage she drove away in her loose black *charshaf*. When she did not return in the evening, I felt that it was ominous; but the next day early in the morning she was back with tears and smiles.

She had got in and had spent the night with Mahmouré Abla. We had of course to hear her adventures. She had left the carriage at a suitable place and walked toward the house. Fortunately the guard at the corner of the street was not there, so granny had only the one guard before the door to deal with. I can imagine her, her white wrinkled face still keeping its perfect oval, her toothless mouth small, pink, and fresh as a child's, her gray eyes full of tears, her bearing calm and dignified, her face clean as only the face of an old Moslem woman who prayed five times a day and washed five times a day could be, and her aristocratic voice saying:

"She is my granddaughter; she has no one; she is shut up with four little ones, and I must find out when the fifth is coming. Let me in, my son, if you have a family and a heart."

She must have actually patted his back as she implored him, and she must have trembled with fear lest Mahmouré Abla, who indicated her presence behind the lattices by excited coughs, should get into one of her usual tempers and scold the policeman or herself for condescending to beg for anything. But the man had looked up and down anxiously and had at last whispered, "Go in, granny, and to-morrow, early at dawn, when I come to take my watch I will let you out; but don't talk loud, for if the other guard knows I have let you in I shall lose my bread; I may even be exiled; so don't ruin me."

"Mahmouré's first word of greeting was, 'Why did you beg a policeman so hard?'" said granny smiling through her tears. But Mahmouré Abla in spite of her pride had wept copiously and kissed her continually, asking about every one of us, and talking loudly about the rough way in which the house was searched and the difficulty she had in getting the guards to buy even medicine for her. Shut up for months in the state she was in, she had of course been suffering, but the guards looked upon the desire for medicine by a woman whose husband and father were in the bad graces of the sultan as luxurious whims. There were hardly three months more before her confinement, and if she were not released she would be condemned to face the ordeal all alone.

My old enemy Insomnia came back and stared at me through long nights, presenting Mahmouré Abla's image distorted in pain and with no one except babies and a very stupid little maid to help her. Why did women have babies any time and anywhere?[2]

The extraordinary court which was sent by the sultan to try the Bederhanis in Tripoli separated my brother-in-law from the Bederhanis, and he was exiled to Jerusalem, which was heaven after the dungeons of Tripoli.

[2] During the first Greek revolution in the Greek provinces of the Turkish Empire, the Turkish people in Istamboul were uneasy about the Greeks, who might rise in sympathy and start massacres, and so the Moslem youth kept guard in the Turkish quarters. Chenghel Tahir Pasha, a strict and wonderfully able man, was appointed to govern Istamboul at the crisis. He issued an order that every one should go to his home after night prayers and that no one was to be seen in the streets. The first night the guards arrested everybody who was found abroad. One of them had gone in search of a *sage femme* for his wife who was going to have a baby. "Tell your woman," said Tahir Pasha, "she must not have a baby at night and at such a time again."

Ali Pasha's military grade was taken from him, and he was condemned to perpetual imprisonment with the rest of his family in Tripoli. He died in the prison in 1907 after a sad and lonely life. Mahmouré Abla was released after two more months, and she had her baby near us. She soon sailed for Jerusalem with her five children to join her husband. They came back with all the other exiles in 1908, and a great reception was given to all the passengers in the boat as having been the victims of the great tyrant.

In the fall of 1906 before we could go back to our place in Pera I had a dangerous internal operation which kept me in bed for six months. I was very near death, but despite very high fever I never lost consciousness. My head was full of strange whims and regrets. I was, as once before, immensely conscious of myself and distant in feeling from every one else. Something was hurting me in an unutterable way. I seemed a foolish child playing with words and as though I had missed the essence of life. What had I missed? I had made a love marriage. I had two babies who made me realize the full ecstasy of motherhood. I could not complain much of the details of my daily life, for they were more or less the same as the daily life of the great majority of other Turkish women. I did not envy the bustle and the empty pleasures of the few more or less described by Pierre Loti. I never had "hat and ball" [3] longings. What I had missed and what I wanted, I did not know. I remember repeating the

[3] That is, to go out unveiled in a hat like Christian women, and to dance.

Turkish expression used for those who die with an unfulfilled desire: "I will go to my grave with open eyes."

In the spring the anxious look on the faces around me relaxed and they talked of moving me to a warmer climate, probably to Beirut; and I also felt hope and desire for life returning. The first time that they carried me into the garden, on a warm day in April, the touch and smell of new grass penetrated me with an absolute sense of contentment, and I seemed to lose all the vague regrets of the past months. The world was after all what it should be; its aspect could be changed according to the use we made of it; its color depended on the lenses through which we looked at it; and its hardness or softness, its painfulness or soothing power, depended on our personal handling of it.

As I could not go to Beirut without the permission of the sultan because of my father's position in the palace, my desire turned to Antigone, the quiet little island in the Marmora where I had stayed in 1901 after my graduation. I wanted a house, an old-fashioned one, with wisteria-covered windows and roses in the garden, big rooms and large halls like the ones in which I had been born but which had been sold some years ago.

There are queer coincidences in life; and a house was actually found in Antigone as like granny's house as two houses could be. The garden was a profusion of rose-bushes; its double stairs had long windows over which wisteria and ivy coiled. It was on raised ground, and below it a steep hill covered with pines ran down to the beach. I went to the place as an invalid and recovered fast both in body and mind. It was the final conquest of my mature self over the foolish whims and the precocious mind of a rather ridiculous young girl. I have gone through great suffering since then, but nothing has ever been able to bring back the mental disorder and estrangement from my kind which I then experienced, and nothing has ever been able to keep me from the enjoyment of the humble things which Allah has put into the world.

We lived in the pine-woods. Every morning we started from the house with the babies, their nurses, and the cook all on donkeys, and we did not return till evening. Reshé had developed into a fine colored lady, dressed in the latest fashion, proud of the attention she attracted, and always taking care to wear a thick veil and gloves, which caused her to be taken for a white woman with a beautiful figure. She took charge of Ali Ayetullah, and Hassan had his old Greek nurse. I lay in a hammock the whole day, body and heart and mind open to the salty warmth of the sea air and the pungent scent of the pines. I was convinced I should get well, for in spirit I felt back in my first childhood. In my new outlook on life the continual intellectual worry had abated. I somehow sensed the human heart better and ceased to be impatient of its foolishness.

As I grew stronger we enlarged our circle of friends, at first with reluctance on my part, but later with real enjoyment. There were some old pupils of Salih Zeki Bey's, some college friends of mine, and some neighbors in Antigone, who included Hussein Jahid Bey and his family. With these we made excursions by boat or went on simple picnics and thus spent a summer of peaceful well-being, oblivious of the throes of the country under its most tyrannical ruler.

The winter of 1907 I passed quietly in Pera. I was deep in old Turkish books, especially the chronicles. I got to reading Naima, the wonderful Turkish chronicler who reaches to the levels of Shaksperian psychological penetration in his very simple yet vivid description. Sometime previously in my nights of insomnia I had begun reading his almost incomprehensible and very formless old prose, and till I could penetrate the hard crust of his language, and till his critical and intensely living presentation of facts emerged upon me, he succeeded in putting me to sleep. But the moment the difficulties of its external form disappeared and I lost consciousness of the form as something apart I had a wonderful vision of individual souls, large crowds, and revolutions in life and action. He was opening my eyes to the psychology of the old Turks, and I found the key which would interpret many moments of psychological importance in our early history, in the bewilderingly fast changes which were now taking place before my eyes.

In May, 1908, we went back to the old house in Antigone, and till the actual Declaration of the Constitution on July 11 of that year we were perfectly unaware of the new life in Macedonia which was blossoming into such tremendous activity.

PART TWO
NEW TURKEY IN THE MAKING

CHAPTER VII

THE PERIOD OF POLITICAL REFORM: THE TANZIMAT, 1839-76

FROM the eleventh century to the fourteenth the new Turkish Empire produced extraordinary sultans, men of great ability and organizing capacity. The fact that the empire governed more justly and humanely than its predecessors, and than the neighboring powers, gave it stability and insured its continuance in a region where the native population much outnumbered the rulers. Able administrators, austere and clean fighters, makers of law, patrons of art, the Ottoman Turks created an Ottoman citizenship which was envied by the members of the neighboring states; and they created an art and a life which have left as much of a mark on the world as any ancient empire, and a greater one than any medieval state.

It is no wonder that the divine right of sultans turned the heads of the ruling dynasty and that they degenerated into tyrants with no ideals except those of personal glory and pomp. The empire lasted for centuries, however, thanks to occasional able leaders and to some wise sultans, and to the vitality of the Ottoman nation.

Besides the internal causes of decay and perpetual wars of aggression so ruinous for the empire, Europe in her feverish progress after the fifteenth century was gaining at a tremendous pace over the Ottoman Empire, for which the seventeenth century saw internal deterioration of every kind, a condition of anarchy at frequent intervals; in the eighteenth century there were feeble attempts to better the conditions of the empire, while its statesmen seemed aghast at the distance gained over it by Europe.

In addition to the serious causes of anxiety which the failing condition of the empire aroused, the French Revolution, which shook political institutions all over the world, quickly sent its loud echo to Turkey.

Selim III (1789–1809), the most progressive sultan in Ottoman history, first declared the desire and necessity for a change, and paid with his life. Gentle and good beyond his time, perhaps beyond ours as well, he was powerless to resist the tremendous momentum of an old and gigantic empire which finally crushed him and his reform. Although his successor, Mahmoud II (1808–39), wrote Selim's progressive ideas in blood and terrorized opposition into mute obedience before he started his reforms, still it took a hundred years more to put reform, even political reform, into shape.

The necessity of reform, born at first in the minds of the few, showed at the same time to these minds the tremendous distance between the Ottoman Empire and the European states, a distance which the empire had to cover as fast as possible. She was so placed geographically that she was pressed by the surplus energies of the Mediterranean peoples and by the growth and upheaval of the Slavs. There is no nation in the world more in need of a cool head, a strong power of defense, and a pacific development of its internal resources.

Change and reform in nations follow two courses: first, the speedy and bloody course of revolution; second, a gradual growth from within, with little apparent disturbance and bloodshed, although the struggle may be long and painful.

The first demands revolutionaries who pull down the entire edifice of a country, who in their bloody rage destroy useful institutions as well as those that are corrupt and decayed. Revolution is the speediest way, it takes a long time to set up a better state in a place which revolution has ravaged. The supreme example of reform by revolution was set by France.

The second, the way of gradual growth from within, is the happier way for a nation which can gradually evolve her reforms, before new ideas take destructive forms or fall into the hands of unscrupulous and ambitious leaders. England has provided the supreme example of gradual reform and change.

Mahmoud II, cruel in temperament, influenced by the French Revolution, frightened by the tragic end of his predecessor, haunted by the vision of the Ottoman Empire crushed between the East and the West, and torn by internal disorder and decay, was naturally led to take the most destructive methods. He therefore began by massacring a whole army of janizaries, who seemed the only obvious obstacle to change.

Mahmoud II is called the Peter the Great of the

Turks, but he deserves as much criticism as praise. Unfortunately he applied the new spirit with the methods of his bloodiest and most tyrannical ancestors. His reign is one of the most disastrous in our history.

It was Abdul Medjid (1839–56) and his remarkable trio of premiers who started a newer and more modern reform.

Abdul Medjid, who was very much like Selim III in desire for reform and in humane temperament, was first helped by Reshid Pasha, a man who had been premier, minister of foreign affairs, and several times ambassador to Paris and London. Reshid Pasha showed himself modern in method as well as in spirit when he instituted his political reform of 1839, the Tanzimat.

Its fundamental principles were the security of life and property, the supremacy of the law, the organization of taxes, the equality of rights of all the citizens. There is a strong and sincere note in the Tanzimat edict, although it is clumsily written, and ends with a naïve curse against those who contravene it.

The Tanzimat was evolutionary and progressive in spirit rather than radical, and it is the sole reform in the history of Turkey which was not only pacific but constructive and effective. Strange to say the edict's final curse seems to have affected all the leaders who have departed from its liberal spirit and have adopted Mahmoud's radical and bloody method.

The first principle of the Tanzimat, security of life, was of supreme importance to the Turkish people.

THE PERIOD OF POLITICAL REFORM

After the time of the wise early rulers who obeyed the law, and who realized the necessity of respecting human life, the people suffered cruelly under later rulers who were intoxicated with power, and wasted human life and property. In addition to the royal caprices which made the finest and best lose their lives by the mere order of the sultan, ministers and governors carelessly and callously wasted human life in Turkey. There are significant anecdotes [1] that illustrate the continual horror which the people felt at the insecurity of life. At last, however, the realization came to the sultan that no growth or stability was possible without security of life, and this was now insured by the Tanzimat.

The equality of non-Moslems appears at first to have been provided for more because of political reasons than of urgent necessity. The non-Moslems had rather enjoyed privileges than suffered from the general social and political disorder of the Moslem communities. Omar,[2] the third calif after the Prophet, at his

[1] A kadi appointed to a province went to make his formal visit to the governor. During the visit the attendants of the governor brought in a man's head freshly cut off and reported that the governor's order to behead his housekeeper had been carried out. The kadi inquired about the man's crime. "The fellow frightened me in my dream last night," was the answer. The next day the kadi gathered his belongings and made haste to depart. When the reason was asked he said, "I cannot prevent myself from appearing in the governor's dream."

A vizir going through the streets incognito was accidentally splashed by some drops of dirty water from a barber shop. He ordered the barber to be put to death instantly. When he was told that the man was his own barber, "Kill some other barber instead," he said; "a vizir's order must be carried out."

[2] The califate, which was in a sense a religious republic during the first century of the Hejira, showed great toleration for the non-Moslems of the conquered lands. Omar's entry into Jerusalem and his treatment of the

conquest of Jerusalem had issued an edict giving to all the non-Moslems security of life and property and freedom with two restrictions: they were required to adopt a special costume, and were not allowed to ride on horseback in the city. Mohammed the Conqueror (1453) after his conquest of Constantinople had confirmed Christian rights and recognized the liberty of the Christians as a community apart. As the Christians were exempt from military service, they held in their hands the commerce of the empire, so that they continually multiplied and grew, for the edicts of the Conqueror and the traditions of Omar were respected. I know of no other country where the minorities were so safe and prosperous during the centuries before they had so-called equal rights.

I have already mentioned that the second part of the reform was of political necessity. When the empire became weak, when it became bewildered with internal and external difficulties, greedy eyes from outside turned to Turkey and found a loophole in the nominal

non-Moslems is one of the most beautiful and humane episodes in history, especially when one compares it with the wholesale massacre of the Moslems by the Crusaders; according to the "New International Encyclopædia," vol. 6, p. 385, "Neither age nor sex could mollify their implacable rage: they indulged themselves three days in a promiscuous massacre; seventy thousand Moslems were put to the sword."

On the other hand, a remarkable story told of Omar illustrates the kindness and simplicity of the man and the spirit of Islam at the period. When the Saracen army entered Jerusalem the patriarch took the key of the city and walked out in order to pay his respects and offer the key to the commander-in-chief. As he approached the camel of the commander-in-chief, the man whom he took for Omar addressed him, saying: "This is Omar's camel, but I am his slave. He has one single camel, and we take turns. It is his turn to walk. Walk on; you will see him coming on foot."

LANDING-PLACE IN SCUTARI

inequality of the Christian minorities. Russia's pretext was found in the Orthodox Christians, as England's was the Armenians later on.

At the time of the Tanzimat, Russia, as the protector of the Orthodox Christians, was pressing Turkey; England, which was at the other side of the political balances, wanted Turkey to hold her own against Russia.

Lord Stratford de Redcliffe, the English ambassador to Turkey, now played an important part in Turkish politics. He influenced Reshid Pasha on many points of policy, and probably the provision of equality of rights for Christians was due to him. The Turkish people were used to respecting the lives and the property of a minority, who were almost like religious trusts to them and who went their way without sharing the military burdens of the ruling race. This tolerance had its roots in the chivalrous attitude of the master to the inferior as well as in the broad spirit of Islam toward alien religions. But the moment the Christians were granted equality by an edict, without sharing responsibility as the soldier citizens of the state, the social order and the old tolerant tradition was upset. Reshid Pasha, knowing all this clearly, evidently undertook the premature consolidation of the external policy of the empire. As I have already said, it was due to the influence of Lord Stratford de Redcliffe, the English ambassador of the time; I will add that he also represented the best and the most lasting impressions of England in the minds of the general Turkish public. He created such a sincere trust and admiration for the justice and the nobility of the English character that neither Abdul Hamid's anti-British policy nor the World War could efface it till the English army occupation, short as its duration was, erased the good impression from the popular mind.

Abdul Medjid was almost alone when he put forth his ideas of reform. The men who stood by him, though few, were strong and determined. Reshid Pasha especially, striving superhumanly to effect the change, knew very well the difficulty, indeed almost the impossibility, of making the masses understand the necessity of the new order of things. As individuals and as classes the Turks were to leap into an entirely different order of things, socially and mentally; and this was not to be done by the old method of bloody terror. In Abdul Medjid, for the first time a sultan of Turkey was going to use moral authority to persuade his subjects. With the example of Selim II before his eyes, Reshid Pasha, on whose shoulders the whole responsibility of the reform rested, was aware of the immediate personal danger in which he stood, for failure would at once have caused the nation to demand his head. On the memorable morning of the day he had to read the edict, he answered his steward, who tried to consult him about household affairs, in this very sentence: "If I return alive in the evening thou canst ask me."

Reshid Pasha and his successors, Ali and Fuad Pashas, all spent their life energy and their extraordinary power of mind and will into converting these edicts of reform and progress into actual fact. It was a hard fight, but all three were men of unflinching courage and tenacity, all three were men of unyielding ideal and honesty, all three died, spent and exhausted before their time.

As progressives rather than as radicals, determined to carry out the reform without the usual method of terror, their difficulties were enormous. Besides internal resistance from privileged classes and persons, they had to face externally the Egyptian question, the Syrian revolution, and the Russian wars. To crown it all, the sultan, although sincere in his desire for progress, objected to the transfer of power from the palace to the Porte, and many were the old pashas who influenced the sultan's mind against the powerful trio. Yet the royal edict worked its way gradually. Half a century later, far on in my childhood, I clearly remember that the equality of races was realized despite the despotic reign of Abdul Hamid.

The Tanzimat period, which brought the first serious political reforms, also produced a wide change in the language, literature, and thought of the country. Modern Europe was furnishing a new current of thought and was creating a new spirit in Turkish writing. The European culture which was most influential in Turkey was decidedly French, the *poètes philosophes*. The nightingale and the eternal rose, the spring, and nature themes of literature were giving way to a wider range of subjects and a new way of looking at man and nature, while the inward change in all directions was leading writers to search for directer and clearer expression in language. Translations from the French were introducing models of French art and thought. It was Shinassi, a poet and author of the time, who first brought to modern Turkish prose a complete change, making it very different from the loose form of the old prose. A younger generation—Namik Kemal, Abdul Hak Hamid, Zia Pasha—blossomed out with a series of dramas, poems, stories, and satires which are considered classical in the Turkish literature of to-day.

This tardy renaissance has not produced masterpieces of world renown in Turkey, but it has produced works which are regarded as great. Besides it represented an admirable effort of human thought and a conscious break from the old in form and spirit, as well as a highly constructive period in Turkish language. There is nothing nebulous or incomplete about the work of these writers. They wrote with a masterly touch and with extraordinary finish; the very translations are a continuous source of surprise to me, so brand-new are they, and yet so Turkish and perfect.

The adaptations, especially that of Molière's "Mariage Forcé," have so recreated the art of Molière that for once a great artist would have been pleased at the perfect shape his masterpieces have taken in an alien culture and language. Ahmed Vefik Pasha, besides being a famous figure of the Tanzimat as a statesman and administrator, is also notable for having most beautifully rendered Molière's work and spirit into Turkish.

Ahmed Vefik Pasha as governor of Broussa put forth

his constructive ability, literary capacity, and administrative genius. He not only conducted the administration so well that the people of Broussa attributed superhuman qualities and loved him as only Turks can love, with a mixture of idolatrous belief and reverence;[3] he also built the great hospital of the town and endowed it with funds, created a theater, becoming its manager, writing the plays, training the actors, and forcing the notables of the town to attend. Through him Molière became the leading influence in the development of the comedy side of the Turkish theater. Molière's spirit, so different from that of the other French classical writers, so human and full of common sense, made an immediate appeal to the simple and sound humor of the ordinary Turk, for not only in "Orta Oyoun" but even in the "Karaguez" one finds the traces of his wit and spirit.

[3] A peasant woman who had lost a watch came to Vefik Pasha. She had heard that the governor could find out anything when he put on his monocle. The pasha, after questioning the woman about the size and appearance of the watch, sent some one to buy a watch from the market. As he handed the watch to the peasant woman he said solemnly, "It is true that I can see everything that happens in this province when I put on my single glass, but the next time you lose something you must come and see me immediately."

CHAPTER VIII

THE YOUNG TURKS

HARDLY twenty years had passed after the Tanzimat reform, and the men who instituted it were still in power, struggling painfully to carry it out, when a younger generation of writers and thinkers went a step further and demanded a constitution. An absolute monarchy with a mere royal edict to guarantee the personal rights of citizens did not satisfy them any more. They demanded representation; they wanted a national assembly. The political ideals of the Reshid Pasha trio appeared old; these men were influenced by the fresher ideals of the French revolutionaries. Under the leadership of Mehemed Bey, Namik Kemal, and Noury (whom I have already mentioned), with some other young thinkers of note, they formed a secret society called the Young Ottomans. Their meeting at Sancta Sophia was found out by the government, and they escaped to Paris to avoid punishment. All the Ottoman students in Paris as well as the French youth who were opposed to Napoleon III joined them, and they were favorably received in French circles. The name of Young Turks was given to the Young Ottomans at this period. The leader and representative of the Young Turks in politics, the man who was to carry out their ideals in politics, was Midhat Pasha.

The political adherents of the Young Turks in Constantinople decided to dethrone Abdul Aziz (1861-76), the successor of Abdul Medjid; and they had an understanding, on which they founded considerable hopes, with Murad, the heir to the throne, who promised to call a national assembly. Abdul Aziz was dethroned and committed suicide in 1876. This was taken as a pretext by the reactionaries and Abdul Hamid to accuse the constitutional reform cabinet of having murdered Abdul Aziz. Sultan Murad V, on whom the Young Turk party depended, became mentally deranged after a reign of three months, which left the throne for Abdul Hamid in 1876. The new sultan affected a liberal attitude and promised to call a national assembly. The Young Turks returned from Paris, and Namik Kemal published the newspaper "Ibret," which became the medium of expression for liberty and progress.

Midhat Pasha as the prime minister called a council to draft the constitution, with Namik Kemal as one of the members. After six months of labor the council presented a draft.

Midhat Pasha announced the constitution to the people by a royal edict of Abdul Hamid, which he caused to be read in the big open place behind the Sublime Porte. The historian Abdurrahman Sheref, who died recently at the age of eighty-four, having lived through the great reform, tells of the event in his "Historical

Talks." "It was a rainy day, but the place was full. I had to push and be pushed by elbows and umbrellas till I found myself a place near the pulpit. The secretary, Mahmoud Bey, read the edict, and Midhat Pasha gave a benedictional speech. It was the only time I had seen and heard Midhat Pasha, and I still remember the tremor and the emotion of his voice. . . . Later on as a young liberal I took an active part in the elections which were to take place for the first time in Turkey. The old men in my quarter were extremely cautious and hesitating. When one of them had to sign the voting paper he said, 'My son, I owe some arrears of tax; will they take it from me if I sign?'"

Although Abdurrahman Sheref by this sentence showed how little prepared the people were for representative government, still as one reads the accounts of the parliamentary discussions and speeches of the first assembly, which lived only a few months, one is struck by the courageous and liberal spirit of the members. Their denunciation of tyranny is surprising and gives one the idea that some of the men at least were ripe for constitutionalism.

Before the national assembly met in Constantinople, Abdul Hamid in a moment of fear betrayed the tyrannical side of his nature by arresting Midhat Pasha and sending him out of Turkey. The assembly, for which Midhat Pasha suffered so much, opened in the last months of 1876 and was dissolved in 1877, the pretext for its dissolution being the Russian war and Turkey's internal diffculties.

In 1878 the general amnesty brought back **Midhat** Pasha; he was appointed governor first to the Rumelian provinces, and then to Damascus and Syria. His achievements as a governor are unique. A series of public works, a real conception of good and just administration unparalleled before and after, a modern attitude toward accepting the equality of individual rights of all citizens are the traditions he has left behind him. But his high ideals and unsullied integrity were to be his undoing, for these were the characteristics that the treacherous and sinister mind of Abdul Hamid most feared and hated. It was while Midhat Pasha was governor of Smyrna that he was summoned to Yildiz, there to appear before the Supreme Court, which charged him with the murder of Abdul Aziz. Forged evidence was brought against him, paid witnesses perjured themselves freely, and Midhat Pasha was condemned to death, when, to the surprise of all, Abdul Hamid, suddenly assuming the guise of the merciful monarch, commuted his sentence to imprisonment for life. He was sent to the dungeons of Taif with some other members of his cabinet. Hardly two years passed when Abdul Hamid, once more frightened at the possibility of Midhat Pasha's release, sent Riza Pasha, who was his minister of war for years; and Riza Pasha had Midhat Pasha, with a few others sentenced at the Yildiz trial, strangled in the dungeons of Taif. Thus died Midhat Pasha, one of the greatest of Turkish patriots, paying the highest price which Turks have paid for patriotism.

Namik Kemal's newspaper was stopped, but he, with Noury Bey, Zia Pasha, and some other Turkish writers, was at the head of the Guedik Pasha Theater, presenting their translated or created plays, when Namik Kemal's "Vatan" (Fatherland) was produced. It caused such an outburst of applause that an enormous mass of people followed Namik Kemal home, applauding and shouting, "Long live Vatan, long live Liberty." The very next night at the second presentation of the play Namik Kemal was arrested and exiled, where he also had to expiate his love and service to his country.

A dark reign of tyranny and of despotism, a system of terror and espionage, is the story of the rest of Abdul Hamid's reign. The words "patriotism," "fatherland," and other expressions of liberty were abolished from the dictionaries; the collections of Tanzimat literature were destroyed wherever they were found and the owners punished with perpetual banishment. A few newspapers were published, beginning with a prayer for the sultan and filling the rest of their pages with lists of promotions and articles on science or travel.

These were the papers I saw in my childhood and early youth. All the great leaders had expired and left the sultan supreme. Most of the Young Turks with some exceptions had lost either their ideals or their hopes. Some used their liberal views as a pretext to extract money from the sultan; it was in some cases political blackmail. In fact very few of the figures who emerged during the revolution of 1908 were found among the political refugees in Europe; they were not Europeanized men such as the Tanzimatists and the first Young Turks. There was an anonymous and strong revolutionary element, with vaguer tendencies of mind, who translated such thought as they had into action with the energy and ferocious power of the Macedonians. At the beginning of 1908 no serious likelihood could be seen that the régime would be opposed. The Turkish people had to grin and bear the existing state of things, which was then of thirty years' standing.

CHAPTER IX

THE CONSTITUTIONAL REVOLUTION OF 1908

ON the morning of July 11, 1908, I was sitting in the spacious hall of Antigone, with my old friends from Beshiktash, Auntie Peyker and her husband Hamdi Effendi. Their son was the young officer who had escaped to Europe and joined the Young Turks, and they often came to me to talk of him and to get his letters, for they corresponded with him through an American friend of mine. They had no hope of ever seeing their son alive. Hamidian rule had a finality and inevitability which made one almost laugh at the idea that it could be changed by a few pamphlets published occasionally in Paris and sent to Constantinople in secret.

I well remember the silence before Salih Zeki Bey came into the hall with the morning paper open in his hands. Granny, who lived with me at the time, was peacefully settled on the corner sofa.

Salih Zeki Bey walked slowly, his eyes on the first page of the paper, and with a strange look of surprise on his face. Then he read aloud the imperial communiqué of four lines. The cringing praise of the sultan was even more exaggerated than usual, but the

THE CONSTITUTIONAL REVOLUTION OF 1908

communiqué was written in concise terms and said that his Majesty the sultan was to restore the constitution of 1876.

As we listened in the old-fashioned hall, with the wide stretch of wonderful blue sea expanding behind a line of dark green pines, consternation overcame us.

The old pair sat in silence, the tears rolling down their wrinkled cheeks. Laconic as were those lines, they transfigured the minds of these old people with the radiant hope that they might see their son again. Granny, who hardly understood the meaning, looked over her spectacles as she asked:

"What does it mean, Halidé?"

What did it mean? I hardly realized that a long scene of heaven and hell was to be enacted in the smothered land of Turkey and that I was to be called to act, to suffer, to knock my foolish young head against the realities of life, struggling endlessly, watching the interminable tragedy to its bitter end. This was to be my education in life after my education in school.

But now to return to our little group. The subject seemed alien and hard to discuss. The word "constitution," after its exile from the dictionary, was now suddenly used again in an imperial communiqué. The indestructibility of thought is marvelous; it is always there, blind to individual suffering and cost, boring its way from mind to mind, leaping large gaps and periods; but triumphant always, it marches on regardless of time, ceaselessly developing and maturing in the mind of man.

Here is a short résumé of the events which had led to the communiqué of July 11, 1908.

Abdul Hamid, in the sham trial and assassination of Midhat Pasha, had dealt a heavy blow to the constitutional ideal in Turkey. His thirty years' reign was a systematic suppression of all hopes of reform, free thought, and speech. Still desire for representative government flickered in individual minds but with no effective result. The Young Turks continued their organization in Paris; but with divided leadership, and with their inability to take any positive action in Turkey, all their labors failed to help the sorry state of things in that country.

Only Saloniki, the central city of Macedonia, which had a special administrative system of its own that was superior to any other in the empire, seemed at all favorable to the expression of freer thought. In fact it was here that the constitutional ideal found its first serious organization in 1906.

It was the secret organization of the freemasons which served the revolutionaries as a model. Talaat, Maniassi Zade Refik, Djavid, Rahmi, Midhat Shukri Beys are some of the best known names of the men who started the secret revolutionary society under the name of Liberty in 1906. The liaison between the Young Turks in Paris and the Young Turks in Macedonia was to be maintained by Dr. Nazim. On his arrival the name of the society was changed to Union and Progress. Some of the young officers of the Third Army Corps joined it immediately and became the vital force of the organization; among the most active of these were Enver, Ismail Hakki, Eyoub Sabri, Kiazim Karabekir, Fethi, Niazi, Moustafa Kemal, Djafer Tayyar, and Djemal Beys. But the names which were most celebrated at the time were those of Fethi, Niazi, and Enver. The only woman member was Eminé Semie Hanum, the daughter of the famous historian Djevdet Pasha, and a well known woman writer.

From 1906 to 1907 it passed through a feverish propaganda period, enlisting new members and organizing its centers in Monastir, Euskub, Resné, and some other towns in Macedonia. The Central Committee was in Saloniki, and the first members included Talaat and Djemal, the two most important figures of the party.

Abdul Hamid heard of it in 1907 and began immediate steps, trying to remove the suspected officers from Saloniki, and sending in his spies, as well as also some regiments from Smyrna, to crush the organization.

The Young Turks immediately passed to action by shooting Shemsi Pasha, who seemed determined and able to fight them; it was also desirable to remove Marshal Osman Pasha from the scene of action, but the fact that he was a national hero and a genuinely fine commander made them wish to spare his life; he was therefore kidnapped and kept out of the way. When the regiments from Smyrna also passed over to the revolutionary camp, things looked serious.

On July 10, 1908, Resné, Euskub, and Monastir declared the constitution under Niazi and Enver, and telegraphed to Abdul Hamid demanding the official declaration of the constitution and threatening a march on Constantinople with the Third Army Corps in case of refusal. The short communiqué of July 11, 1908, was its outcome.

The history of the first two years of Union and Progress deserves to be carefully written. Its spirit and its message to Turkey, which turned the tide of events for good and evil, must be recorded in its own virile and forcible tones. Although I have known most of the leading figures well and for a long time, and some have told me its early history, still in 1908 I was totally ignorant of its existence. It is for them to tell the story of their pioneer years. I go back to my hall in Antigone and take up the moment when Salih Zeki Bey read the communiqué.

What was the effect of this thunderbolt in the city of Istamboul? How would the city act, or how had it already acted? These were the enigmas we tried to solve that morning.

It was Hussein Jahid who brought us the news in the evening. The city had looked hesitatingly at the constitution so suddenly and simply announced. The people gathered at street corners and tried to talk in undertones, but there was a feeling of uncertainty, even of distrust, a vague questioning as to the meaning of this sudden change; some went so far as to take it for a trap in which to catch the people of Istamboul. Hussein Jahid had written enthusiastic editorials for

A VERY OLD STREET IN SCUTARI

THE CONSTITUTIONAL REVOLUTION OF 1908

"Sabah" and "Ikdam," the two prominent papers of the capital, for the next morning.

We had a sleepless night, sometimes talking but mostly thinking. I wandered restlessly in the large hall, walking out into the warm July night that was so sweet and balmy. Something invisible and new in the air haunted us. We had queer dreams and visions about the terror and blood which accompany revolutions, but we did not allow them utterance.

The words "equality, liberty, justice, and fraternity" sounded most strange. Fraternity was added on account of the Christians. The great ideals of Tanzimat, expressed as the Union of the Elements, had taken this familiar form. There had never been a more passionate desire in the peoples of Turkey to love each other, to work for the realization of this new Turkey, where a free government and a free life was to start.

Poor granny was restless. "No good comes out of new things. What you call constitution was given at the time of Midhat Pasha, and he lost his head for it," she said.

In the evening of July 12, Hussein Jahid brought us news from the city once more. Usually so impassive and calm, he also seemed affected by the enthusiasm of the city. The papers might have been printed on gold-leaf, so high were the prices paid for them. People were embracing each other in the streets in mad rejoicing. Hussein Jahid smilingly added, "I had to wash my face well in the evening, for hundreds who did not know me from Adam, hundreds whom I have never seen, kissed me as I walked down the road of the Sublime Porte; the ugly sides of revolution, vengeance and murder, will not stain ours."

The next day I went down to see Istamboul. The scene on the bridge caught me at once. There was a sea of men and women all cockaded in red and white, flowing like a vast human tide from one side to the other. The tradition of centuries seemed to have lost its effect. There was no such thing as sex or personal feeling. Men and women in a common wave of enthusiasm moved on, radiating something extraordinary, laughing, weeping in such intense emotion that human deficiency and ugliness were for the time completely obliterated. Thousands swayed and moved on. Before each official building there was an enormous crowd calling to the minister to come out and take the oath of allegiance to the new régime.

As I drove along the Sublime Porte the butchers of Istamboul were leaving its austere portals in their white chemises. They also had come to get assurance from the highest that this new joy was to be safeguarded and that they, the butchers, also were going to share in this great task.

In three days the whole empire had caught the fever of ecstasy. No one seemed clear about its meaning. The news of the change had come from Saloniki through several young officers whose names were shouted as its symbol. To the crowd the change in its clearest sense spelled the pulling down of a régime which meant oppression, corruption, and tyranny, while the new, whatever it was, spelled happiness and freedom.

I went down to the city twice that week and came back stirred to the very depths of my being. The motley rabble, the lowest pariahs, were going about in a sublime emotion, with tears running down their unwashed faces, the shopkeepers joining the procession without any concern for their goods. There seemed to be no thieves and no criminals. Dr. Riza Tewfik and Selim Sirry paraded their handsome figures on horseback, solving the judicial difficulties of the people with long speeches. It looked like the millennium.

In every street corner some one stood up on a chair or on the box of a carriage and made a speech to an admiring crowd. One man with a long red beard harangued the people near the bridge with those words: "I have a beloved wife and five children. I swear that I am ready to cut them to pieces for the sacred cause as I would have done for his Majesty."

I wondered why he did not cut himself rather than his wife and children and why he felt so deeply in love with his Majesty at this particular moment. The man was our neighbor and became a deputy for Siverek in the elections. I believe that it was sheer hysteria which made him speak so at the moment. But the most popular speaker of the day was Riza Tewfik. As the Hamidian police were entirely cowed by the fear of the mob and did not dare to interfere, it was Riza Tewfik who marched on horseback and kept in order the mob which followed him, by speaking all the time. He was perfectly hoarse at the end of the week, so much so that when he came to see us in Antigone he spoke in whispers. A young friend of Salih Zeki Bey's who had heard him speak to a crowd of Kurdish porters in Istamboul used to mimic this whole scene with great effect. Here is some of the speech as he purported to have heard it:

"Tell us what constitution means," the porters had shouted.

"Constitution is such a great thing that those who do not know it are donkeys," answered the speaker.

"We are donkeys," roared the porters.

"Your fathers also did not know it. Say that you are the sons of donkeys," added Dr. Riza Tewfik.

"We are the sons of donkeys," roared the porters again.

In the general enthusiasm and rebirth I became a writer. Istamboul in the enchantment and beauty of the first days reminded me of a line of Tewfik Fikret, from his "Mist." He had written it in secret, and it had circulated from hand to hand in the old days. The poet, looking through the enchanted mist of Istamboul, had seen all that was incurable, unclean, and evil in the hearts and lives of its dwellers, and painting it in lurid word-coloring, he had asked, "Among the millions who live in thy heart, how many spirits will rise pure and luminous?"

The mist with all the evil and unclean spirit had dispersed, and the people were in the throes of a marvelous spiritual rebirth.

THE CONSTITUTIONAL REVOLUTION OF 1908

The newspaper "Tanine" appeared on July 20, 1908. Tewfik Fikret and Hussein Jahid edited it together, and they had a staff composed of the ablest and best known writers of the day. Salih Zeki Bey was to collaborate in its scientific departments, and I was to write in its literary columns.

The paper had almost all the writers of the Edebiati-Djedide (New Literature) school. They were considered the great writers of the period, and their greatest figure as man and poet was Tewfik Fikret.

Edebiati-Djedide, which arose in the worst part of Abdul Hamid's reign, when the very words with which to express free ideas could not be used, was still in spirit a continuation of the Namik Kemal and Tanzimat schools. They continued transfusing Western culture into Turkish ideas as best they could. Halid Zia, the first modern Turkish novelist, a follower of Paul Bourget but an original and powerful short story writer, and Jenab Shehabbeddine, a clever prose writer and a remarkable lyric poet, were in the staff of "Tanine."

Riza Tewfik had read and made me acquainted with the school, through their writings in "Servet-Funoun," a popular literary magazine of the time. Hussein Jahid as the strongest and most powerful critic, indeed the unique critic of the last twenty years, was also one of the personalities of the literary school. Although his prose was considered in the first rank, he appeared to me in his literary attempts to be either too sentimental or too didactic. Hampered in his style and fettered in his thoughts by the censor, as he himself expressed it, he realized his powers fully in his political writings during the Unionist régime after 1908. The school was fiercely attacked by the old writers for its imitation of European culture, and had been equally criticized by my contemporaries for lack of personality. But it must have succeeded in transmitting a new message and a new life in its work, for the new age looked up to it as the intellectual representative of the day.

To my mind neither Edebiati-Djedide nor the younger writers of whom I shall speak more fully later have recreated, in their writings, the Turkish life of the times and its inner psychology, so well as some of the oldest Turkish chroniclers had done of their own time. Naima shows in one single revolutionary scene a singular power of representing the setting as well as the thoughts and the feelings of his time, with an understanding which would sound true and real in any age, although the Turkish prose of the period in its loose and primitive form of the day was hardly a fit instrument to express such a perfect picture of real life. Both Edebiati-Djedide and my own contemporaries lacked that supreme genius which creates life from within without binding itself to schools, styles, or tendencies in fashion.

To me, at the time of which I speak, it was flattering to collaborate with the famous writers of the day; I was entirely unknown and was just at the beginning of my career as a writer.

"Tanine" appeared as an event in the country. No other paper had such a brilliant position, such an enor-

THE CONSTITUTIONAL REVOLUTION OF 1908

mous sale and popularity; but before three months had passed the entire hatred of the opposition focused against it. The reading of the consecutive issues of "Tanine" in 1908 and 1909 would give one a very fair idea of the new life, the good and the bad tendencies which started with the revolution.

Tewfik Fikret and Hussein Jahid were the leading forces of the paper in the first years. It sounds strange to write in 1925 that I have never seen Tewfik Fikret. I was not emancipated enough to go to the newspaper offices, and I saw only a few men among the most intimate friends of Salih Zeki Bey and my father; but I have carefully followed Fikret's career, which had throughout an important effect upon the currents of thought in Turkey.

The personality of Tewfik Fikret was that of an apostle. His passionate belief in humanity and international understanding allied him more with the first promoters of the constitution and with the Tanzimatists rather than with the Young Turks of 1908. He stood for the Ottoman ideal of the Union of the Elements, or the fraternity doctrine. He was a great patriot and believed in a high standard of Ottoman citizenship; he never fell under the influence of the nationalist tendencies which, from different causes and events, shaped Turkey in the later years. Tewfik Fikret's personal austerity and lofty morality made him a very effective example for the youth of Turkey. He presented the spectacle of a clean and very moral man without religion, which is a rarity in Turkey.

Tewfik Fikret attacked above all else these two things: tyranny and religion. Being a man *sans peur et sans reproche,* he did not realize the social and individual value of religion, its importance in human morals and culture, its historic necessity to complete the social evolution in the early stages of human society. He saw only how men in general suffered from the tyranny and the narrow rule of the churches, how men rent each other in the name of religion all over the world, and what political use they made of creeds and of their gods. His famous attack on religion called "History" aroused a tremendous storm in religious circles, and he was mercilessly attacked by the clericals, both during his life and after his death.

He shared, however, one trait with the Unionists and the reactionaries. He was as narrow and as merciless as they were to those who deviated from his own line in politics and in principles of every kind, and he fought them down as ferociously as did his opponents. The inflexibility and the rocky resistance of the man constituted both his force and his weakness.

His later attacks on the Unionists, formerly his friends, were quietly received. They had indeed deserved his bitter reproaches after the Galata Serai affair of which I shall speak later, and the personal respect which the Unionists had for him, both as an old comrade and as a great man, made them tolerant of everything he wrote or said.

So we see that "Tanine" had the benefit of this

THE CONSTITUTIONAL REVOLUTION OF 1908

gigantic energy to fight down the old state of things in 1908 and partly in 1909.

After Fikret had left "Tanine" the second living force was Hussein Jahid. An ardent admirer and disciple of Fikret in his philosophical tendencies, and a fanatical believer in the necessity of the westernization of Turkey, he put forth all his intellectual forces in the cause of progress. Personally calm, well balanced, and reserved, he became ferocious in his polemics against the conservatives during the first period of Unionist power. His ardent advocacy of the new life and progress developed in him to the utmost degree the power for sharpness of attack. The antagonistic tone of his writings has since mellowed down to a more moderate and calmer but much more effective pitch.

He had the same intense feeling against the separatist influence of religion that Fikret had. He seriously believed in the separation of church and state but was not able to stand up for it in his paper on account of the immense reactionary passion which his publications and the revolution aroused. After the Balkan War he showed decided nationalistic tendencies which separated him from Fikret.

The Unionists had come to a superficial understanding with two different minority revolutionary societies: the Tashnaks, the Armenian revolutionary leaders; and the Macedonians, led by their famous chiefs, Sandoski and Panitcha.[1] The Albanian and the various Arabic

[1] He was recently killed by a Bulgarian girl in Vienna during a theatrical performance.

revolutionary societies were in the making and had not been considered at all. In fact the active and vital elements of the Unionists were largely influenced by the narrow and somewhat violent principles of the Tashnaks and the Macedonians. The Armenians massacring the Turks in Eastern Anatolia and Adana, the Turks massacring the Armenians in the same regions, the Bulgarians massacring the Turks in the Balkans were animated by the same spirit. On the other hand, Russia or any other imperialistic power of the West that needed free and unoccupied ground for economic and political penetration inflamed and encouraged the conflicts of the Near-Eastern races with all the means at its command.

The Young Turks stepped into power without having studied the strength of the separatist tendencies, or the way to deal with them in case the constitution of 1876, which they were restoring, should fail to solve the fearfully complicated Ottoman dilemma. Turkey was an empire; the new leaders were at heart unconsciously empire men with a moderate constitutional ideal which accorded representation to all; and they did not realize their responsibilitiy in any other important issue. The fixed idea, that once representative government is established all the old evils will be cured, blinded them to a clear study of the political situation in Europe and in their own country. The enthusiastic wave of approval and sympathy which the peoples of Europe sent us created a sense of security at first, and no one saw that behind the generosity of peoples there is the

THE CONSTITUTIONAL REVOLUTION OF 1908

rapacity of governments, till Turkey began to be attacked on all sides in the very midst of her reform struggles. The annexations of Bosnia-Herzegovina, Crete, and the Rumelian provinces and the invasion of Tripoli succeeded each other in a bewilderingly short time.

During the first weeks of the revolution a large number of newspapers appeared, each putting forth a new idea at random and each fighting the ideas of another paper. It was almost impossible to disentangle and detach ideas clearly and analyze their significance. Some have developed into forces for good and evil, and others have disappeared equally for good or evil.

Among the progressive thoughts which "Tanine" advocated and which aroused the bitterest opposition was that of emancipation of woman. The very mention of giving her an equal chance in education and of elevating her social status enraged the conservatives. They did not realize that "Tanine" was not yet a party organ and that its ideas about the emancipation of women and the complete westernization of all the Turkish institutions were put forth on its own responsibility.

The young leaders of the revolution on the other hand were politically occupied, struggling to change the cabinets which did not suit them and spreading their organization all over the empire in a way which was changing the center of the executive power, taking it from the government organizations and passing it on to the party centers.

It is important to note that the duality of the executive power, only the semblance of which was in the government while the reality was in the hands of the party centers, was heading Turkey for the first time toward a party dictatorship. A very old and ardent Unionist returning from Russia in 1922 told me humorously that the Union and Progress was copied in Russia. "Nothing new in Russia," he said. "The system is ours whatever the principles are. Except that they have added the Cheka and do not possess our governing capacity."

The Fascist system in Italy and the People's party in Turkey are now two rather violent types of the Unionist system, with a single man at the head of each, instead of the triumvirate and the immediate circle around it which ruled the Unionist régime.

The purely Unionist publications of the party had a military and primitive character, and they consisted of violent papers with very destructive names: "The Thunderbolt," "The Gun," "The Bayonet," etc.

The elements of the opposition, which started within a few months after the revolution, were these: the conservatives, who sincerely feared a radical change which might entirely upset the old social order and tear the country to pieces; the clericals, who sensed a lay tendency in the new order of things; the political institutions of the minorities, including the patriarchate, which feared the complete loss of their authority if the Union of the Elements principle were realized; and the powers, who, having made their spoliation plans, feared the loss of their strategic grounds, if a serious parliamentary

THE CONSTITUTIONAL REVOLUTION OF 1908

government were established and the minorities were satisfied. The common and the most explosive weapons they used were reactionary, women and religion being the supreme ones. Every politician who wanted to arouse popular feeling against the new régime, and all the interests which were concerned to fight down the spirit of the revolution, united in playing on the fanatical fervor and the reactionary tendencies of the Moslem communities. There were, however, a few useful tendencies in the opposition, the most important being that of Prince Sebahheddine's Decentralization, but it got lost in the general whirlpool of ideas and the conflict of the newspapers.[2]

The classification of the Unionist forces at the time would be something like this: writers like Fikret or Jahid who either belonged or did not belong to the Union and Progress but stood up for the new order of things on account of their progressive ideals; the organizers of the Union and Progress, military or civil leaders who did not occupy important posts officially but interfered in the operation of the government and did not allow it to function independently; a spontaneous propagandist class moving all over the country, giving lectures, opening schools and night classes for the people, and literary clubs; finally, the floating class of men who were spies under Abdul Hamid but liberals and business men under the Unionist régime—in short men with no color or conviction who pass from one party

[2] The spirit of his program was partial autonomy for different races of the empire.

in power to another so long as there is some material interest to be gained.

In October we returned to the city. We took a house in Istamboul near Nouri-Osmanie, which is central and near the schools and the university where Salih Zeki Bey taught. As all the printing houses and the newspaper offices as well as all the intellectual institutions were there, one felt the immense throbbing moments of Turkish life around one. I had become a very busy journalist and writer in three months. I received a great many letters on widely varied subjects. Sometimes my correspondents asked social questions, sometimes political ones, but each took care to send me a long exposition of his own views. Some of the letters were about family problems and secrets; no Catholic priest could have received fuller and more candid confessions than I did during those months. I carefully burned them with professional discretion. All my correspondents may be assured that their personal secrets are safe.

Besides these letters I received visits from a great many women belonging to different classes who came to me with their personal troubles and asked advice. It was through these visits that I first became aware of some of the tragic problems of the old social order. I am indeed grateful to those humble women who brought to me their difficulties in their relations to their families and to society. I got much valuable life material from their stories. The surface of the political revolution was of passing interest, but the undercurrents of life, which started in the social depths of Turkey, drew me irresistibly into its whirlpool.

October saw the beginning of the elections, and the elections were the panacea put forth by the new system for holding the empire together, and for silencing the far-off voices of danger which thundered on the horizon.

The leading figures of all the national groups were chosen as deputies in the new parliament. We never had an assembly composed of so many daring and famous men; when they gathered together, the atmosphere thus created lacked harmony. Ideals and personalities clashed immediately and inevitably. All that was alive, vital, and energetic in the country had been hurled into the parliament. Though there was good will and simplicity in the power which sent them there, there was also ignorance about their conflicting properties. The Young Turks had every intention of creating a series of columns to hold the structure of the empire up, but the columns were so varied in size that they finally permitted the complete crumbling away of the imperial edifice they had sought to uphold.

"O country, O mother, be thou happy and joyful today," sang the large and mixed crowd, passing from under the windows of my house in Nouri-Osmanie. No one who heard it sung in the ecstatic tones of the crowds could keep back his tears, so much did it express of sincerity and joy. Masses of people followed the election urns, decked in flowers and flags. In carriages oat the Moslem and Christian priests, hand in hand. Christian and Moslem maidens, dressed in white, locked in childish embrace, passed on, while the crowd that followed sang enthusiastically, "O country, O mother, be thou joyful and happy to-day."

The memory is so intense that to this day I cannot think of it unmoved. I think of it as a final embrace of love between the simple peoples of Turkey before they should be led to exterminate each other for the political advantage of foreign powers and their own leaders.

I found granny crying each time the weird music, the singing, ecstatic crowd, passed, and each time she shook her head and said:

"It means the end of everything. No good will come out of it; I cannot help crying. It gives me a creepy feeling down my spine as if I heard the Mevloud" (the sacred poem of Mohammed's birth chanted in religious ceremonies).

I felt exactly the same religious emotion as if I too heard the Mevloud chanted. But, alas, the holy babe was destined to turn into a monster before it could stand on its feet.

The election quarrels stormed high and low, blackmail tainted the opposition, while the Unionist press took a truculent and threatening tone. The voices of discord were shrieking their loudest while the representatives elected by the peoples and the national groups assembled for the parliament—a parliament consisting of the most revolutionary spirits of the time, and opened by one of the greatest despots in history.

Alexandre Pankoff

IN ISTAMBOUL

CHAPTER X

TOWARD REACTION; THE ARMENIAN QUESTION

THE official entry into the parliament of the new representatives, in their simple black coats, side by side with the brilliant uniforms and the jeweled decorations of the Hamidian officials, marked the visible passage of Turkey from the old régime to the new. As one watched the splendid procession with its streak of men in black, one's heart cried out, "Behold the coming régime!"

Around that coming régime the storm gathered. At first the opposition was concentrated against the political organizations and the political writers, but the moment was coming when every writer who stood for progress without taking sides with any political party was to be attacked. For the moment the opposition really barred the way to any kind of new thought. Instead of concentrating against the rather raw, impetuous, and tactless politics of the Union and Progress, the opposition attacked persons and progress. The Byzantinism and Levantinism of the opposition went to such depths that the non-party element and the progressives who were shocked by the intolerance of the Unionist party in its narrow attitude nevertheless rallied around it, so bitter and personal did the method of the opposition appear. On the other hand the party in power became deaf and intolerant to even sincere and well meant criticism. Lack of liberalism on one side and lack of principle on the other gradually destroyed the party dictatorship in Turkey.

It was in January that I received the first but not the last danger-signal in the form of an anonymous letter. In all my writings I had clearly stated my belief in a gradual educational change, in the study and understanding of the difficult social problems of the country, and in the necessity of giving the greatest consideration to educational reform. As these principles, frankly expressed, kept me out of party politics, it was a great and an unpleasant surprise to me suddenly to find myself mixed up in them.

Among the many envelops I have received in my life this one stands out in my memory as clearly as if it lay before me as I write. It was white and small and contained a card and two small square bits of blank paper. On the card there was first an order that I was not to write any more to "Tanine," and then followed the threat that if I did not obey "the punishment will be terrible." I have received many letters of that sort and have actually read my own death sentence in official print, but I have never before or since been so terror-stricken. My hands were cold and damp, and I actually felt weak in the knees.

I can honestly say that I have never felt so cowardly and yet so brave, for I did not capitulate before the physical terror. I had a clear conviction that those who sent me the note were fighting not only the Union and Progress but any form of new thought. I realized next that it was not only my life which they threatened but something else even more terrible for a woman in my position.

When I tried to overcome the physical fear of death and the moral fear of being blackmailed in public in Old Turkey, I saw my little ones—Hassan Togo building a house in bricks, shaking his golden curls happily, and Ali Ayetullah watching my face with his wonderful deep eyes. I was only twenty-four, and this was the price of the literary fame I had acquired in a few months.

I do not know how I lived through the physical and mental horror of the succeeding months but I did live and write for "Tanine" and the other papers as usual. Youth imagines death as an unbelievable horror, but youth is difficult to cow even with the vision of death and disgrace. It was about this time that I came to know a lifelong, honored, and beloved friend in the person of Isabel Fry. I had written a letter intended as an appeal to the "Nation" which attracted her attention, and we exchanged letters. Salih Zeki Bey, who was in London at the time, had called on her, and he gave me his impressions.

"She is a fine woman, but she will be disappointed in you if she comes out to Turkey," he said.

"Why?" I asked, rather piqued.

"Because you look young and foolish, and wear ruby-colored velvet dresses," he said, smiling and pointing at my new frock.

I always think of that ruby-colored dress in connection with Isabel Fry, but I did not have much longer to wear bright-colored dresses at home. (Turkish women of a certain class did not at that time wear colors out of doors.) Miss Fry, who had taken me for an elderly woman from the tone of my letters, happily did like me despite my ruby-colored velvet dress.

She came to Turkey in February, 1909, for the first time and stayed three weeks. We went to see some Turkish women who were interested in reform, and she visited a few schools as well. She wrote an excellent article for "Tanine" on women's education.

The political passion reached its climax in March, 1909, when Hassan Fehmy, a journalist on an opposition paper, was shot on the Galata Bridge. This was the first political murder of the new régime, and it had a very bad effect on every one. The opposition used the funeral as a demonstration against the Unionists. From the corner of my house I saw a bier wrapped in a Persian shawl, with the Arabic verse from the Koran, "One martyr is enough for Allah," written in large letters over the coffin and a white-turbaned crowd following it like an immense daisy-field. The ominous silence gave me the impression of what it must have been like in the old days of Fatih,[1] when thousands of

---

[1] Fatih, as the center of great theological colleges (*medresses*), was always opposed to westernization. Great mutinies in Turkish history were led by the eminent hodjas and the theological students at Fatih, and these mutinies put forth the religious pretext, their usual war-cry being, "We want Sheriat," meaning the holy law.

theological students with their white turbans rose and broke up the reforming tendencies before these tendencies were ripe. I spoke of it to Salih Zeki Bey, who smiled and said: "The Unionists have the chasseur regiments from Saloniki, the founders of the revolution. They need not fear a reaction." At the end of that very month the same regiments supplied the leaders of the counter-revolution from among its sergeants and the corporals.

"Beware the ides of March," I said to myself as I was awakened by unfamiliar and far-off firing on the morning of March 31, 1909. There was a feeling of intense gloom and oppression, although the weather was bright and sunny. A deadly silence reigned in the usually bustling streets, broken only by occasional irregular steps, with the clink of military spurs.

The meaning of this unaccountable firing was announced to us by our old man-servant Hussein. He had been with us since our school days, and I had taught him how to read and write. His education, such as it was, had given him a passion for politics, and he followed cabinet changes and the political quarrels of the papers and parties more than I did. He hated the Unionists and reform, and he would gladly have seen even his own masters torn to pieces on account of their progressive ideas. But he was an old servant and in a strange way my pupil, although he was twice my age, and so we treated his politics as a joke.

I well remember his glee as he knocked at the door of my bedroom that memorable day and said:

"Wake up, Effendim, the army has risen, the bloodstreams carry deputy corpses, Ahmed Riza and Hussein Jahid are torn to pieces before the parliament in Sancta Sophia." (The parliament first met in the Ministry of Justice at Sancta Sophia Square.)

Inconceivable as it seems, in the first moments of Unionist misfortune he had run up to our bedroom door in great joy to tell us of the death of two men both known as radical reformers, although one was our friend and the other a very respected and admired personage.

In his extreme excitement he began from behind the door to tell me about Dervish Vahdeti, the leader of the reaction. Hussein had evidently followed him about as he spoke to the soldiers. Vahdeti was a reactionary and fanatical hodja who preached the wholesale massacre of all the Unionists and of the young students and officers favorable to reform; he considered them the real enemies of the holy religion. He published a paper called "Vulcan" in which he asserted that the British and Russian governments would be far more favorable to the holy law than the existing Turkish government, and that the government, with the Unionists, must be exterminated. This outburst of antinational Islamic fanaticism appeared suspicious, and he was thought to be the paid emissary of the British embassy, a tool of Mr. Fitzmaurice, the first secretary of the embassy, whose name was involved in the counter-revolution of 1909. I did not study the evidence against Vahdeti, for I was absent during his trial, and so I cannot say whether or not there proved to be any truth in this. Anti-patriotic and anti-national church supporters have always existed throughout the history of the Christian Church. Vahdeti might have been a Moslem instance of the same thing. But there has been a change among the fanatics of his sort since then: no Moslem reactionary advocates a foreign occupation now, and the Islamic churches in and out of Turkey have become much more nationalistic.

Salih Zeki Bey went out hastily to find out about the extent and importance of the rising. The next thing I remember about the day is the coming of my father with Dr. Djemal, an old friend from Sultan Tepé. The counter-revolution, they reported, was a very serious one. Mehemed Arslan, the deputy from Lebanon, had been lynched, and Nazim Pasha, the minister of justice, shot before the door of parliament by infuriated soldiers, who took them for Hussein Jahid and Ahmed Riza Beys. The soldiers were shooting their officers, as well as any one else whom their organizations pointed out as a liberal or a reformer.

Tewfik, the son of Auntie Peyker and Hamdi Effendi (the young officer who had returned from Europe after the constitution was declared, but had joined the opposition and was now with the reactionaries), sent word that I must escape to some safe place and that my name was on their black-list. Dr. Djemal asked me to leave the house in disguise and hasten, but I thought that I was safe in my own clothes in Istamboul, for no one would know me there. I took the boys with me and immediately started with my father and Dr. Djemal for Scutari, where I could find a refuge more easily. As we drove along the Sublime Porte firing was going on, and the people were moving like condemned shadows, while solitary soldiers were running hither and thither. We took a boat from Sirkedji, the only one that was available.

I left the boat at the landing in Scutari and had started to walk into the town, holding tightly the hands of the little boys, who were convulsively clutching at my skirts, when suddenly a human hurricane hurled itself on us and flung us apart. It was soldiers from the Selimié barracks, who, after killing their officers, were rushing down to take the boat and join the counter-revolution. I found myself flattened against a shop, Ali Ayetullah was pushed into a coffee-house, and Hassan was thrown against a wall. They were trembling and half fainting with fear but were miraculously unhurt in the brutal stampede. It was my first contact with the mob.

In the meantime father's house, as that of a Unionist, although neither an important nor a very well known one, was in danger. Some Unionist houses were attacked. During the day and the night, Sultan Tepé, so lonely on the top of the green hill, was a scene of shouting, rioting, drum-beating, and firing, while the rifle-shooting from Istamboul rose to a frenzied pitch. The mob with lanterns and drums continued their demonstrations all night, and each time they approached we expected the horror of the final moment. The whole night I sat watching and waiting, the babies crawling around my knees, clutching me as the firing and shouting became louder.

The next morning strange-looking men stood by the door and watched the house. Opposite the garden walls of Sultan Tepé is the *tekké* of the Euzbeks; the sheik as well as his children were friends of my father. That evening in the dusk a young man from the *tekké* jumped over the garden wall and came to the house without being seen by the men at the door. It was he who said that I must escape, for a cousin of theirs, an influential reactionary, was trying to find out if I was in my father's house. An hour or two later under the cover of the night I escaped with the boys through the back door to that holy refuge. The young men of the *tekké* kept armed watch that night, and I rested two nights in that quiet and comparatively safe shelter, but as the reaction grew wilder and as the city was moved more and more by the spirit of massacre, I was no longer safe. When the reactionary cousin, knowing the liberal tendencies of the youth of the *tekké* as well as my father's friendship with the sheik, began to inquire whether I had taken refuge there, I had to leave the sanctuary and seek refuge in the American College, which was then in Scutari.

In leaving the *tekké* I had to take further precautions. As I had grown up in the place, every one knew me, and the boys as well as I had to be disguised. I put on granny's loose black veils and dressed the boys in the oldest clothes of the gardener's children. I walked along the hills above Sultan Tepé, and Nighiar, my sister, who was a student in the college, came with me; before we had gone far from the *tekké,* the sight of two unusually brutal men running on the hills frightened her so much that her knees gave way. I could not help laughing in spite of my own anxiety, for she fell on her knees like a young camel.

On reaching the American College, Dr. Vivian, who had Dr. Patrick's place for the time, received me with great kindness. Her calm strength and friendly reception brought back to my mind for the first time since the beginning of the horror the imminent danger in which the new ideals and the country stood. These I had forgotten in my terror. Before I could greet Dr. Vivian I sank on a chair and began to sob passionately.

I stayed in the college four nights, hidden in the very room in which as a little girl I used to sit and repeat my childish lessons to Miss Dodd. All that seemed ages ago now, as I read the papers and listened to the incessant firing in Istamboul. There was a rumor that an army was coming from Saloniki to suppress the counter-revolution. How strange it sounded! A hundred years ago another Turkish army had marched from Macedonia under Alemdar Moustafa Pasha to save the young reformer Selim and his reform from the mob and the army which had risen against it. Was history going to repeat itself in another form?

I heard in the meantime that Young Turks were being protected by the Russian embassy and helped to escape. The Russians in and out of politics have behaved with real humanity and chivalry. The Russian embassy, although no friend of the régime, gave asylum to revolutionary and anti-revolutionary with equal generosity.

A rather mysterious phase of the reaction was the Armenian massacre in Adana. It seemed that the party of reaction, which was killing the Young Turks in Constantinople, was killing the Armenians in Adana. The Armenian and foreign sources declared the massacre to have been prepared by the Young Turks themselves. But the Young Turks, who were powerless and hiding for their lives, were hardly likely to be able to direct any such movement. The causes were deeper and more complex.

As I have already mentioned, the Young Turks had come to a superficial understanding with the Tashnaks, the Armenian revolutionary leaders. The Unionist program, which involved a centralized representative government, was accepted by all the minority leaders, and some of the Armenians were sincere Unionists. But some, indeed even the majority of the Armenian leaders, still kept their separatist tendencies, and these were anxious and watchful. The Armenian Free State, which was a mere political game to Russia and England, was a real political ideal to some leading Armenians; and they needed continual trouble and a martyred Armenian nation in Turkey as a pretext to attract the attention and the sympathy of the European public and to induce European interference in the internal administration of Turkey.

The Young Turks in their first understanding with the Armenian Tashnaks had allowed them to keep their arms till the new régime should be firmly settled. This was the apparent cause of the massacre of Adana.

In Turkey massacres are set in motion by a mutual feeling of distrust and fear. It happens in some such way as this: In the Turkish quarters the rumor would go around that the Armenians were going to use their bombs and kill the Turks. As a rule the Turks were without arms in those days; hence bombs in the hands of a revolutionary minority made them nervous. The same rumor would go round in Armenian quarters, and the potential fear and hatred, already worked upon and accumulated by the politicians, would explode, the leaders would disappear, and the people would proceed to throttle each other. Thus the discovery of arms in the Armenian quarters and a personal quarrel between two individuals started the great Adana massacre. Djemal Bey (later Djemal Pasha) was sent as governor after the reëstablishment of the Unionist régime; he restored order and became immensely popular especially in the Armenian quarters.

During my stay in the college the street massacres, the anarchy, and the lack of any control over the mob became so dangerous that my family sought for me a safer refuge out of the country, and I had to leave for Egypt with my little boys in the midst of the counter-revolution of 1909.

CHAPTER XI

REFUGEE FOR THE FIRST TIME

THE name of my boat was *Ismailie*. Two berths were found with difficulty in a second-class cabin containing in all six berths. I was again heavily veiled in an ample and old-fashioned *charshaf* of granny's, and my sons were disguised in the old suits of the gardener's boys. In this guise we were smuggled into the boat by Miss Prime and the cavass of the Russian consulate. The anarchy of the city had made the police careless, and so I do not think it was as difficult as we supposed it would be. Miss Prime gave me a sewing-bag which she herself had made for me, containing all kinds of sewing-material. In the whole course of my life I have never received a more useful gift. The stockings and frocks I have darned and mended with its contents are beyond counting. I still keep it almost reverently. A large box was also smuggled into the depths of the boat. I myself could only carry a bundle which would be in keeping with the class to which my dress made me appear to belong, and which would therefore arouse no suspicion. Salih Zeki Bey gave me a letter from an Armenian professor addressed to some Armenian revolutionaries in Alexandria, and the boat started.

I sat on my berth, the boys clinging close to me. It was smelly and dark with a large amount of queer luggage piled up everywhere. For a long time I did not trust myself to think of anything but the immediate present. With two babies and but little money, I was thrown into the unknown, leaving my people behind me to an uncertain fate. I cannot deny that there was also a sense of the relaxation of tension. No more should I have to face the probability of being torn to pieces before the very eyes of my little ones; no more might the little ones be trampled under the feet of the furious mob of Istamboul. It was soon dark in the cabin, and before the light was lit the plump figure of a woman stood by the door of the cabin and said in English, half to herself and half to me:

"What is that black bundle?"

I was the black bundle. I opened my veil and removed the long upper mantle of the *charshaf;* I felt much comforted by the friendliness of the voice.

"Good evening," I said.

I remember the joy in her face as she found that I spoke English. When the light was on I saw to my surprise that my new friend was a chocolate-colored American negress, with a round face, the friendliest imaginable, and very fashionable clothes. What she saw was a figure of a woman sitting cross-legged on the lower berth and bending her head to prevent it from knocking against the low ceiling of the upper one.

I must have looked like a vision from the grave after

the misery of the preceding week. Thinking that my long hair would be a hindrance to me as a refugee woman, I had cut my hair, and it was my short hair that brought her to me with a spring. Kneeling down before my berth she looked hungrily at my face:

"Oh, oh!" she said, "you are Susie's very image. She is just like this—the thin face and the eyes and the hair. She is my daughter, Susie is, but she is white" —this with pride—"her father was a Frenchman."

After some intimate details about Susie's white father and Susie's fairness, the mother put her plump arms around me and kissed my cheeks over and over again.

In ten minutes I knew all about her. She was an "artist" from a place in Pera called Cataculum, perhaps a night bar. Whatever else I forget I shall never forget that funny name. The terror of the revolution was driving her away. She was throwing up a profitable contract, she told me, and flying from Constantinople. She had in America the sixteen-year-old daughter who looked like me, according to her description. Besides that warm passion (which spent itself in hugging me constantly) she loved another Frenchman called Monsieur Nickol. I am afraid Susie's father had been dead for some time. The man had promised to marry her. She herself was thirty-two, a fine smart colored woman of the stage and as gay and coquettish as she could be. She seemed to have Reshé's color and Nevres Badji's affectionate heart; and her odor was very different from either, for she used Parisian scents of the strongest sort, which, mixing with the unpleasant odors of the cabin, took on a strange quality. The dirty stuffy place brightened up with human affection and gaiety, and the little boys laughed and kissed her and treated her with affectionate but slightly condescending familiarity, in the selfish manner of little white boys who have black nurses. Reshé used to be haughty and had succeeded in making herself respected by the little ones, while this one, despite her fashionable clothes, rings, and ear-rings, spoiled the boys, running about and playing with them like a little girl. The second day she fell rather badly in love with the head waiter, but in spite of this she did not neglect the boys, taking them daily on the deck.

The morning took an eternal time to come in that cabin, and no sleep was possible amid the snoring and the smell, but when it did come the first note of brightness was struck by the colored lady. She began her toilet with a song in the half-pathetic half-humorous tone peculiar to her race, and she used a great deal of eau de Cologne, which at least was familiar. Powdered and rouged, she approached my berth and began again to tell me about Susie, and going on to Monsieur Nickol, imitating with a queer American negro accent his French jokes, after which she finished by helping me to dress the boys in that dirty little hole—no easy task.

The journey to Alexandria took five days, and as the the days passed I became increasingly conscious of her vulgarity and wondered what people would think if they saw me with a bar artiste from Cataculum. On the fourth day I accidentally saw her being kissed twice by the handsome Italian head waiter, which not only shocked me but also made me shrink a little.

The Armenians, who had received a telegram from the professor in Constantinople, came to the boat to fetch me, and they took me to a hotel in Mohammed Ali Place, owned by a motherly Frenchwoman called Madame Bonnard. Shinorkian, one of the Armenians whose name I well remember, had the refined manner of the gentlemen of the Tanzimat period, which has left its mark on all the racial elements of the empire. He had left Turkey during Armenian troubles in the time of Abdul Hamid and had never returned. Whatever his sentiments were, he had the perfect manner of the Turkish gentleman, which soothed and comforted me.

In the square before my hotel the hurdy-gurdies played the same tune again and again, and I can hear that tune now. Italian girls with white or colored kerchiefs over their heads sang and gathered money in a little plate; Arabs, in silk gowns, shining shoes, immense gold chains over their jackets, and rigid fezzes with tassels on one side, filled the place. Some sat on the benches; others walked up and down the street. On the right of my window stretched a European street, and on the left the blue sea washed the shores. The noises reached their climax as night drew near.

The color and noise of Egypt, so different from Turkey, the mixed crowd with its lively tunes and perpetual gestures, affected me strangely.

After the strain of the last weeks in Constantinople, the novelty of the place charmed the boys; and if my visits to the American consulate, where I hoped to receive letters from home, had not been fruitless, the new atmosphere would have made me very happy. The Arabic I had learned from books did not help me much, and no one spoke English, but I soon discovered to my great surprise that Greek was the language most spoken in Alexandria.

The city was going through an epidemic of scarlet fever and measles, and there was a very high child mortality. On the fifth evening of my arrival in Egypt as I undressed Hassan I found him hot, and on closer examination I saw red spots on his body, which put me in a panic. A Greek or Italian doctor who was in the hotel told me that it was scarlet fever (it proved afterward to be measles) and said I must send Hassan to a hospital. I remember sitting on a chair and staring at him stupidly, as if he had struck me a blow on the head. My utter despair must have touched the old man, for his fat face kindled with pity and he said: "*Corimou* [my daughter], I will not declare it. Don't let any one come to the room, and keep the other boy away from the bed of the sick one. I will call it influenza."

How terrible—and cut off from every one who belonged to me! Still there was this kind old man, who was doing a thing which would have brought him punishment if it had been found out.

I had an ugly week of anxiety. As I had not heard

from home I was afraid to spend money, and I daily washed all the clothes myself. I was wondering whether all who belonged to me had been killed, and how long I and the children would be able to live with the little money I had brought with me. I washed on clumsily, rubbing the skin off my hands, and thinking hard. Ali Ayetullah tiptoed about, hanging the clothes on the rails of the beds, and putting things in order in the wardrobe, standing on a chair to do so. As his little body moved round the room, his large eyes never leaving my face, I felt a strange sense of dependence on him. Every day just for a little while I took him out into the fresh air, but he pulled my hand all the time, wanting to go back to his sick brother. He had a queer way of squatting on a chair at a distance and telling stories to Hassan.

When Hassan was better again I walked to the consulate in the hope of letters; there were none. As the secretary walked with me to the door, the black lady of Cataculum with a white gentleman entered the room.

Was it the presence of the man, or the exaggerated rouge on her cheeks, or my bourgeois soul of those days? I cannot tell, but I know that I walked out of the room without giving any sign of recognition. The strange and startled look in her eyes as they flashed at me seemed to say, "No longer so miserable or so thankful for human kindness!" Before I reached the streets, I was longing to run back and make reparation for the cowardly feeling which made me act as I did. I knew it would be a long remembered shame of my soul. But I did not go back somehow, and the memory still haunts and hurts me.

It was about three weeks afterward when I got a letter from home, but I was so miserable that I wired to Salih Zeki Bey and asked him to come to Egypt at once, telling him about Hassan's illness.

He arrived about May 1; but by that time, although Hassan was still in bed, he was out of danger, and Ali had not caught the measles.

Salih Zeki Bey brought news from Constantinople. An army from Macedonia under the command of Mahmoud Shevket Pasha had marched on Constantinople and entered it. There had been little fighting between the Macedonian forces and those of the sultan. Abdul Hamid was dethroned, and Mohammed V had ascended the throne. Abdul Hamid was exiled to Saloniki. The new cabinet was formed mostly of the old elements. Hussein Hilmi Pasha was the prime minister. Talaat and Djavid Beys were the first Unionist members who entered the cabinet, one for the interior and the other for finance. Martial law was declared, and there were a great many executions; the reaction was drowned in blood.

In the meantime I received a letter from Miss Isabel Fry inviting me to England, and Salih Zeki Bey urged me to accept the invitation. Although I was interested in England, I could not bring myself to be separated from my sons, and the idea of traveling alone to England frightened me not a little.

Salih Zeki Bey not only urged me to accept the invitation, but he also undertook to be personally responsible for the boys in my absence. So after a rather happy fortnight spent in sight-seeing and getting used to wearing a hat I started from Egypt all alone for England, and embarked at Port Saïd direct to Tilbury.

If I were to go over the details of that voyage, even a little Turkish girl of twelve would laugh at me. I was utterly upset with timidity and misery. The journey passed somehow, and I landed safely on the English shore. The dear little house of Miss Fry in Marylebone Street stands out as the first familiar impression. She had prepared a full and interesting program for a Turkish woman who had as yet no public experience.

I will speak only of the impressions which stand out in greatest relief during that visit. One is a scene of Mr. Masefield's "Pompeii," which he read to me in Miss Fry's farm-house at Hampden. It was not published then, and I have not read it since, but it impressed me as most forceful. Another impression is of Mr. Dillon speaking on Irish Home Rule; I heard him in a debate in Cambridge, thanks to the kindness of Professor and Mrs. Browne, who took me there. The sincerity and personal charm of the old man stirred me strangely. I remember leaning over the railing of the gallery to hide my tears, so deeply was I moved, and I have elsewhere publicly owned that his speech was one of the emotional causes which started me on the road of nationalism. The British parliament was the next thing, and it inspired me almost with pious emotion. As the oldest parliament, it had been a symbol to us in our bloody struggle and effort for representative government.

Mr. Nevinson perhaps is the last but the strongest figure that stands out in my memory. He struck me as one of the few true idealists I have met in life. No philosophy is lonelier, no principle so fruitless as idealism from the material and personal point of view, and I have sadly learned to question the personal motives of most men who profess an ideal or a principle, but Mr. Nevinson's I have never questioned.

In October I returned to Turkey.

CHAPTER XII

SOME PUBLIC AND PERSONAL EVENTS, 1909-12

I HAVE a painful memory of my home-coming to Sultan Tepé on my return from England. The little boys stood with their backs to the garden wall, holding hands. Whether it was fancy or reality I could not tell, but the peach-like coloring of Hassan's face seemed to have assumed a delicate tinge, and his usually round cheeks looked sunken. That very night I realized fully what a bloody revolution means to a child's delicate nervous system. In the middle of the night I woke with a start to hear Hassan talking deliriously in his sleep. It was a frantic appeal to the soldiers not to kill me, and he repeated it all the time with the accent of unutterable misery and fear which only a child can have in its voice. In the morning he had a very high fever, and it proved to be typhoid. This time I was so completely occupied with nursing the child that I slipped out of the world of affairs and barely realized the great and exciting change which the new régime was undertaking.

I wrote "Sevie Talib" during the long watches of the night. Hassan's case was not very dangerous, but on account of the shock he had received his nerves were in a deplorable condition. His delirium and his helpless terror brought me nearer to understanding children in similar cases of suffering in later years.

The book was published in the winter. The fact that I had dared to expose social shams and conventions brought down on my head a volley of criticism. But the book's popularity was equal to the severity of the attacks. It was about this time that I had an invitation from Prince Medjid to visit him and his wife in his house near Chamlidja. Prince Medjid was the most popular prince then in Turkey. A clever musician and painter, a highly cultivated man, both in Oriental and European literature, a skilled horseman and a tender-hearted human being, these attributes made him very much to be desired as a ruler. But he was rather far down the line of succession, being then the sixth I believe. His invitation to me was not merely an invitation to a writer, it was to an old acquaintance. When I was three years old and he quite a young man we had known each other. I had a blurred memory of a wonderful chandelier, very spacious halls with heavy silk furniture and gilded mirrors, and a young man who wore his fez very much on one side and who held me on his knees and teased me calling me "naughty," while tall women in long trains and high head-dresses glided about silently on the highly polished floors. I seemed also to remember an immense garden, a pond, weeping willows, and several swings with fair Circassian girls swinging in them. Somehow after I went to see the prince and the princess in their palace

I could never locate these places, though the memory of them still haunted me.

I shall never forget the feeling of uneasiness and of being entirely out of place in a palace which overwhelmed me. When I saw that the prince and his stately wife were quite as nervous as myself I recovered. Prince Medjid seemed agreeably excited over the new régime, which allowed him to meet people and move about like any ordinary human being. So far he had been buried in his library and had only been able to ride about within the limits of his own large park.

"I feel like a new doll taken out of a box and told to move and speak," he said. I was glad to be once more confirmed in my early belief that however great the position of a man may be it is wrong to remove him too far from the habits and lives of his fellow-men.

Although the kind and affectionate manners of the prince and the princess never changed, I felt oppressed whenever I visited them in Dolma-Bagtché. They quietly dropped out of my life after the prince became heir to the throne, though I did see him again in sad circumstances of which I shall speak later.

I was at that time writing a series of articles on the educational question of the day, which was the subject that interested me more than any other. The articles had evidently attracted the attention of Saïd Bey, who was the counselor of the ministry of education, and he called on me one day and tried to persuade me to give some of my time to teaching. He especially wanted me to see the normal school for girls and to propose some changes. I had never thought of teaching and did not care much for the idea, but it seemed to me that the call to the educated Turks to teach in the era of reform was like the call to military service. It led me to go to the normal school and study its conditions.

I visited and studied the school with Nakie Hanum. She was an old graduate of the normal school and had been for some time a teacher in the American College, where she had assimilated during her training there all that was best and most applicable to school management in Turkey. Endowed with intelligence, character, and constructive ability, she developed into one of our best organizers. Her natural understanding and knowledge of the students and of the teachers of the time fitted her especially for the task. She was appointed director of the normal school, and it was with her that we carried out the reform which the ministry of education accepted in my report.

At first the school was in Ak-Serai, an old dilapidated building, and its dominant teaching features were Arabic, Persian domestic science, and a thorough instruction in religion. It needed a curriculum with a newer and more scientific spirit, a living language, and a more modern atmosphere and equipment. The most vital change was to be the development of a new spirit in the Turkish student. A new sense of responsibility and of coöperation, a new self-respect in the child, as well as a more earnest and open-minded and less autocratic attitude in the teacher were necessary before the new education in Turkey could take shape.

No one could have done it better than Nakie Hanum. She knew her human material so well that she was able to evolve the new spiritual liberty of the child without too much destruction or exaggeration. Time has shown us that the point of equilibrium between the teacher and the taught is very delicate and of most vital importance. If it is too much on the teacher's side it creates an autocratic, tyrannical, and repressive system of education; if it is too much on the student's side it creates complete anarchy. Without a proper adjustment of the relations between teachers and students, without the right degree of discipline and order, one can neither teach nor learn seriously.

Nakie Hanum's teaching corps showed real self-abnegation and made very serious efforts, conscious as they were of the importance of their part as pioneers in a new realm of education for women. I entered the school as a teacher of the principles of education, and my first contact with the teaching and student classes in Turkey began at that time.

It was a year of liveliest interest. In two years the educational department saw the necessity of a girls' college, and as the normal school had shown real progress it was turned into a college, and a new normal boarding-school was opened in another part of Istamboul.

For five long years I was a teacher in the girls' college, teaching the history and principles of education and ethics to the young and some other things which one teaches behind the lines, things which are necessary if one means to build new country. If I taught I also learned, and in the give and take my students formed and molded me as much as I did them. It was with the help of some of the students of those years that we were able to modernize and organize the mosque schools some years later with Nakie Hanum, and it was with the aid of the same element that I organized the schools and the orphanage in Syria, of which I shall speak in coming chapters.

Before I pass on to another subject I must say that Saïd Bey—the counselor of the ministry of education, several times minister of public instruction, and a well known professor in the University of Istamboul—must have the honor of being the pioneer advocate of the modernization of women's education in New Turkey.

After bitter moments caused by the severe repression of the reaction, the Hakki Pasha cabinet came into power in 1910 with a big program actuated by the spirit of reconciliation. Hakki Pasha, who was an authority on international law, and who had stood the test of Abdul Hamid's reign, seemed the proper person to take the responsibility for the moment. Neither too young to antagonize the old, nor too old to stand against new ideas of progress, he had the confidence and the respect of all. A limited number of the extremists of the Union and Progress were the only people against him.

SOME PUBLIC AND PERSONAL EVENTS, 1909-12

In announcing his program he gave as his motto the following verse from the Koran: "Allah has ordered to rule according to justice and mercy." But he had no time to carry out this axiom. The Tripolitan trouble —the sudden seizure of Tripoli by the Italians—roused the popular anger against him so violently that he had to resign immediately. He was accused of not having foreseen the event in time, and of not having taken any diplomatic or military action to prevent it.

The constitutional reform in Turkey, which aroused the general sympathy of the world, somehow disappointed the powers, who had so neatly planned the division of the sick man's estate. One after another they hastened to snatch from Turkey what they could. During the first months after the establishment of the new régime in 1908 Austria had broken the feeble thread which bound Bosnia-Herzegovina to Turkey. An immense excitement broke out through the entire country, followed by acute disillusion. It was the first shock to the childish belief that once a New Turkey arose the powers and the aggressive little nations who surrounded her would allow for the difficulties of the reform period, and give her at least a short time to find herself. I remember the wild demonstrations in Istamboul, the speeches and street gatherings, the discarding of fezzes because they were of Austrian manufacture. Solemn vows of the eternal boycott of Austrian goods appeared in all the papers. Everywhere in Turkey the crowds had worn picturesque red tops; now they wore home-made white caps. Although it was difficult to imagine anything in the way of military action against Austria, still Kiamil Pasha's practical way of arranging the dispute with Austria by accepting two millions of Turkish pounds angered many people as the first commercial act in Turkish history where a question of honor was involved. The Turkish government as well as the nation was used to fighting for lost causes, at whatever cost of Turkish lives, money, and other resources. The supreme point had always been the safeguarding of national honor. The Turks so far had never conceded land without fighting for it. The vast lands which they had had to yield up had always been watered abundantly with Turkish blood. Consequently the practical old man, when he showed realism in politics instead of the traditional patriotic idealism, aroused a passionate resentment.

Before the sore feeling about Bosnia-Herzegovina had been calmed, the Cretan assembly declared the annexation of the island of Crete by Greece. This aroused another wild outburst. I measure the general disappointment from the pain I personally suffered. A strong patriotic literature blossomed out from every poet's pen. What would sound chauvinistic and exaggerated now then represented emotion of the sincerest kind. "Crete is our life; let our blood flow," shouted the youth of the country for months. Then the Italians seized Tripoli, and the burden of the song changed again.

So in 1910, Turkey, on top of everything else, was to

face the loss of vast lands in Africa. The practical settlement of Bosnia-Herzegovina, the helplessness of the government before the annexation of Crete, had already filled the cup to the brim. Action became inevitable before the outburst of public feeling.

At first there was the usual boycott, though with even greater emphasis than usual. "Tanine" was one of the papers which went into perfect hysteria over Tripoli. A large list of signed vows appeared. "I will not buy Italian goods; I will not eat macaroni; I will not speak Italian . . ." was the strain in which it went on. In the first edition of "Handan" my editor was obliged to announce the change of her vacations from Sicily to Corfu. I even had scolding letters from Saloniki, the center of the revolution, for allowing a hero of mine to play Verdi.

"I will not eat macaroni" cost Italy a good deal, for Turkey until then had consumed a great amount of Italian macaroni, and the opening of macaroni factories in Turkey probably begins at that time.

The Tripolitan affair not only somewhat diminished the Unionist prestige but, what was more important, it made the man in the street realize that reform and the ideal of a westernized Turkey were the cause of all the trouble.

The isolated position of Bosnia-Herzegovina and the Austrian rule that was already established there had put it out of the reach of the Turkish army; the island of Crete with its Greek majority and the very poor condition of the Turkish navy [1] made attack in that direction impossible; the same reason made active measures in Tripoli seem impossible when one considered the superiority of the Italian navy and the modern equipment of the Italian army that landed in Tripoli. Still every one thought that if the impenetrable desert and its fighting folk had been better organized and prepared, the Italian attack might have been rendered more difficult. Yet the geographical position of Tripoli was such that after Turkey had ceased to be a powerful empire and lost her supremacy over the seas, it was doomed to fall into the hands of any Mediteranean power which was suffering from a surplus population and had a modern navy. But this fact did not diminish the bitterness felt at the series of blows dealt so cruelly to Turkey, or the indignation at the Italian massacres of the defenseless Tripolitan people.

The Young Turks saw very well that the next blow would come from the Balkans, that Turkey's Macedonian provinces would be snatched away from her. Therefore they had to think and act instantly toward organizing a modern army and toward doing all they could to hinder the Italian occupation. With this end in view they smuggled a few leading Turkish officers into Tripoli, who organized the native forces and made Tripoli uncomfortable for the invading Italian army.

This course was very much in keeping with Turkish

---

[1] Abdul Aziz had almost ruined the national budget in organizing a navy, but Abdul Hamid had ruined the navy by personal intimidation. The ships were practically imprisoned and rusted in the Golden Horn.

THE MOSQUE OF FATIH

temperament. If the defense of Tripoli was not of the highest wisdom, it at least savored of the old days of chivalry. From the historical point of view one may find three reasons which led the Young Turks to undertake the defense of Tripoli as they did: first, the warlike spirit of the Tripolitans and the atrocities committed by the Italians in Tripoli; secondly, the loss of Unionist prestige, which demanded some show of high courage and sacrifice if it was to be regained; thirdly, the feeling that if no action was taken the series of spoliations would go on forever.

Before long Enver Bey, the military attaché in Berlin, and Fethi Bey, the military attaché in Paris (both heroes in 1908), came to Tripoli, and a bold defense was begun under their leadership.

The Tripolitan war is the first of the great and disastrous wars which the New Turkey has sustained within the last fourteen years. Without sending out any large forces of men or of warlike resources, with a handful of idealistic young officers thrown, as it were, into the desert, the national honor was insured and the Tripolitans were helped in their struggle against the Italian occupation, the beginning of which had been so bloody. The war appealed to every one in Turkey. Young men known as bitter anti-Unionists volunteered and fought under Enver and Fethi. The popularity of these young leaders once more rose to the height it attained in the first days of the revolution. Enver's fame as the hero of Islam, and his pan-Islamic ideal, date from the Tripolitan struggles. His organization of the desert forces and his relation with the Senussi leaders were such that if he had wished he could have been easily made the sultan of the Tripolitan Arabs with larger prospects of expanding his domains. But at the end of two years the Balkan war began, and the disaster of the Turkish arms in Macedonia brought back Enver and Fethi and their brother officers to defend their country.

In the very midst of the Tripolitan excitement the Turkish papers took up the Galata Serai incident, an incident which would have passed unnoticed had it not been that the names of Salih Zeki and Tewfik Fikret were involved.

Galata Serai was one of the greatest schools for boys in Turkey, and including Tewfik Fikret it counted most of the great poets and writers among its graduates.

Tewfik Fikret after retiring from politics had turned to education as the president of Galata Serai, and he was successfully reorganizing that establishment and putting his own marvelous spirit into it. He was very much influenced by the new school movement in France, and was in favor of an individualistic Anglo-Saxon educational ideal, somewhat in the line of Desmoulins' principles. In fact Desmoulins has affected very strongly a certain set of politicians and intellectuals in Turkey who were called Decentralists, and their leader was Prince Sebahheddine.

Tewfik Fikret had obtained very fine results from his work in Galata Serai when an administrative difficulty involving a difference of opinion with the minister of public instruction made him resign. The minister at the moment was, as a savant, an equally prominent man, and the Young Turks maintained a neutral attitude toward the disagreement between Fikret and the minister, Emroullah Effendi.

Emroullah Effendi begged Salih Zeki Bey to accept the post vacated by Fikret. In those days there was a strict tradition about the presidency of Galata Serai; only men prominent in letters or science could fill it. Salih Zeki Bey, after asking Fikret if his decision to leave the school was final, accepted. The public opinion divided itself into two camps, the old students of Salih Zeki and the followers of Tewfik Fikret. A long and violent series of discussions occupied the newspapers. It was called the "difference between the poet and the savant." Salih Zeki kept the post till he became the rector of the university and the counselor of the ministry of public instruction. But this made Tewfik Fikret's separation from the Union and Progress final.

In 1910 I was having serious domestic trouble. I felt that I was obliged to make a great change in my life, a change which I could not easily force myself to face. Salih Zeki Bey's relation with and attachment to a teacher looked serious enough to make it seem conceivable that he contemplated marriage. A believer in monogamy, in the inviolability of name and home, I felt it to be my duty to retire from what I had believed would be my home to the end of my life. But knowing Salih

Zeki Bey's passing caprices of heart and temperament I wanted to be absolutely sure, before breaking up my home, of the stability of his latest attachment. I therefore took the little boys with me and went to Yanina near my father with the intention of waiting there for a few months.

At my return Salih Zeki Bey told me that he had married the lady, but to my great surprise he added that polygamy was necessary in some cases, and he asked me to continue as his first wife. There was a long and painful struggle between us, but at last he consented to a divorce, and I left what for nine years had been my home.

It was a cold April night when I drove with the boys to Fatih, to the big old-fashioned house of Nakie Hanum, where I stayed till I found a suitable house. What now seems an almost ordinary incident in a woman's life was then of supreme importance and the cause of great suffering to me. My foolish heart nearly broke. I think the women of Turkey must be more used to divorce nowadays, for one hears little of broken hearts in the many divorce cases that now take place there.

Nakie Hanum's house was in a narrow street with other typically Turkish houses with low eaves and many windows, but it was the highest in that street, and from the room where for some time I lay sick I could see the upper part of a single dark cypress over which the needle-like tops of the minarets of the Fatih mosque pierced the blue sky. I heard the continual creak of wood as an old donkey turned round and round drawing water from some deep well in the opposite gardens. Besides this primitive melody and the call from the minarets of Fatih, there was virtually no sound in the street.

Before long I found a house in Fazli Pasha, a steep but broad street on the southern part of Istamboul leading to the sea. I could look out from my bed upon the expanse of grayish sea with the blue haze at its horizon and the ruddy glows of the sunsets over it.

I had been in low health for the whole year, feeling feverish and very tired, but I had not paid much attention to it. A medical consultation, however, showed that it was rather a serious chest weakness, and my continual fever and troublesome cough as well as my severe headaches obliged me to stay in bed for three months.

Salih Zeki Bey's second marriage had aroused such personal curiosity that every eye probed me hard to see how I bore my own trouble after having written so much about other people's. I remember one fat woman in particular among my acquaintances who used to come with stories about the love-making of the new couple and watch my face with obvious curiosity. I neither questioned nor commented; I had a strange feeling of wonder at her apparent desire to see me suffer. I passed the test of vivisection rather successfully I believe, for my calmness and apparent lack of interest made her after a time drop the subject. Still it was a great pity that every one spoke of me as having consumption at this moment of my life, for consumption is ridiculously associated in the public mind with disappointed love.

I allowed myself no sentimental self-analysis or morbid philosophizing at this time, such as I had occasionally indulged in during the other serious illnesses I had gone through. I meant to conquer all physical ills, and I meant to make a home for my sons equal to the one they had had to leave, and to surround them with a happy and normal home atmosphere. I was determined to live, and not to leave them to the sort of life which children have when their mother is dead or crushed in spirit.

As I write these lines I feel as if I were writing of the life of a young woman who has passed away. I see her lying on a simple bed of high pillows; I see her struggling to write her daily articles or short stories; and I hear her cough continually. Then the evening lights blaze over the waters, the little boys come back, and she makes painful efforts to conquer her wild desire to kiss and hug them. They chatter about the American school they attend, and finally they go down to dine with granny, while she is left alone in the twilight room, with the utter mysterious loveliness and strange longings of the evening. She looks at pain with a quizzical smile, while she listens to the voices of the evening in the streets. The sellers of yogurt, cadaif, the chanting of beggars, the footsteps of workers who pass down to Koum-Kapou, and at last the call of the childish voices and the patter of small feet scampering in the dusk in those large, lonely streets.

My own favorite among the voices belonged to a blind Arab beggar, and it was only on Friday evenings that he came. I knew that he leaned against the corner of the house, one hand against his cheek, while his guttural melody lengthened into an infinite wail, which yet had something of the desert and its lonely passion as it penetrated the evening air. It was mostly a religious chant, a wail and a complaint in wondrous simple melody, calling to the Prophet, *"Ya Resoulallah, Ya Resoulallah."* The "Allah" was long and died away in a hissing sound. In no other musical experience have I ever had this almost uncanny contact with the musician. I was perfectly aware that he felt some one listening to his guttural melody, for sometimes he would stop for a moment and murmur searchingly and low, as if he were trying to reach out for the soul-contact which had snapped for a moment: "Where art thou? Art thou listening?"

Then his stick struck the pavement, and he staggered on silently in the manner of the blind.

Six months later when I was traveling and for the first time was not there to hear him, he said to the cook, who gave him the usual coin, "She is not up-stairs any more."

In the autumn of 1910 I was once more going on with my lectures and lessons, and the cough and fever had gone. Besides my lessons and writings I had become a busy public speaker.

CHAPTER XIII

PHASES AND CAUSES OF NATIONALISM AND PAN-TURANISM IN TURKEY

I CONSIDER the time from 1910 to 1912 as a prelude to my final plunge into nationalism which took an intense form after the disaster of the Balkan war. The campaign in Tripoli and its chivalrous spirit had vaguely and almost agreeably flattered the nationalistic tendencies which had hitherto been nebulous. Perhaps if the unfair treatment we received from without after the disaster of the war had not knocked us so hard, we might never have been awakened and developed into very enthusiastic nationalists.

It was the beginning of my acquaintance with Youssouf Akchoura and Keuk-Alp Zia which led me for the first time to our racial past, and distinctly further away from the Ottoman past. I had been always strongly drawn to folk-lore and to the unpretentious but elemental beauty of the popular literature, and so the early days of the race allured me as perhaps the purest sources of the unwritten poetry and stories of the nation. Cultural curiosity as well as the tyranny of external events was throwing most intellectual Turks back into an intense study of the beginnings of the race.

Nationalism in Turkey has more than one phase and

name as well as definition; besides, taken as a whole, it presents the key to important events in recent Turkish history, so that it is necessary to give a short survey of some of the phases of the movement.

Turkish nationalism unconsciously and culturally began with the simplification of the language long before 1908. But it was a movement belonging distinctly to the Ottoman Turks. In writings of Riza Tewfik and Mehemmed Emin, who first began to use the Turkish meter in poetry and to adopt simple language of the Anatolian Turk, one saw that they felt clearly the difference of the Ottoman Turk from the other Turks in general. Nationally analyzed, the Ottoman Turk appears entirely different. He came to the Near East and Europe, and there he acquired in his blood and in his language, as well as in every particle of his ego, something new, something special. Although one may try to go deep into the elemental force and character of his race, one is obliged to recognize that things have been added to his spirit and physique which have altered him from what he was when he had first come to the land which is called Turkey to-day. In short he was the Ottoman Turk and had to be considered as such, and everything contrary to his individual development in language and culture could not be lasting. To force his language back to Chagatay would be as artificial as forcing it into Persian or into French. Hence his simplification and nationalization would take the line of his own national genius.

During the last twenty-five years the Ottoman Turk

has been reviewing his language and evolving it toward a subtler, richer, and more comprehensive capacity, containing expressions and possibilities of an advanced language, a language which can create and propagate science and philosophy. The Turkish dictionary had already been consciously simplified on these lines by Shemseddine Samy Bey and Professor Naji. From 1910 forward another conscious effort was put forth by the Turkish writers on similar lines. They tried to stabilize scientific expressions, and they simplified the Turkish grammar, separating it from the Arabic and Persian. Keuk-Alp Zia, Naim, and Fiza Tewfik Beys may be mentioned among the foremost who worked to find the scientific and philosophical terms, while Hussein Jahid wrote the modern Turkish grammar which is now taken as a model. This was creating a language, a national spirit, and a comprehension of culture belonging to the Ottoman Turks.

Arrived at this point, nationalism in Turkey, with its vastly mixed and acquired characteristics and blood, could only be cultural and social in the truly popular sense so long as the nationalist Ottoman Turks were definitely bound to be democratic in their political ideal.

Pan-Turanism was a larger understanding and definition of the nationalism expressed by Keuk-Alp Zia and some well known writers from the Russian Turks, such as Ahmed Agayeff and Youssouf Akchoura Beys. At first it was purely cultural, but it was developed into a political ideal by some leaders of the Unionist party, especially when the Turkish arms passed into old Russia during the World War. But politically speaking Pan-Turanism never had a clear boundary or a crystallized expression or an explanation. Talaat Pasha pleasantly and humorously remarked at times, if any one criticized it, "It may lead us to the Yellow Sea." What was the real basis of Pan-Turanism? Was it the political unity of all the Turanian people? Had the Christian Turks any place in the Pan-Turanism expressed by the Ottoman Turks? Or was it only meant for the Moslem Turks, which would be some form of the Pan-Islamism of Enver Pasha, who would add racial unity to the religious unity he vaguely imagined to bring forth, and failed.

I differed from Keuk-Alp Zia in his political conception for uniting the Turks. I believed and believe that nationalism is cultural and regional in Turkey, and that it would not be possible to unite the Turks in Russia to us politically in the way we then thought was possible. They themselves follow distinct and national lines, and differ from us very much. Besides they would object to being interfered with by the Ottoman Turks, however much they may admire our literature. The elements and influences which are building their culture are distinctly Russian, while those of the Ottoman Turk are distinctly Western. The utmost possible and perhaps the most desirable political connection in the far future, between the Turks up to the Caspian Sea and the Ottoman Turks, would be that of federal states, giving a large and free margin to both elements to realize their individual culture and progress. But if such a time ever comes, I am not sure that Armenia and Georgia and even Persia will not be ripe to join the Turkish United States and form a strong whole to protect their integrity from Russia, as well as from European invasion and domination.

Keuk-Alp Zia was really one of the great thinkers of the Unionist régime. Although it is difficult to say who really effected the passage of Pan-Turanism to a political ideal, whether it was Zia himself or the leading politicians of his party, it is clear that Zia at first began it as a purely cultural ideal. He was trying to create a new Turkish mythology which would bridge the abyss between the Ottoman Turks and their Turanian ancestors. He wrote a great many charming stories and poems for children; he tried to popularize his knowledge of the origin of the Turk, and the new ideal of life which he was trying to bring into being. In some of his first works he used words which were archæologically Turkish, but which sounded dead and artificial. He soon realized his mistake, and in his last works he uses the popular Turkish of the country.

He became the patron of many young writers and caused a large number of books on sociology and philosophy as well as on history to be translated into Turkish. Fuad Kuprullu, the scholarly young writer, owes his great compilation of historical data on Turkish ancestry to Zia's influence, and it was Zia who caused the ministry of public education to buy and collect most of the available publications on Turkology.

It was in the beginning of 1911 that Zia came to Constantinople from Saloniki, bringing his literary and philosophical activities with him. He started an intellectual movement in Saloniki with the review called the "Young Pens," and he had a talented staff. Zia was a member of the central committee of the Union and Progress, which had been transferred from Saloniki to Constantinople. For the time being he used his influence for the best in the Unionist party. He very often came to visit me in my house in Fazli Pasha, and we enjoyed an intellectual friendship till 1915, after which differences in educational as well as in political principles drew us apart.

He was originally from a well known family in Diarbekir, a family which has produced learned men and poets. In his early youth he had worked on the origin and the grammar of the Kurdish language which had given him in some quarters the reputation of being a Kurdish nationalist. But he had come to Constantinople for higher schooling in the time of Abdul Hamid, where he became a very ardent Young Turk, and he was arrested several times as a student who read the works of Namik Kemal. He was in Saloniki during the organization of the Union and Progress and became a highly honored member of this political society.

He was a fat, short, and very dark man, with a mark like the sign of the cross on his forehead which caught one's attention at once. It was the freak of a bullet which he had tried to lodge in his brain at twenty, but whose effect he had somehow survived. He had strange eyes looking beyond and away from the people and things that surrounded him. He had the air of a stranger, who patiently submits to a strange environment, yet he was easily influenced and changed his ideas through intercourse or reading much more than people who seem outwardly absorbed in their environment. His chief interest was fixed in sociology and philosophy. He held it to be his mission to guide the social reform more than the political reform of the Turks, according to the historical data he could gather from the social and political institutions of the Turks in their pre-Islamic stage. He believed that Islamism, as founded by the Arabs, could not suit us, and that if we would not go back to our pagan state we must start a religious reformation more in keeping with our own temperament. He was a warm admirer of the Protestant Reformation, which perhaps truly began the nationalization of the European peoples. He published the "Islamic Review" in which he gave rather a good translation of the Koran in Turkish. In his ideas of religious reform he was greatly influenced by Moussa Bikieff, the Tartar Moslem religious reformer in Kazan.

His most charming work at the time was the "Children's World," a paper for Turkish children, the first simple attempt of its kind in Turkey. The "Review" translated a great many stories about animals and fairies from English successfully. He published at the same time his simple Turkish stories, taken from the unwritten lore, and put into every popular Turkish verse.

As I think of him now,[1] sitting under the green shade of my lamp, smiling mildly and indulgently at the sharp and rather sarcastic remarks of Youssouf Akchoura, dreaming of a better state in religion, in literature, in moral beauty, for a better state for Turkish women and children, I can hardly believe that he tolerated and even developed the materialistic philosophy of the Union and Progress during the last years of the World War.

In spite of his opposition to hero worship which he expressed in a line, "No individual, but society," he yet wrote epics to the military and civil leaders of the Union and Progress, and in later years to those of the Nationalists. These epics are quoted as among his inconsistencies.

He was very much under the influence of German philosophy, especially under Durkheim. But his last oracle was Bergson. He was, however, very consistent in one point, and that was about the direction of Turkish progress. He believed that the Turk must be Westernized at any cost. Among the many definitions which

[1] He influenced me not a little in my writings during those days. So far my novels had been dominated only by the ordinary psychological problems of life. In 1910 I published "Ruined Temples," and in 1911 "Handan." Although I could without false modesty say that "Handan" achieved the greatest success of its kind, I was far from being satisfied. However immature and unsatisfactory I now consider it, I am doomed to live as its author. Keuk-Alp Zia told me that he did not like it, and added smilingly, "She lives too much in Europe." I was perfectly miserable the moment it was in the hands of the publisher. "New Turan" soon followed and was not only an outcome of events and thought trends of the day; it was also largely affected by the apostolic sincerity and austerity of Keuk-Alp Zia.

he tried to give the Turks, the best is his last one: "I am of the Turkish race, Moslem religion, Western civilization." His book called "Turkization, Islamization, Westernization," contains his philosophical and sociological ideas.

Parallel to Keuk-Alp Zia's Pan-Turanism was the Pan-Islamic ideal of Enver Pasha and his followers. If in the late years of the World War they seemed Pan-Turanistic it was because the Turanians whom they thought of uniting with Turkey were Moslems. But the ideal had as little influence as Pan-Turanism, politically speaking. The separatist tendencies of the Moslem units such as the Arabs and the Albanians discredted Pan-Islamism. Besides, the young and the reforming elements feared it as an element of reaction and fanaticism. An intelligent understanding of the aspirations and the needs of the Moslem minorities might have helped to justify Enver Pasha's Pan-Islamism. As it was, only the Moslems outside of Turkey showed any interest at all. The fear of the Allies about Pan-Islamism was quite groundless, and their attribution of all movements of self-assertion among their own Moslem subjects to Turkish influence was and, above all, is groundless. It has amused me not a little to see how the movement in Hedjaz by Ibn-Saoud is considered in the "London Times" (in one of the April numbers of 1925, I believe) as being encouraged by Angora. It would please Enver's soul, but it would seem irony to the almost fanatically secularized Turkish government of to-day.

TURKISH WOMEN IN NINETEEN EIGHTEEN

Nationalism found its first external organization in Turk Yourdu, a kind of literary and cultural club formed by the Turkish students in Geneva in 1910. As it had some fine students from among the Russian Turks, its spirit was Pan-Turanistic, at least culturally. It issued non-periodical reviews and continues to do so, some of which contain unusually fine literature and studies on Turkology. The club passed a resolution calling me the Mother of the Turk, a tender tribute of the Turkish youth, which not only touched me but has also molded me in the responsibility of a real but humble mother to my people. I am glad of this opportunity which allows me to own the godfathers of the title, which was generally attached to my name in the Turkish world, and which is the greatest recompense I would have asked, had I been given my choice, for my insignificant services to my people and country.

Another Turk Yourdu was founded a year later by older research students, among whom was the eminent jurist and statesman Youssouf Kemal.

The capital soon followed the example. The founding of Turk Yourdu in Istamboul was chiefly and primarily one of the many intellectual undertakings of the Union and Progress, but men who belonged to it confess that although they endowed it with funds they never tried to make a political tool of the organization. The organization published a weekly which goes on to this day. It was edited by Youssouf Akchura, who was openly and decidedly anti-Unionist, although an avowed and sincere Pan-Turanist. He made a great success of the paper, and it had perhaps more readers among the Turks in Russia than in Turkey. Akchura, a believer in the superiority of the Russian Turk to the Ottoman Turk, advocated warmly the necessary cultural unity of the Turks. He wrote interesting articles on this subject, but it was amusing to note that the Turkish he uses was that of the Ottoman Turk of an older period rather than that of the very recent nationalistic Ottoman Turk. Keuk-Alp Zia, Mehemmed Emin, Ahmed Hikmet, Riza Tewfik, as well as the nationalists of the later and younger school, contributed to it.

The external expression of nationalism went one degree deeper and propagated itself among the younger generation, especially the students. It first originated among medical students. The medical faculty has the historical honor of starting almost every new movement, especially when it is directed against personal tyranny of despots and régimes, or the tyranny of reaction and ignorance. It had given the greatest number of victims to Abdul Hamid's tyranny. But it would be interesting to note in this instance how and why the Turkish student has thought of himself as something separate and different from the other Ottoman students of the empire.

After 1908 all the non-Turkish elements in Turkey, Christian and Moslem, had political and national clubs. When the Turkish students of the universities saw their fellow-students, whom they had so far identified with themselves, belonging to separate organizations with national names and separate interests, they began to wonder. The non-Turkish youth were passing into feverish activity about their national affairs, as something different from that of the Turk.

The Ottoman Turk so far had been a composite being, an Ottoman citizen like any other, his greatest writers writing for all the educated men of the empire, his folk-lore and popular literature passing from one generation to another, unwritten by the educated, but powerful in the minds and memories of all the simple Turkish-speaking Ottomans. For the first time reduced to his elements and torn from the ensemble of races in Turkey, he vaguely faced the possibility of searching, analyzing, and discovering himself as something different from the rest. How was he different from the others? Where was he being led in the accumulation of other desires and interest? Cast out or isolated in his own country, he not only saw himself different, but he had also the desire to find out wherein lay the difference.

The first separate organization formed by the Turkish youth in this sense was called the Turk Ojak (Turkish Hearth). So it was in 1911 that the first national club was founded. The founders were a few medical students who kept their names secret. The fundamental spirit of equality and fraternity of the Ojak was an established tradition then. No member allowed himself to feel superior to any other. The club was helped by some writers and famous doctors as well as by the Union and Progress.

Two dominant clauses which were never allowed to be altered by the general congress, and which show the tendencies and the spirit of the Ojak are: first, the Ojak will help the cultural development of the Turk; second, the Ojak is not a political institution.

To those clauses the old members of the Ojak have been fanatically faithful from 1911 to 1924. Neither the extreme Unionists during the ascendancy of the Unionist régime, nor the anti-Unionists after the decisive downfall of the Unionist régime in 1918, could alter these clauses and drag the Ojak into party politics.

The most active period of the Ojak began when Hamdullah Soubhi Bey became the president. By his great oratorical powers he obtained tremendous influence over the youthful members, and his tenacity and diplomatic ability made him persuade all the great men and all the governments to come to his aid either with funds or in some other way. Besides the majority of young students, the majority of Turkish writers and leading men also belonged to it, and worked with admirable idealism for the cultural development of the Turk. Lectures and free lessons were opened to the public by well known men, among whom Keuk-Alp Zia was the most prominent. Men belonging to all shades of political creeds and ideals gathered in sincere understanding under its roof.

The clubs helped the Turkish students from all over the Turkish world to obtain their education in Istamboul. The Ojak, which showed Pan-Turanistic tendencies culturally, was against Pan-Islamism, but in a few years Pan-Turanism also gave way to a regional nationalism, which can be defined as belonging to Turkey proper and the peoples who live in it.

In 1912 the general congress elected me as its only woman member. It was in 1918 that another congress chose a council of eleven to modify its constitution. I was in the council, and we modified the constitution with a new clause which made women members eligible. Many Ojaks have risen all over the country since then. The situation of the Ojaks in the present time, after the alteration of their constitution in 1924 in Angora, wants an entirely different treatment.

As nationalism is considered a narrow ideal by those who aim at the welfare of humanity and hope to obtain it through internationalism, I have often been reproached by my international friends. And as I have not ceased to work for the happiness of my kind, especially of those who are nearest to me, I have honestly tried to analyze the inner meaning of my nationalism, whether it can hurt others who are not Turks, whether it can hurt in the long run the family of nations in the world to which Turkey also belongs.

The individual or the nation, in order to understand its fellow-men or its fellow-nations, in order to create beauty and to express its personality, must go deep down to the roots of its being and study itself sincerely. The process of this deep self-duty, as well as its results, is nationalism. I believe with all earnestness that such a national self-study, and the exchange of its results, is the first and right step to international understanding and love of the peoples and nations. It is after I have loved my own people and tried to understand their virtues and their faults with open-minded humility that I begin to have a better understanding of other people's sufferings and joys, and of their personality expressed in their national life.

I will also admit that there is a narrow, negative, and destructive nationalism in the world, which has deluded itself with the belief that a nation can only grow and thrive by exterminating and oppressing the peoples under its rule, or by conquering and suppressing the nations around it. Both are forms of wrongly understood nationalism which can be called by the names of chauvinism and imperialism. And the peoples who exercised them have themselves suffered materially and morally more than the peoples whom they have tried to hurt. One must admit at the same time that chauvinism and imperialism are not the only outcomes of nationalism. The internationalism of Soviet Russia has shown itself both chauvinistic and imperialistic in certain ways.

The leaders of a nation—and the philosophers, who are perhaps more effective in the long run—have distorted principles by following the good or the evil of the very first man. There are those who believe in the positive action of the good, and try to adjust the good of their own people with that of the other nations and get their support from the best and the highest interest in human nature. It is this idea which is bringing into existence the League of Nations, and gathering nationalistic people as well as international ones around it.

There are those who believe in the domination of material interest only and seek their ends by exciting the worst in their fellow-men, and by leading them to perpetual conflict within and without. I shall repeat here a conversation I once had with a leader. I shall not mention his name, but he will recognize himself if he reads these lines. My readers will also recognize the methods of those great men and régimes who use all means and ways in order to retain their power.

He was the brother of the chief of the most powerful revolutionary band in 1920 in Turkey and was an extremely intelligent man. As we had not then been able to organize a regular army, that particular band was supreme and held the destiny of the revolution in its hands. I asked him the methods by which he and his brother got so much power over their men.

"The essential and dominating motive of man is self-interest and fear," he said. "Wherever you govern, you must have a strong minority whom you hold by those forces."

"How do you do that?" I asked.

"The spoils are mostly divided among those, and they must be so much involved and so much richer and more powerful than the majority that they must be ready to go to any length of sacrifice, and fight for the chief against the majority whenever it is necessary. They must know that the community will not tolerate them if they lose the favor of the chief."

In Paris only some months ago, a Rumanian youth, whom I accidently met, told me about the interior politics of Rumania, the banks, the corruption, the monopoly of national riches by the political party in power. It sounded exactly like the ruling methods of the revolutionary band, but on a larger scale.

My own conclusion is to teach to all the coming generations the love of our kind, the constant struggle for a higher state of national morality, a better adjustment and greater equality among all peoples; these are the only fundamental conditions which can make life possible and lasting on the globe. It was the selfish and materialistic philosophy of the latter part of the nineteenth century which brought the greatest of human disasters in the form of the World War. Its consequences are not yet at an end. The hypocrisy and personal unworthiness of many of the world's leaders, whether national or international, can lead to a complete and final destruction of all that has been the outcome of infinite suffering and experience for thousands of years. The renaming of ideals, which is too often a mere political game in the hands of unscrupulous leaders, is not enough; it is the rules of the game that must be changed.

CHAPTER XIV

THE BALKAN WAR

I GOT a clue of the coming of the Balkan troubles while visiting my father in Yanina, through a Turkish officer called Sabit Bey, who himself died in the Balkan war. He was one of those simple big dark Turks, with the innate sense of justice and goodness of his race. He was a very close friend of my father and very anti-Unionist at the time, on account of the drastic measures of the Unionists in putting down an insurrection in Albania. He hated tyranny, and during his visit to Albania he was shocked by the severity of the Unionist régime in Albania. Macedonia and Albania were the fields where the seeds of war were sown, not only by the external policies of the powers but also by the contradictory national desires of the inhabitants.

In the meantime the Unionists were having their own internal difficulties in 1911, especially within the parliament. They were not only losing their majority in the parliament, but the popular feeling against them as freemasons and radicals was such that their prospects of success in a new election were very doubtful. The immediate if short-sighted solution of the difficulty was the dissolution of parliament, and the use of the sultan's power to consolidate their position; both of these courses were reactionary according to the principles the Unionists had professed in the constitutional revolution of 1908.

The first step was to strike out the thirty-fifth clause of the constitution, which had been added in 1908 in order to modify the thirteenth article of the constitution of 1876, the article which gave the sultan the right of dissolution, by means of which Abdul Hamid had dissolved the parliament of 1876. Now the Unionists wanted to give back the right of dissolution to Sultan Mehemmed Reshad, who was playing safely in their hands. The parliament refused to vote the abolition of Clause 35, and so the Young Turks had to persuade the senate to step in and take advantage of the difference between the government and the parliament, which seemed insoluble, and to use their prerogative of voting the dissolution. The first Young Turkish parliament was dissolved on Jaunary 5, by the Young Turks themselves, but the result of this first reactionary step was destined to recoil upon themselves. For before three months had passed over their new parliament, a semi-revolutionary and military organization called the Saviors of the Nation gathered in Maltepe and demanded the dissolution of the new parliament and the formation of a cabinet composed of impartial men. The senate once more dissolved the parliament, and what is called the Great Cabinet was formed under Gazi Mouhtar Pasha, with a large number of old

THE BALKAN WAR

grand vizirs and other members known for their hatred of the Unionists.

The Great Cabinet, as well as that of Kiamil Pasha which succeeded it, representing the opposition, the Entente Liberale, retained power about six months. It was a period of utter disillusion. They repeated every single misdeed of their political rivals, and the only motive which seemed to dominate them was their hatred and mistrust of the Unionists. I believe that it was their utter incapacity and lack of ideals and their repetition of courts martial and imprisonment which made the best of the Turkish world cast in its lot with the Union and Progress.

In June I once more went to visit Miss Isabel Fry in England, and it was during this visit that I wrote the "New Turan."

As Miss Fry left for Dublin before the end of my visit I took a flat in Cambridge Terrace, where Dr. Riza Tewfik had lived before me. In the solitude and the discreet half-light of the English atmosphere I worked well. The noise which one may expect of the great traffic of London is so smooth and even, and the life of the great city is so softly tuned down to a strange order, as if all passed through a padded screen before it reached you, that it throws one entirely into oneself. No atmosphere is more restful and favorable to creative work than that of London for an unknown and young writer. The isolation is so complete that one is forced to dig into one's inner resources.

Every day about noon I walked out into the streets.

It was my only plunge into the city, and it made me feel like a drop of oil on the surface of an ocean, always apart and unassimilated despite its infinitesimal size. I was much criticized, mostly by the allied press, because of "New Turan," and I have often smiled to think of the place where I wrote it. No book has been more misunderstood. In the outer world it has been held largely responsible for the faults of the Unionists, while in Turkey it was taken to represent a formulated doctrine of nationalism.

The book is a political and national Utopia, but not so far away from possibilities as one may suppose a Utopia to be. It looks forward to a New Turkey where a chastised and matured Union and Progress has taken the reins of power, where women have the vote, and where women work with the qualities of head and heart which characterize the best Turkish women. The simplicity and the austerity of their lives have become different since the magnificent days of the Ottomans, with the unhealthy luxury and parasitic tendencies of a class of women which only a high but degenerate civilization like the Ottoman creates. The highest ideal is work and simplicity. There is not only a Turkey that is nationalized in its culture, but there is also a Turkey that is liberal and democratic in politics. Above all, there is no chauvinism in the administrative system. The book, which has the usual love-story, has not much pretension to art, but its practically worked out ideals will, I firmly believe, be at least partly realized.

About the end of August, 1912, Turkey entered the

THE BALKAN WAR

Balkan war. The splitting up of the internal control and the loss of Turkish prestige in Albania hastened the Balkan alliance, and Turkey received the famous ultimatum. The war was declared by the Great Cabinet.

Mr. Asquith's government officially declared that the status quo would be respected, whatever the results of the war should be.

The result was one of the greatest defeats in Turkish history, with the massacre of three thousand Macedonian Turks and Moslems—one of the greatest massacres of the last hundred years.

The declaration of Mr. Asquith's cabinet was evidently a simple precaution in case of Turkish victory, and the massacres did not arouse one quarter of the indignation which the Armenian massacres had done. These facts spoke bitterly in Turkey against Europe, and in the Islamic worlds in Asia. I believe that the two different measures meted out by Europe to the Moslem Turks and to the Christian peoples in Turkey keenly intensified nationalism in Turkey. They also aroused the feeling that in order to avoid being exterminated the Turks must exterminate others. As the Bulgarian victory made the world overlook the crimes of her revolutionaries—crimes of which the Bulgarians themselves surely did not approve, for they are a kindly race—so any other nation in the East could hope to have all her massacres forgotten, so long as she could impose respect with her victorious force. I am sorry to put the case so brutally, but I am only relating the effect on the

Turks of the European diplomacy of those days, and its responsibility for the bloodier development of later years.

On the other hand, there has never been a worse managed war than the Balkan war. The lack of sanitary organization, the badness of the service behind the lines was deplorable. The sheep starved in the cars, and the flour rotted at the depots, while less than a mile away men died of hunger. When the Turkish refugees flocked in panic to Constantinople to escape from massacre, when cholera broke out among the immigrants and in the army, when one saw an entire population dying in the mosque yards under the icy grip of winter, the sight of the misery in Constantinople seemed too grim to be true.

Granny went over to Scutari, which she considered holy ground, being on the Asiatic continent, where Mecca is. My servants left for their own country, and I sent my children to Broussa. The march of the Bulgarian army on Constantinople seemed more than probable. My sister arrived among the refugees from Adrianople and passed on to Scutari. Most of the families left Constantinople. I stayed in Fatih at Nakie Hanum's house and worked with the women of the Taali-Nisvan Club for relief and nursing.

We, with some teachers and some educated Turkish women, had formed that first women's club. Its ultimate object was the cultivation of its members. It had a small center where the members took lessons in French and English. It also opened classes for a limited number of Turkish women to study Turkish, domestic science, and the bringing up of children. We had Mrs. Marden, of Guedik Pasha school, and Mrs. Bowen, who helped us in the teaching of English, as well as in lending us the Hall of Guedik Pasha school, where we opened a series of lectures for women. There was a feministic tendency in the club, but as a whole it kept within the bounds of usefulness and philanthropy, and we tried to maintain a quiet tone, avoiding propaganda, which becomes so ugly and loud and offers such an easy way to fame for any one who can make sufficient noise.

The club organized and opened a small hospital with thirty beds in Istamboul. A young surgeon and a chemist, both husbands of club members, volunteered to help; the beds and equipment were provided by the members; and one member lent a house. We took only privates. As the Balkan war saw Turkish women nursing men for the first time, any little human incident became a tremendous scandal.

I came every morning from Fatih and returned to it late every evening. The streets were deserted except for the refugees shivering in the mud, and sick or wounded soldiers who had arrived late, staggering, or leaning against the walls or each other for support.

I realized then the extent of my affection for my people and for my land. I cannot make out which I loved best, but I felt my love was personal and incurable and had nothing to do with ideas, thoughts, or politics, that in fact it was physical and elemental. Very often

I was the only woman crossing Sultan Ahmed Square. I had on my loosest and oldest *charshaf,* and often I would stand in the middle of the square and think with infinite sadness of an alien army marching toward it. I had a foolish desire to stoop and kiss the very stones of the place, so passionately did I love it. No force could have dragged me away from Constantinople. I belonged to the place, and whatever its fate, I meant to share it.

I bought the newspapers every morning, though they reported nothing but a series of national disasters. But I had to go to the hospital with a calm face. I knew beforehand how those Anatolian eyes would look at me, proud in spite of the tragic curiosity and anxiety in their childish depths.

"Good morning, sister. How are you to-day?" I knew what it meant, but I went on with the usual work, the early visit of the doctor, and the painful dressing of wounds which followed.

There was an Angora man who stayed in my mind rather as a symbol of the Anatolia of those days. He must once have been a fine specimen of manly beauty. He had those dark greenish eyes and long lashes and the tall physique of his region, but now he had turned into a huge skeleton. He had gone from Albania to Yemen, and after seven years of it he had been sent home three months ago, broken with malaria and hardship, his intelligence almost extinguished. Hardly had he arrived in Constantinople when he was sent to the Balkan front. He was wounded in both legs, and both were in danger of gangrene. He had to be isolated, and the surgeon meant to go through a series of operations before giving him up to amputation. His heart was not in a state to bear chloroform, and he had to go through it all as best he could.

Then I saw how an ordinary Turkish soldier who has lost all except his sense of manhood bears pain. He had almost forgotten his mother-tongue in the desert and had not learned much Arabic; somehow he had ceased to need speech. The doctor made him understand that he was not to move his leg during the operation.

He remained rigid, as if he were a piece of unyielding iron. He closed his eyes, clenched his teeth, and lay as still as a dead man, crushing my hand, which he always humbly asked to hold in his.

In a week the danger of gangrene was over, and we transferred him to the common room, where we fought against his malaria. During the last days of his convalescence he recovered his memory and interest in life to a certain degree, and got me to write his letters to his village. He was going back and wanted his fields got ready for barley sowing.

Another case which twined around my heart was of a Macedonian. His legs were both wounded, and his arm had been broken in great pain after what was probably a bad setting. He asked to be allowed to sit up in bed, and he would rock himself to and fro. I soon found out that the rocking and the hardly audible moans were not for the arm. He had left a little girl and a wife in Sketché, and the place had been taken by the Bulgarians. The usual stories about the massacres and atrocities had been circulated, and his people had not turned up yet. There was an immigration commission in the municipality, and to it I used to send some one regularly to find out about the baby named Hadije, aged four, and the woman called Eminé, aged twenty-five. Each morning I had to go into the room and face the dumb despair in that man's eyes. Sometimes I said: "It is a long way off. They may turn up yet. She could not walk like the others with a child."

"She has an ox-cart," he would say through clenched teeth and go on rocking.

The resigned and pathetic patience and the dumb dignity of the suffering of these men was past belief. They were so much ashamed of their defeat that they received every bit of kindness, even nursing, with apologetic gratitude.

Every evening as I left the hospital I heard the newspaper boys shouting their special editions, which always contained a new Turkish disaster. That desolate march of the defeated Turkish army through hostile races, hunted and starving, freezing, only a few of its members reaching the capital, seemed like a nightmare without end.

It was on one of those gloomy evenings when I felt well nigh at the end of my tether, that a letter arrived from Derne in Tripoli. It was a letter from six officers, in our one and only machine-gun detachment.

It was written by their chief officer, who called himself Ishildak, and all the six signed as the officers of the New Turan.

It was a delirious declaration of love, but love to their land and people. They were feeling that supreme emotion which one feels at the suffering of a very much beloved being. It was the same sort of thing which made me want to kiss the muddy streets of Istamboul. They had come back to the defense of the mainland of Turkey after their hardships in the desert. The letter was so wonderful that I used it in the story which I wrote during the Gallipoli period called "The Dream of Ishildak." Although the name "New Turan" had become the rage, and some shops already called themselves by it, and I had letters from Kazan and Tashkend on the subject, still I shall always love the book most, because it supplied those isolated young soldiers with the enthusiasm which makes men forget their suffering.

I found out that Ishildak was one of the first members of the Ojak, but I never met him. I followed his career, which was a series of battles. He wrote one last letter from Mesopotamia asking me to give ten copies of "New Turan" to ten graduating officers, instead of giving prayers for his soul, in case he died. And he died in Mesopotamia.

Izzet Pasha's return as well as that of the young element from Tripoli added a new strength to the defense of Chatalja, and the Bulgarian army after heavy losses saw the impossibility of entering Constantinople.

But the event which soothed the national pride, writhing under the shame of a sweeping defeat, was the raid of the *Hamidie,* the adventures of the phantom ship, as the European press at the time called her. The Turkish crusier *Hamidie* had been to Varna and had bombarded it at the beginning of the Balkan war. After receiving a severe wound on her side, she had come back. Although her return to Constantinople in her sinking state was considered a great naval feat, no one had dreamt of seeing her emerge from the docks in the Golden Horn and venture out again for fighting purposes.

Hardly four months had passed, and when every one was discussing the gathering of the Greek fleet in the Dardanelles we heard of the *Hamidie* bombarding the island of Shira.

It was a miracle how she had slipped out in the dark through the Dardenelles and through the Greek fleet which was closely watching at the mouth of the straits. Then the Turkish as well as the European press began to revel in the real or imaginary exploits of the phantom ship. The Greek fleet went in immediate pursuit, but the *Hamidie* went on her way, bombarding the coasts of the Adriatic and the chief Greek islands, sinking Greek transports, but saving the lives on the sinking ships with scrupulous humanity, and leaving the rescued on any coast which the *Hamidie* could approach without risk. In technique, in chivalry, and in fantastic feats of courage, it is perhaps the most perfect episode in the fighting annals of the Turkish sea battles. The great modesty of the commander, Captain Reuof, did not allow him to pose as a hero. On the contrary, his strong belief that all the glory was due to the high courage of his men, and that the Turkish people are always the victims of hero worship, especially in military affairs, made him fight down his own popularity in Turkey.

In the meantime an organization of a semi-official character was trying to raise money to help the refugees and the hospitals. The Taali-Nisvan organized a meeting of women in the University Hall in Istamboul, both to help the refugees and to send a protest to the queens in Europe asking them to use their influence to stop the massacre of the non-combatant Turks and Moslems in Macedonia.

There were about six women speakers, and the hall was more than crammed. Before the meeting was over women were throwing their jewelry to the pulpit, tearing their furs off to be given to the refugees and the sick. The meeting chose two women delegates to go to the embassies in Pera, to ask them to convey the protests to the queens.

On January 2, 1913, I was so weak and reduced by heart-trouble that I was obliged to go to the German hospital. On January 10 I was wakened by the head sister, who entered my room in a hurry and ran to the balcony which overlooked Istamboul. She was so much excited that she was waving her hands and talking aloud to herself.

"What it is?" I asked.

"The Unionists have carried out a *coup d'état*," she said. "They have taken the Sublime Porte by force, and there has been shooting; Nazim Pasha, the war minister, his aide-de-camp, and a Unionist called Moustafa Nedjib are dead."

The circumstances of the *coup d'état* were these: The powers had presented a collective note to the Porte demanding the cession of Adrianople to Bulgaria. The cabinet of Kiamil Pasha decided to accept the allied demand on January 9. Adrianople, however, had not yet fallen, and its long and gallant defense made the public bitter against abandoning the city while its continued defense was still possible. The Unionists took up the popular side and proposed at all costs to prevent Adrianople's surrender. They came to an understanding with Nazim Pasha, the minister of war, who was opposed to the cession of Adrianople, promising him the office of grand vizir. On January 10, Enver and Talaat led three hundred men to the Porte, meaning merely to quietly ask Kiamil Pasha to resign. But in the general excitement two of the Union and Progress party, Yacoub Djemil and Moustafa Nedjib, fired, and Nazim and Pasha and his aide-de-camp and Moustafa Nedjib were killed. This is the Unionist version. The opposition insisted that Moustafa Nedjib had orders from Enver to fire. As Moustafa Nedjib himself died in the general firing it is difficult to verify either version. Mahmoud Shevket Pasha's cabinet was then formed.

THE BALKAN WAR

Adrianople fell very soon after, and the London conference on May 30, 1913, saw the Young Turks sign the cession of the fallen city for which they had carried out their *coup d'état*. Their excuse to public opinion was that they had ceded it after its fall, whereas Kiamil Pasha was going to cede while it was fighting.

On June 2, 1914, Mahmoud Shevket Pasha was assassinated by the opposition.[1] He was a man of really high principles, great honesty and capacity, as well as a moderate and kindly man. He was mostly attacked by the opposition for faults of his party for which he was not responsible.

Djemal Bey, the military commander of Istamboul, arrested the murderers as well as the conspirators. About twelve men, among them a pasha the son-in-law of the sultan, were executed, and a large number were exiled to various parts of Anatolia.

Djemal Bey had called on me with his wife, whom I already knew, after the publication of "New Turan" and had warmly declared himself a New Turanist who would try for the realization of the ideal. He appeared so delicate and sensitive that it was impossible to foresee the ferocious energy he was to put forth in reducing the opposition. I must confess that I did not like the

[1] The opposition had planned a *coup d'état* similar to that of the Unionists which had been carried out on January 10, 1913. They meant to assassinate a large number of Unionists, but the immediate and severe measures of the Unionists after the assassination of Mahmoud Shevket Pasha broke the opposition in its organization. Riza Nour Bey, then an influential member of the opposition, and now the deputy from Sinope, speaks of the plan of the opposition in his book called "The Inner Secrets of the Entente Liberale," published in 1918.

drastic measures which were taken to punish the political offenders. Djemel Bey (afterward Pasha) gives his reasons for all his political acts in his Memoirs. I asked him at the time to do something for Tewfik, the son of my old friends in Beshiktash, who had been arrested as one of the conspirators. He promised to do something, and he accordingly helped Tewfik to return from exile.

Taking advantage of the differences which had risen between the governments of the Balkan states that had fought against Turkey, the Turkish army marched once more on Adrianople in July, 1913, and recovered it without much difficulty. Thus ended the Balkan war.

CHAPTER XV

MY EDUCATIONAL ACTIVITIES, 1913–14

THE years 1913–15 of the Unionist régime deserve to be appreciated for the sincere and hard struggle put forth for constructive change in the country. I have so far told about the first political difficulties of the Unionists, their desire to hold power at any cost, their blunders, and their reforming energy and courage. But now they began to display a certain ability to govern relatively better, and they laid the foundation of modern reform, which has continued ever since despite all obstacles.

The most serious reforms were those of the army and of finance. Djavid Bey, the greatest financier whom New Turkey has had so far, coöperating with French advisers, chief among whom was Charles Laurent, transformed the finance department from a medieval into a modern institution both in spirit and in function. The customs were organized by our old friend Sirry Bey under the supervision of Sir Richard F. Crawford, one of the ablest foreign advisers Turkey has ever had.

Enver began the reform of the army when he was hardly thirty-two. He called in a German military commission to set the change afoot. Apart from the political complication into which this influence led

Turkey at a later period, the Germans also accomplished their immediate task with admirable conscientiousness. Enver was an admirer of the German military system, which he had studied in Berlin during two years when he was a Turkish attaché there. His reorganization of the Turkish army was one of the most successful of the reforms undertaken, because of the military aptitude of the people. I could cite many staff-officers, to-day in prominent positions, and very anti-Enverist, who admit that the reorganization of the Anatolian army of independence was possible only because of the sound basis that Enver had laid. His unflinching determination to organize a younger and more efficient staff, his absolute disregard of political considerations where promotion or punishment was concerned, are admitted by his opponents as well as his admirers.

Comte Roubilant modeled a new gendarmerie, and a number of other foreign advisers did excellent work in the public works. Admiral Gamble and later on Admiral Limpus were called to reform the navy. Admiral Gamble has left a name which is still spoken of with respect and affection among the young element, especially among the common sailors.

Comte Ostrorog unfortunately could not stay long as an adviser in the work of judicial reform. After a very short service, with the exception of Hussein Jahid almost all the important members of the Union and Progress came to consider him very anti-Turkish.

The ministry of public instruction had no European

MY EDUCATIONAL ACTIVITIES, 1913–14

adviser for years. Both the opposition and the conservatives showed themselves jealous and ferociously critical of the direction of that department. Many well known men of the empire came to be ministers of public instruction one after another, but there appeared a lack of clearness about their aims and principles.

Emrullah Effendi was the first man who had a clear idea of what he wanted in the field of public instruction. As he believed in the importance of higher education he tried to advance the universities, and also to send a large number of students to European universities.

Hussein Jahid, who was one of the strongest intellectuals of the party, always refused the post, conditioning his acceptance on the adoption of the Latin characters, which the government would not do.

Shukri Bey, who became the minister of public instruction in the cabinet of Saïd Halim after the assassination of Mahmoud Shevket, was the first successor of Emrullah Effendi who had decided ideas and the energy to carry them out. Although I resigned from the educational department on account of a difference of opinion with him on the principles of education in Turkey, still I can sincerely admit that his work deserves consideration.

When I first went into the department I saw that there were a few educational centers which had their own tradition, culture, and quality; these were Galata Sarai, Mulkie, Dar-ushaffaca, and the two other colleges in Istamboul. They had provided educated citizens for the empire and for the new régime, few in number but valuable in quality. Now we had to keep up the standard and increase the number at a time when we had very little teaching material of the desired quality. The education of women seriously speaking was begun by the new régime, and in 1913 we had a good college—and a normal school. I felt that our efforts must be directed toward slowly increasing the numbers without endangering their quality, that the normal schools should be fused with the colleges and that several of these should be united in order to economize teachers and equipment, and thus keep up the standard, which was falling low in the many normal schools and colleges which we opened all over the country, and which were only nominally what they should have been.

I worked out my project with precision and had an appointment to see Shukri Bey at the ministry during the very first week of his ministry. I went to Broussa for the week-end. On my return I saw a statement in one of the papers that two teachers who were not present at an inspection (they had no classes in the school on that day) were to be reprimanded. Although there was no name I found that I was one of them, and I immediately resigned. The ministry had no control over me on the days when I had no lectures to deliver. Probably it was merely a foolish mistake of some very old inspector, but I felt that I had to do what I did.

Before the week was out Talaat Pasha, Keuk-Alp Zia, and Dr. Nazim Beys called on me.

It was the first time I ever saw Talaat Pasha. I was

immediately struck with his simplicity, humor, and geniality. At first he spoke on many different subjects, but he came to the point in a way which showed both delicacy and cleverness. He had come to induce me to recall my resignation. Somehow he made me feel that I was sacrificing my life-work for personal pride, and when he saw the effect his words had on me he took up my resignation and handed it back to me with a smile. "It lacks a stamp," he said. "Do take it back, and do not give up your pupils so easily." There was intelligence and a lack of the consciousness of pride and power about him which so often characterizes men who attain power as fast as he had done.

From this time he called at the Bairam festivals regularly and at other times occasionally. He continued to do so when I was bitterly criticizing his personal politics and the policy of his party, and he kept up his friendliness to the last. His frugal ways, his modest life, and his charm of the true democrat kept my respect and admiration for him as a man throughout. However one may criticize him, one is obliged to admit that he was the truest of patriots, and that no act of his was either for personal gain or love of power. He lived and died a poor man, proud to be poor, and ready to endure all for what he believed to be best for his country.

He succeeded during those years in creating a much better department of the interior, and he fought mercilessly against corruption and abuse. He used to say in those days, "We began as revolutionaries, but the time has come to make the law supreme in this country."

All this gave way during the last years of the World War. Every one seemed to be possessed by one single idea, the final victory. No one can fully realize how much principle, high purpose, and human feeling, as well as material wealth, have been sacrificed and damaged for victory all over the world, and what a long struggle is necessary for moral and material reconstruction.

Three months after this event I resigned for good. Shukri Bey clearly showed that his educational policy was to obtain quantity at the expense of quality. He wanted to have the largest possible number of men and women who would read and write, and he did not care for the rest. He went on multiplying schools and calling them by names to which the education they provided in no way corresponded. In 1915 he also called in German professors and advisers who did some good academic work for the university. Much as I was and am against his basic principle of quantity against quality, I must admit that the large number of people now able to read and write in Turkey is the outcome of his work. Had he stayed longer in power he might have had a more lasting effect on the higher education of the country.

Nakie Hanum resigned a few months after me. She had created a girls' college which was notable from every point of view and had proved herself to be a serious educator. Before she had had time to rest, she received an offer from the education department of the

MY EDUCATIONAL ACTIVITIES, 1913–14

ministry of *evkaff* (pious foundations), to which all the mosque schools belonged.

Hairi Effendi, the great sheik-ul-Islam of the Unionist régime, had began a series of interesting and serious reforms in *evkaff,* which was under his control. The department had in its charge a large number of theological schools (*medresses*) of an extremely scholastic and reactionary kind as well as all the primary mosque schools, mixed or unmixed. A great deal of money was spent on these institutions. Hairi Effendi began an able and drastic reform in all of them. The *medresses* for the first time were to have modern science taught by modern teachers instead of the old scholastic curriculum and the old teachers. The mosque schools, which so far taught only the Koran and which were housed in little holes, were to be modernized, and a dozen schools were amalgamated in one big and up-to-date building in an important center. Each was to have a modern staff with a modern curriculum. The boys' schools were organized by Ali Bey, a very capable and progressive section chief in *evkaff*. The girls' schools as well as the small mixed ones were to be organized by Nakie Hanum as the general director. I became their inspector-general and adviser.

Nakie Hanum soon succeeded in creating a hard-working, sincere, and capable body of teachers. She was greatly helped by the young graduates of the college whom we had ourselves trained. Her schools immediately became the best primary schools in

Istamboul. The best specialists on educational subjects offered to train her teachers, and her own central school in Sultan Ahmed acquired an atmosphere of learning and happy camaraderie among the old and young elements of *evkaff*. Hussein Jahid, Adnan, Edib, Djavid, and Youssouf Akchura Beys were among the staff who regularly lectured to her teachers.

Keuk-Alp Zia was numbered among the friends of the school. But when Shukri Bey advanced the theory of unity of education, using the expression in a sense which means centralization, that is, to have all the schools under the ministry of public instruction, Keuk-Alp Zia favored the idea, as well as Shukri Bey's plea that no schools should be under the *evkaff*, which is a religious institution. But the curriculum of the *evkaff* schools at the time was more secular than obtained in the schools of the public instruction.

The school centers were in the poorest and farthest quarters of the city, in places where I had never been, and I got on close terms with people with whom I should never have come in contact except in my capacity as an inspector who made weekly visits to those quarters, studied the little ones, and got to know their parents.

There was also at this time some change in my household. Mahmouré Abla, with her five children and her husband who had returned from Adrianople, came to live with me. Nighiar, my sister, who graduated in 1912 from the college and had become a teacher to Nakie Hanum's school, came to me also.

There were seven pairs of childish feet that wore out

MY EDUCATIONAL ACTIVITIES, 1913-14

the oil-cloth on my stairs but brought a new world of life, youth, and joyful bustle to the house.

Granny was living with me as usual, but I had lost the old sense of nearness to her for the moment. I was constantly out for lessons and lectures, the club demanded much of my time, and my circle of friends had had a great deal happen to it.

My writing I had to do after ten o'clock at night when the noisy little house slept and left me quiet in my room. Granny also enjoyed those quiet hours; she came to me for talks then. She was much shocked by the new women. Their talk, their walk, their dress, and their general aspect hurt her. She felt lonely, like a stranger in a world where she felt she had stayed too long, like a visitor who has outstayed his welcome; it was as if the newly arrived guests had taken all the room, and they looked ever so different from her. She suffered because they shook their arms as they walked, looked into men's eyes, had loud voices, and smoked in public; above all they did not iron their clothes as she did every morning. In spite of every difference we found certain inner contacts where we met on common ground and understood each other.

In the middle of a difficult passage when my heroines had to be tended through their hysterical outbursts and follies (I had a special capacity for describing folly) she walked into my writing-room and said, "Let us talk, Halidé; I have not opened my mouth for days." Sometimes we did talk to her heart's desire, but at times I could not talk; the heroine or the hero absorbed me more than granny, and then she walked back to her room with a sadness which spoiled my work, even kept me awake with remorse. She was eighty years old by this time but still appeared in good health, and always clean and dainty with a very correct taste, her clothes beautifully ironed; and she never missed any of her five long prayers daily.

Now and then she spoke of her longing for the old houses with the wisteria, the spacious rooms with many windows, and the blazing lights of Istamboul seen through clean white curtains, with simple divans about. The chairs and heavy curtains and the little rooms of my house distressed her. I must have had some secret longing also, for we set out in search of big old houses with large gardens. We both knew that I could not change my house in Fazli Pasha. It had its own associations, its particular scenery; it had helped me to stand on my feet at a moment when I was broken physically and spiritually, and I had written the youngest and most passionate if not the best of my work there.

Once we found a house in a little street behind Sultan Ahmed which answered the description—the double stairs, the wisteria, the bath-room with old and beautifully carved basins, and the pointed door covered with red cloth and golden clasps.

We did not take it, but we talked of it, of the bath, of the double basins, and of Sultan Ahmed Mosque, from which one could hear the evening prayers and see the lights on its minarets in Ramazan nights.

Very early one morning I was awakened by a queer

noise outside my door. I walked out almost into Mahmouré Abla, who spoke in undertones:

"It is granny," she said.

She had fallen at my door with a fit of that horrible thing, apoplexy.

She could not talk or move, but her eyes had their comprehending look, intensified with new knowledge, which made her regard the ignorant ones around her with a sort of pathetic pity. Her unfailing humor still flickering in her eyes, she moved her right hand (she could still do that) and made the sign of three with her fingers. It was her usual sign in her other sicknesses, signifying, "I will live only three days." I telephoned to the doctor, but I also sent for hodjas who would chant the Koran softly and breathe its healing effects over her, which soothed her and made her feel safe on her road to heaven.

The only doctor she could tolerate was Dr. Adnan, the family doctor and friend whom she loved as a son, both on account of his old-world manners and for an imagined resemblance to Uncle Kemal. It was hard to get him at once.[1]

---

[1] As Enver Bey had come back from his march to Adrianople with a severe attack of appendicitis, Asnan as his friend stayed with him through his illness and its two grave operations.

Dr. Adnan was intimate with Enver in Germany, and he speaks of Enver in those days as a man of incredible purity of life and spirit. No force of feminine charm, no amount of temptation and pleasure, could draw him away from his hard-working life and priest-like abstinence. He was engaged to Princess Nadjie, whom he saw during this illness and married a few months later.

Dr. Adnan's intimacy with Enver stopped very soon afterward. He buried himself in the organization of the Red Crescent and in his lectures

I well remember taking Dr. Adnan to her room for the first time after her attack of apoplexy. I saw a look of horror in her face instead of the pleasure I had expected, and it puzzled me greatly. But he walked to her bed, took her white veil, which had been taken off to put ice on her head, and covered her head, which immediately brought back the usual look to her eyes.

After the third day she fell into a nervous agitation; it was as if she was ashamed of not having kept her word to die promptly on the third day. In the days when she had seemed far away from death and had spoken to me of it I used to think that her death would not make much difference in my life, but when I saw the moment of her final departure so near I suffered atrociously. I realized how much I wanted her and what a link she was to all that counts so much in a poor human's past.

On the morning of the ninth day of her illness she seemed calm, and I had hopes of her recovery, a hope she seemed to read with gratitude in my eyes. I am sure that she wanted to feel that she had not been a burden, a feeling which all the old carry so pathetically in the depths of their childish hearts. She called me with her eyes as I entered. I ran and laid my cheek against her cheek. That wonderful clean and personal perfume, which only the old women of her class and

---

in the medical faculty. He was obliged to perform his military service as the assistant *ad interim* to the chief of the field sanitary department, where he came under Enver's command. Their relations never resumed the old footing. The beloved Enver Bey of 1908 and of Tripoli was now the hated military dictator. Dr. Adnan often repeated the saying of our famous writer Suleyman Nazif, "Enver Pasha has killed Enver Bey."

generation had, penetrated me. I knew that I would never experience it again; it was passing away with her. An instant of infinite tenderness, something like religious ecstasy, enveloped both of us. I kissed her hands reverently, with the chastened and repenting pain which I still have at times, wondering if I had done all that it was in my power to do for her happiness in her last days.

As I left her room I thought of something she had said in the late hours of the night.

"I am afraid," she had said, "of the earth in death, but somehow the little cemetery on that Sultan Tepé hill, the cemetery of the Tekké"—the monastery where I have taken refuge twice—"would not be so lonely. I would not mind being there."

None of her beloved ones were buried there, but it was the tiny cemetery of the Euzbeks, where a few of the homeless Euzbeks from Tashkend and a few sheiks belonging to the order were buried. The place has infinite space, quiet, and beauty. As death then had seemed a myth to me in the undying energy of my youth I had said, "I will come there too, granny, and we shall have the midnight talks over again."

This had soothed her and she had confidentially added, "Even in a cemetery I hate crowds and bustle."

This conversation haunted me that night. That same night she passed away, and we buried her in the humble cemetery on the lonely hilltop.

It was Kurban Bairam the next day, and I had the room full of friends who offered me more than a Bairam felicitation. Keuk-Alp Zia was the last to leave, as Dr. Adnan entered. I was glad to see that the doctor could steal away from Enver Bey for a Bairam visit and for condolence. But I was pinned to my chair when I tried to rise by the strange pain which I had had during granny's illness, and I groaned involuntarily.

"What is it?" he asked.

"The pain in my side," I answered.

"It must be appendicitis," he said laughingly. "There are dozens of cases that I know of in the city—quite an epidemic."

It was in fact a grave case of appendicitis, with high fever and the familiar severe pain. I felt very grateful for the attack, which left me alone with myself during this time.

Eight days later I was transferred to the German hospital to be operated on, and Dr. Adnan took up his watch by my bed. I was up in a fortnight, although I stayed on for another week in the hospital. The expressions of sympathy and interest which I received during my illness touched me deeply.

Talaat Pasha called with Dr. Nazim and laughingly declared that he was sent by the Committee of Union and Progress. Then he fell into a childish mood about Adrianople, which they had recently recovered. He had paid the recovered city a visit that very week, and the impression of it was fresh in his mind. However patriotic a man may be for the whole of his country, there is always one town about which he must be sentimental, and Talaat was sentimental about Adrianople.

"I come from a village near Adrianople," he said, "and I shall never forget my joy at the sight of Selimié Mosque when my father drove me to the city for the first time. When I went there this time I felt just the same." I looked away, that he might give free play to his emotion, which was evidently such a rare thing with him. He looked like the simple boy of the days when he was driven to Adrianople in his father's cart, at the sight of the matchless minarets of Selimié.

Some months before the outbreak of the World War Talaat Pasha called on me with an unusually happy expression.

"I have good news for you," he said. "We have begged Miss Fry to come to Turkey to organize women's education. She has agreed to come and study the situation before taking any decisive step. You see that we are really serious enough about education, so I beg you to persuade her to undertake the work."

I told him firmly that I should stay on in the *evkaff* schools but said I would do my very best to persuade Miss Fry.

When Miss Fry arrived I was rather miserable with the after-effects of appendicitis plus a weak heart. But it was a great joy to have her. Talaat Pasha and the other leaders of the party who met her were charmed with her simplicity and sincerity and hoped that she might stay. But she was unable to come to an understanding with Shukri Bey on certain points which she regarded as essential, and she left Turkey after a month's visit. Little did we think when we parted that an endless stretch of war years lay between us until the time when we should meet again.

When we opened the schools of *evkaff* in September, 1914, I went to see Hairi Effendi, the sheik-ul-Islam, to discuss some changes I wanted made in the schools. The building of Sheik-ul-Islamat was one of those old and very Turkish departments looking over the Golden Horn. The chief secretary, a young man with an immaculate turban and graceful manners, introduced me to the state room of the sheik-ul-Islam.

It was an immense square room along three sides of which stretched a low couch. The floor had a red and blue carpet. There was a big bronze brazier in the middle of the room, and a single beautiful crystal chandelier hung from the middle of the ceiling. The sense of space, simplicity, and comfort was only disturbed by the modern American desk, which seemed out of harmony and too small.

Beneath the windows the Golden Horn stretched out; numberless old sailing-boats danced on the waters, sails down and masts waving in the sun. Hairi Effendi's tall figure cut strangely across the view, as he walked down the room in the immense folds of his black gown. He had a dark face with a long, hooked and crooked nose, bright black eyes, and his white turban very gracefully wound around his fez.

In spite of the unusual beauty of the place and the picturesque garments of the sheik-ul-Islam, there was

Alexandre Pankoff ON THE WATERSIDE

something so simple in his handclasp and cordial manners that I immediately sat down by the desk and took out my note-book. He leaned forward and listened (he was slightly deaf), one hand busily taking notes as I spoke. When I had finished, he read his notes and told me which of my proposals were possible and which were not, in clear and businesslike language. I took leave of him with an immense respect for his wisdom and practical sense. It is a great pity that he also was beaten by the military policy of the Unionist régime. Rarely had a régime such a large collection of able and intelligent men at its command, but its narrowness and short-sightedness, fostered by the clique who wished to snatch material advantages from the ugly scenes of war, caused it to annihilate its own chances as well as those of Turkey.

My last meeting with Hairi Effendi was in 1922 in the tiny room of my house in the village of Kalaba near Angora. He had the same sort of picturesque gown and turban, and he was as stately as ever, bending gracefully in order to get under the low ceiling of the room. He had come back from Malta, and I believe he paid me the first visit he paid to any one then. It was just before he retired to his own place in Anatolia to die. He had that mystic knowledge of life which made him fly from it. He would have been of infinite value if he had stayed and worked in the forming of the new government. "I am ill and on the verge of the grave," he said sadly but resolutely.

It was on a winter's day in the same year that I had something of an adventure in one of the back streets of Istamboul. The street is called Arasta. A series of old holes-in-the-wall, which are used as habitations by a certain class of poor of the city, form the street, and it is an adventure to go through it. I left Nakie Hanum's school rather late in the afternoon with her, and we tried to take a short cut through Arasta in order to get to the main road and a carriage. Perhaps we were also prompted by curiosity.

I had the fashionable black *charshaf* and veil of my class. On my inspection tours in the farthest corners of poor Istamboul I used to wear a loose old-fashioned *charshaf,* and I never pinned the cape so tight as to make the form of my head and hair apparent; and I took care to have my face open, although I carefully hid my hair and neck. But I had not thought of going through Arasta on that day.

Up and down walked a series of little girls as we entered the narrow street. They had print dresses of the poorest sort, and bare feet shod with wooden clogs which they dragged painfully, but they had a saucy and aggressive way of walking in spite of this impediment. One had a dirty baby in her arms, half her own size, and the baby's nose was running all the time. Another had a broken silk umbrella, which must have had a prosperous past and was evidently stolen property. All lifted their dresses in mock imitation of the chic women of the city; all strutted in a make-believe promenade of great ladies. I must admit that they made me ashamedly conscious of how ridiculous our class could be. There was finished mockery and insult and the bitterest irony in their every gesture, when with my fashionable black *charshaf* I found myself in their midst.

"Oh, oh, look at her!" shouted the girl with the umbrella—there was neither rain nor sunshine. "On her head she has a caldron,[2] a *peshtemal* [3] around her belly has she. She has a well-ring around her throat and wrists,[4] and her shoes are bath-clogs." [5]

A unanimous shout of laughter, accompanied by savage and significant movements, inimitable imitations but openly hostile to me, greeted her speech. It appeared to me like a delicious piece of realistic comedy, and I would have given anything to throw off the offending garments, which displayed my class, at whose expense they were laughing, and join in their play. As it was, I was in real danger of being badly stoned, or of having my dress torn in a way that would have been worse than inconvenient.

I immediately lifted my veil and joined in the conversation. The human face, especially the human eyes, have their force among their kind. A human being whose eyes and face are invisible is easier to attack.

---

[2] This was meant for my hair, which was piled on my head. The women of the people sensibly plait their hair and leave it on their back.

[3] A silk or cotton shawl which women wrap around the body rather tightly in public baths.

[4] White cuffs and collars which showed through my veil and which they likened to the marble rings around old wells in Turkey.

[5] This was aimed at my high heels. Bath-clogs are very high, very different from the low clogs which the poor women and children wear in the streets.

"What a beautiful umbrella!" I said admiringly. This sobered the owner of the umbrella, who was strutting about, her thin body in mock contortions of the fashionable walk. My back against the wall, I faced her thin face with its sharp vicious outlines and feverish eyes. Calm, amused, laughing with them at their gibes and sarcastic remarks, I disarmed the little crowd for a moment. But the moment I made the slightest show of movement they all bent down, picked up stones from the old pavement, and got ready in case I should escape. I had to advance very carefully, keeping them amused with my conversation. The little girl carrying the big baby in her arms became my enemy instantly. She resented my compliment to the umbrella, whose owner she evidently disliked.

"She has a caldron on her head," she began again, repeating the rest in a very clever rhythm.

The owner of the umbrella interfered. "Thou shut up, thou faceless [shameless] one. Thy sister has also a tight *charshaf,* a red one. She goes to the mosque in it. She puts powder on her face and paints her cheeks."

"Of course. It suits her. She will do as she likes. What is it to thee, thou monkey-face?"

This was from my adversary. But the umbrella was equal to anything.

"Thou art a monkey-face. Thy sister is black, and she looks like egg-plant with yogurt over it when she puts on powder."

"Her lover gives her all that. Does thy sister have a lover? Answer that, or I throw stones at thee."

"She cannot," said the umbrella to me consolingly. "She has that Gipsy bastard in her arms."

The pantomime and the comical quarrel had drawn the little mob's attention away from me, so I talked and edged along the wall, still facing the crowd. So long as they were not aware of my efforts to escape they did not attack, but the moment they realized the meaning of my movements they united against me.

"Shame to thee! Thou hast taken sides with the stranger" (every one outside Arasta is a stranger); this was from the little girl with the baby to the umbrella.

I stuck fast to the umbrella and flattered her shamelessly. "Who is her sister's lover?" I asked.

The other one answered with rage: "What is it to thee? It is the driver Noah. He brings her the powder and the red *charshaf*. Does her sister have a lover? Tell me now."

They nearly came to blows over Noah, but we were now near the corner. The butcher and the seller of pickles ran with sticks as they saw us coming with the queer little mob after us. At sight of them the mob dispersed with wild shrieks.

The butcher looked as proud as a medieval knight who had just rescued a lady. "Never pass along that street when it is dark, especially dressed as you are," he said. "They stone and tear people's clothes. I have saved a number of people."

I did not believe in the heroic rescues of the butcher, but I thought his advice both sound and useful. In the streets of Fatih, Jihanghir, and Kassim Pasha I always took care to let my dress resemble that of the other women of the neighborhood, and I never closed my veil. I made friends with many children similar to those of Arasta, and they even gave me their henna-covered but dirty little hands and led me through the intricate back streets, telling me about their people and their personal affairs and calling me "lady aunt" in a sweet and slightly protecting way.

None of the old teachers of *evkaff* lost their place when Nakie Hanum undertook to modernize the mosque schools. She trained them, giving them only Koran, domestic science, and sometimes history courses to teach. They made a great effort to accustom themselves to the new atmosphere, for material reasons at first, but later on because the warm fraternity of the organization attracted them genuinely. In some ways the older ones seemed more familiar with the peculiar needs of the children and their families than did the younger ones, and some of them had the charm of old-fashioned Turkish manners, which one rarely found in the new generation of teachers, although the younger ones had better and more up-to-date training.

There was one little school in Jihanghir with a woman at the head who came from an old family and had gone into teaching for financial reasons. She had the old Arabic and Persian culture and was well trained in Oriental history. Her name was Fikrie Hanum, and I can never forget the clear pious expression of her face, so mild and so serious and tolerant.

MY EDUCATIONAL ACTIVITIES, 1913-14

Her school was always full of flowers, and the old bare boards were always scrubbed and clean, while her white curtains were always gleaming. Her little ones had acquired something of her personal charm of manners; they were individual little women and little men instead of only students. They took care of the flowers in the garden, felt proud of their happy little place, and talked to one with unconscious grace and freedom. Their garden was like an eagle's nest, perched over the wonderful beauty of the Bosphorus, with countless ledges of brightly colored earth and here and there plantations between the garden and the foaming blue waters of the narrow winding Bosphorus. The garden was full of geraniums and carnations, lovely bright reds; and the place had wooden stools made by the little boy students, where one could sit and watch the children play.

Nakie Hanum gave her a young assistant who introduced more scientific teaching, while she went on with the general care and religious teaching. Youth and change had appeared to her harsh and ugly at first, but in time she became one of Nakie Hanum's most loyal and loving hands. The little schools with three grades had usually these older ladies with young assistants; but the six-graded ones, which were being newly opened in larger centers with modern buildings, were run with completely young staffs. It was good to see them grapple with their problems and meet their successes and failures.

An event in the old school which we had left with

Nakie Hanum brought about a public discussion between Shukri Bey and myself, which made our breach wider. We had tried to create a discipline on more positive lines, based on the responsibility and the self-respect of the students. The old system of the punishment and exposure of youthful sins and faults was avoided, and a relation of much greater friendliness and respect was springing up between the teacher and the taught when we left the school.

Nakie Hanum's successor had brought in the system of the convent with its exposure of faults and public punishments. The resentment which followed had broken out into what was almost rebellion when a foolish and inexperienced young teacher called the graduating class "rude donkeys." The indignation of the students developed into a regular riot, and the teacher had to fly through a back door to a carriage, the students pursuing.

The inspector who went to inquire into the cause of the trouble ended by fastening the blame on five of the first class and expelling them. These students would have had only three more months to finish their course, and all belonged to a class of people who are obliged to work; the disgrace would mean lifelong unemployment. Knowing this to be the case the inspector called on them and told the students that if they would sign a paper stating that Halidé and Nakie Hanums had had the riot arranged, they should have their diplomas. As the girls had not seen either of us for months, they honorably refused to sign such a false document, though the inspector tried hard to make them do it. I cannot believe that

Shukri Bey would have stooped to such a low trick. The inspector, knowing our difference with Shukri Bey, probably wanted to get promotion by this means. A public discussion between me and Shukri Bey in the papers made Shukri Bey keener to get the schools of *evkaff* into the ministry of public instruction through the pretext of unity of instruction. A violent propaganda for this change began. Hairi Effendi being a moderate and Shukri Bey an extremist in the party in those days, Shukri Bey gradually carried his point, and Hairi Effendi resigned.

I met Shukri Bey personally in 1924. His efforts with German aid for the improvement of the higher schools and the university since 1916 had resulted in raising the standards. I saw that with years he had also realized the importance of the quality of his teaching, and he was doing his best. I sometimes think that it might have been worth while for Nakie Hanum at least to have come to an agreement with Shukri Bey.

In 1914 I wrote a little play for Nakie Hanum's children. It gave me much childish joy, and it took me only six hours, one single evening, to write it. It was called "The Shepherds of Canaan." The subject was the story of Joseph and his brethren. It had three prologues and three acts. It was never published in book form, except in a much shortened form as the libretto of an opera composed by Vedi Sabra, a celebrated Syrian musician.

Yahia Kemal, the purist poet of the Turkish

language, rehearsed the children and I worked with Ertogrul Mouhsin, our famous actor, to design the stage and the costumes. The stage was white, as well as the curtains. A single archaic white arch was the entrance. In the background there were real palms in the first act. These, with Pharaoh's throne in the second and third acts, were the only furniture on the stage. The little ones had gorgeous colored mantles in every brilliant shade, head-dresses, and bare feet. The glare of mixed color against the white background, and the childish groups moving and acting as only children can act, satisfied me completely. A few artists and intellectuals found pleasure in the setting, but the play was criticized by the general public. The performance took place in the Turk Ojak before a very large audience. It had caused us some hesitation to put a prophet and a passage of sacred history on the stage, but there was no public displeasure over this.

The Ojak pulpit and hall were during these years open for lectures, plays, and concerts meant to elevate the taste of the general public. It was here that the custom of mixed audiences was first begun. Thanks to the discreet and really perfect manners of the young men then in the Ojak the event passed without any gossip or criticism. It is in that same hall that I addressed a large audience of men. Within a year this came to seem quite natural, and I had to do a great deal of public speaking to audiences of every description in and outside the Ojak.

MY EDUCATIONAL ACTIVITIES, 1913-14

It is in that hall that I came to know Goumitas Vartabet, the Armenian priest, musician, and composer. He was one of those musicians, actors, and lecturers of fame whom the Ojak invited to address its weekly audiences.[6]

Goumitas had become very famous with the Anatolian songs and the music of the old Gregorian chants which he had collected during years of patient labor in Constantinople and Anatolia. He had trained a choir of the Armenian youth and was considered a great leader among the Armenians.

As he appeared in the long black coat of the priest, his dark face as naïve as any simple Anatolian's, and his eyes full of the pathos and longing which his voice expressed in its pure strong notes, I felt him an embodiment of Anatolian folk-lore and music.

The airs were the ones I had often heard our servants from Kemah and Erzeroum sing. He had simply turned the words into Armenian. But I did not pay any attention to the language; I only felt the inner significance of that tender and desolate melody from the lonely wastes of Anatolia.

The acquaintance that began that day continued, Goumitas often coming to my house to sing. He continued to come even after the Armenians and Turks were massacring each other. We both silently suffered

[6] Opinion was divided in the Ojak about the program for the weekly performances. Some wanted only Turkish things to be given, while others insisted that it would have a more widening effect to have the beauty and the culture of other nations. The latter point of view triumphed at the time.

under the condition of things, but neither of us mentioned it. Mehemmed Emin and Yahia Kemal Beys, both great poets who had always taken a humanitarian view of nationalism, were interested in his personality and came to hear him. Youssouf Akchura also came, prompted by his love of music, but he declared that Goumitas had done a great harm to the Turk by stealing his popular culture in the form of music and songs.

Goumitas came from Kutahia and was of very poor parents. They knew no Armenian, and Goumitas learned it only in later life. His parents were probably of Turkish descent, from the Turkis who had joined the Gregorian Church. The Byzantine rulers had called in Turkish tribes to form a barrier against the Saracenic invasions, and though these were mostly put along the southern frontiers, some might have moved elsewhere.[7]

Goumitas's voice had attracted the attention of the Armenian church leaders in Kutahia, and he was sent to Rome very early to be trained in music as well as to be made a priest. He was an Armenian nationalist whether his origin was Turkish or Armenian, but in temperament and heart he was a real Anatolian Turk if unconsciously. His musical vein was inherited. I remember the very words he spoke which gave me the clue.

[7] A great number of the Christian minority, mostly Greek and some Armenian, spoke only Turkish and looked very Turkish. It was a mistake I believe and not good policy to let them enter into the exchange in the Lausanne Conference. If a Turkish church had been recognized independently of the Greek and Armenian churches, there were enough conscious Christian Turks, and a very valuable element too, who would have stayed in Turkey.

"I inherited from my parents a pair of red shoes and a song," he said. "The shoes were from my father, but the song was from my mother; she composed the music, and made the words."

It was a simple song about two white pigeons, and in the purest Anatolian dialect. To this day it is the women in Anatolia who compose songs and make folk-poetry. It goes from mouth to mouth, and the best naturally survives.

As a man and as an artist Goumitas was of a quality one rarely meets. His asceticism, the pure and beautiful simplicity with which he taught the Armenians, might well have been imitated by other nationalists. His way of expressing Anatolia both in song and in feeling was profoundly worth hearing.

Goumitas one day sang an Ave Maria in Armenian which belonged to the sixth century, a thing of rare mystical beauty; and the utter ecstasy and religious emotion of the air so fascinated me that I asked him if he had set any of the Psalms to music.

"Yes," he said, "the one-hundred-and-first."

"Are you too tired to sing it?" I asked.

He had thrown himself into the low chair near the piano, and his face was white and full of strange lines of pain.

He began singing without moving from the chair. As he began to sing I felt that the air had none of the sacred and humble beauty of the Ave Maria. It began like a hissing curse, bitter, rebellious, and angry; as he went on he rose slowly, looking like the apparition of Mephisto in "Faust," drawing himself to his full height as he reached the last words. Then with his arms raised, his face like a white flame, and his eyes like two black flashes, his tones ended like a peal of echoing thunder. It awed me and made me feel strange. I instinctively took the Bible from the bookcase near me and found the last stanzas of Psalm 101.

I will early destroy all the wicked of the land: that I may cut off all wicked doers from the city of the Lord.

It was the cry of the hatred and vengeance of his soul for my people. He had such a look of madness and suffering that I tried to be absolutely calm and quiet, but he looked embarrassed; he knew that we had looked into each other's souls. We were seeing each other, with the Armenian and Turkish blood, and Armenian and Turkish suffering, as an increasing flood between us.

In 1915 the Ojak generously used its influence to have him spared from deportation, but in 1916 he had a serious disturbance in his mind, which gave way under the strain of those horrible times. Dr. Adnan begged Talaat Pasha to allow him to go to Paris for a cure, and this was accorded to him. He is still in an asylum.

He was not the only one to be afflicted by politics, translated into human wickedness. I saw in Angora in 1922 a Turkish woman from Erzeroum, who had pitched a frail tent by the waters of Tchoubouk. She had been a refugee since 1917 and had been wandering all over

Anatolia with her husband.[8] I see her now, tall, her weather-beaten face like a piece of wrinkled leather, only the brilliant blue eyes and their black fringes denoting her youth. I remember her very words as she told me how her four boys, the eldest eight and the youngest two, had been massacred, how she had had to leave them among flames and blood and escape with her life, and how she heard their call every night. She did not sing her pain in Psalms, but it was the selfsame pain of Goumitas in my room at Fazli Pasha. I know a man, an Erzeroum member of the first national assembly, who would not hear of mercy to the Armenians because seven members of his family, including his young wife and his sister-in-law, had been butchered by Armenians. I knew a poor Armenian in Syria who had lost his speech and wandered in the night crying like a dumb tortured animal because he imagined his two boys, who were separated from him, had been shot. I know . . . never mind what I know. I have seen, I have gone through, a land full of aching hearts and torturing remembrances, and I have lived in an age when the politicians played with these human hearts as ordinary gamblers play with their cards.

I who had dreamed of a nationalism which will create a happy land of beauty, understanding, and love, I have seen nothing but mutual massacre and mutual hatred;

---

[8] I have written her story as she told it to me under the title of "A Woman from Erzeroum." The women of Angora became very much interested in her and visited her and tried to help her. She left for Erzeroum in one of the groups of refugees that were sent back to their country by the government.

I have seen nothing but ideals used as instruments for creating human carnage and misery.

There were great idealists and lovers of humanity in Russia who have suffered and died in order to demolish the barriers between classes and nations and to bring brotherhood and happiness to their kind. The result is just as ugly as what I myself have seen.

When will true heart and understanding come to humanity?—not merely in name and principles. Now I can only say with Kant, "Ce n'est pas sans une violente répulsion que l'on peut contempler l'entrée en scène des hommes sur le théâtre du monde; encore plus grande que le mal fait aux hommes par la nature est celui qu'il se font réciproquement."

CHAPTER XVI

THE WORLD WAR, 1914–16

IT began with the assassination of the Austrian crown prince and ended with the declaration of the World War. No one in Turkey during those first days dared to imagine that it would end with such world-wide disaster. I will not discuss the responsibility for it in the general sense. If the economic and military growth of Germany as well as its materialistic philosophy were among the contributing causes, we have since learned that there were causes and long preparations of equally materialistic and aggressive kind on the part of the Allies.

But it is most interesting, although extremely painful, to review the pros and cons on our own side which led us into the general catastrophe that resulted in the lengthening of the war by four years in the Near East, to the discomfort of the world in general and to the cost of Turkey in particular of many lives and much avoidable suffering. Before giving a rough outline of our reasons, I want to draw the attention of my readers to three of the principal works which are illuminating to the greatest degree. The first one is Professor Earle's "The Bagdad Railway," which was published in 1923. Having a non-prejudiced mind and a desire to see the truth, and writing at a period when the thick cloud of propaganda on both sides has thinned away with time, he sees matters very clearly; and as the work is purely economic, any one who wishes to understand the economic dilemma which led to the great struggle finds an excellent and unbiased authority in the book.

The second is the "Le Sort de l'Empire Ottoman," by A. Mandlestan, the first dragoman of the Russian embassy in Constantinople till 1914. The book was published in 1917. He has gathered an extraordinary amount of data on the Young Turk régime and on the causes which led Turkey to enter the war on the German side. He has one single aim, and all his data is grouped and even twisted to prove his point. It is more or less the point of view blindly, passionately, and narrowly held by the allied world in those days. The spirit of his arguments is that the Ottoman empire must be torn to pieces, and the Turks must not be considered as ordinary human beings, and the Young Turks are ordinary criminals, having massacred the Armenians. There is a detailed account of Armenian massacres and a series of exaggerated accusations with reference to the other minorities, whom he asserts the Turks meant to exterminate. I do not, however, find a word about the great massacre of the Turks by the Bulgarians nor its accompaniment of atrocities in 1912, not a word about the great massacre of the Turks by the Armenians who entered Oriental Turkey in 1915 with the Russian army, which has been simply told by the Russian officers of the same Russian army who revolted against the Armenian cruelties. The book, in spite of its data, made me see for the first time the incurable narrowness and one-sidedness of the European mind of those days concerning my country and my people, and for the first time I saw clearly that the arguments of the Young Turks had real force. However, the declarations of a former grand vizir,[1] which he puts into his book in order to refute its contents, possess very strong and irrefutable arguments and data on the Turkish side.

In opposition to Mandlestan's views is the third book called "Les Causes de la Guerre," by Boghitchevitch, which has recently appeared in Paris. This work gives a detailed account of the principal policies dominating the world before the war, that of czarist Russia which had aimed at the crushing of Austria and Turkey in the Balkans, and that of France which upheld Russia in order to crush Germany and recover Alsace-Lorraine. Boghitchevitch, as an old Serbian diplomat during the preparation of these policies and during the World War, gives interesting political documents on the subject.

I am against war in general, and so I cannot defend our going into it on any side, but if one disentangles the mass of knotted political arguments of the day and tries to see clearly the psychology of the Young Turk leaders who entered the war, one sees these causes: First, the desire for complete independence; that is, the abolition of the capitulations. The Young Turks tried hard, but in vain, to enlist the sympathies of the Allies.

[1] "Le Sort de l'Empire Ottoman," p. 106.

But the Allies wanted their neutrality without paying anything in return. Secondly, the inherited and justified fear of Russian imperialism. Whether Constantinople was promised in 1914 or in 1916 to Russia, the Young Turk leaders believed that England must use Turkey as a bait to catch Russia, to whom she was a traditional and political enemy. Thirdly, the deplorable financial position of Turkey. Even to insure neutrality she needed financial aid, and she could not procure it from the Allies. A well known statesman of to-day told me once that after the refusal of England to pay for the war-ships she had confiscated, the government was strongly carried away by the pro-war element. If this is not the whole of the truth it is at least a significant part of it, and it shows the sore need of Turkey for financial aid. Fourthly, the decided and openly prejudiced pro-Christian attitude of the Allies, who always helped the Christian minorities to gain economic, even political predominance against the interests of the Moslem and Turkish majorities. Fifthly, the psychological insight of Germany into the weak spots of the Turkish situation, and her cleverness in seizing the right moment.

The Young Turk leaders used all the available arguments to justify their entry into the war and to turn the Turkish people against the Allies, who were still very popular in Turkey. It is queer to observe that public opinion turned against the Allies and began to feel the arguments of the Young Turks justifiable only after the Young Turks had passed out of power. The

Greek occupation and atrocities under British patronage, and the Armenian atrocities against Adana under the patronage of the French, were talked of as the symptoms of the allied justice and rule in Turkey foreseen by the Unionists before the war.

In 1914 not only the masses but most of the intellectual and leading forces of the Unionists were against the war. Only Enver Pasha and a certain convinced military group, along with the profiteers, were in favor of war. Somehow the war seemed an impossibility, although a great many people feared it and felt uneasy, knowing the strength of military dictatorship in Turkey.

I received two different visits and had two memorable conversations during the first days of October. First came Djemal Pasha, the minister of marine, who took tea in my house with Madame Djemal Pasha.

"I am afraid our government is drifting into war," I said point-blank.

He laughed as if I had said something absurd and childish. I remember the determined expression of his face as he said these very words:

"No, Halidé Hanum, we will not go into war."

"How will you manage that?"

"I have power enough to persuade them not to. If I fail I resign. It would be extreme folly."

Three days later Djavid Bey called. He had an air of despondency and looked seriously troubled.

I asked him the same question.

"If they go into war, I resign," he said. "It will be

our ruin even if we win. There are others who will resign as well, but we hope to prevent it. Talaat is against it at the moment."

On the eighteenth of the same month Turkey entered the war.

Djavid Bey with some of his colleagues resigned. Djemal Pasha did not resign.

He called soon after to take leave. He was appointed commander of the third army; that is, on the Russian front. He seemed in good spirits and tried to explain his change of opinion. His chief argument was the Russian one. He already believed that Constantinople would pass to Russia if the allied forces won, and as the Allies did not give sufficient guarantee in return for our neutrality, the supreme duty of the Turkish army was to help the side opposing Russia; and in the event of German and Turkish victory, in which he firmly believed, he thought that the Turks would be free as they have never been before, and that the capitulations and foreign interference generally would cease.

It is very sad to think to-day that if the Allies had consented to the abolition of the capitulations and given some assurance about Constantinople the military party could not have driven Turkey into war.

Djavid Bey was in disgrace and was keenly watched. He did not leave his house for some time. He was sharply attacked and even called a traitor by the extreme Unionists.

Djemal Pasha's destination was changed to Syria as the commander of the fourth army. He was to attack Egypt and try to keep the English busy and make them concentrate great forces on the Syrian front.

The terrific defense of Gallipoli was the first great event of the World War in Turkey. I will not speak of its almost superhuman heroism and sacrifice. For me, all the honor is due to the common Turkish soldier whose name no one knows and who cannot appear in moving pictures as the hero of the day. Mr. Masefield's book, "Gallipoli," makes one realize the great human and great war material which such a nation as the British has lost, and it makes one realize at the same time the fighting value of the Turkish army which could successfully defend Gallipoli against the allied forces and fleets. There was a keen sense in the men of defending the gates to the main Turkish lands; there was a more than keen sense of fighting against the Russian hallucination projected in their brains by the allied forces.

With the allied attack on the Dardanelles, many families once more left Constantinople, and I had to send my children away to Broussa.

It was about the time of the great battle of March 5 that Youssouf Akchura invited the nationalist writers to gather in the offices of "Turk Yourdu" and seriously discuss their future plans if the Allies should force the straits and enter Constantinople. They were to decide in case of such disaster whether they were to stay on in Constantinople and go on keeping the ideals of nationalism in the hearts of the people or pass on and work in safer and more favorable lands.

There was a series of lengthy gatherings and long discussions, which in the end took a somewhat melodramatic turn. But they never lost their hot and passionate character. Dr. Adnan was asked to preside as the most cool-headed person present.

First every one was to define his nationalistic creed. The younger writers, Kuprulu Fuad and Omer Seifeddine, declared that nationalism was the search and the discovery of a nation's ego, and the teaching of it to the individuals of the nation. As to the fundamental elements of the national ego, they were vague. Omer, who became my friend in later years, confessed to me in his humorous way that Keuk-Alp Zia, their master, who was not in Constantinople then, was always changing the fundamental elements of the national ego; they could never be definite for fear they might be called on to formulate something quite different on the same subject.

Aga Oglou Ahmed, as an old nationalist, declared that nationalism was a common mentality composed of four different elements; namely, language, religion, origin, and common customs. And around these four elements and the order of their importance the discussion raged. As political tendencies in Turkish nationalism depended very much on the order of their importance, it made the discussions instructive and illuminating. Hussein Zade Ali, a venerable old unionist and nationalist, declared that religion and language were

WHEN THE MOSQUES WERE FULL THE FAITHFUL PRAYED OUTSIDE

the foremost elements, and origin came next. "A Moslem negro who speaks Turkish and calls himself a Turk is nearer to me than the originally Turkish Magyar," he said. Thus he stuck to Pan-Islamism in a mild way, while the younger generation insisted more on origin and language, regarding religion as the least important, and thus stuck to Pan-Turanistic tendencies.[2]

Finally the meeting tried to decide with rather melodramatic speeches whether or not the writers who symbolize Turkish nationalism should stay on in Constantinople or go elsewhere. It was then that Mehemmed Ali Tewfik, a young journalist, made a most emphatic speech full of rhetorical effect enthusiastically suggesting that these writers should not only stay but should even find some way of being martyred, and thus seal the sacred cause of nationalism with their blood. Although in those days it was easy enough to get oneself killed, still the writers thus complimented as being worthy of death looked a little queer. Mehemmed Emin, whose name was the first, sat with his hands folded, contemplating, and my humble self, who was also among the chosen, wondered what sort of death Mehemmed Emin contemplated. There were twinkles in many friendly eyes. And I really think that it was the supreme joke in those tragic days.

---

[2] Although the younger nationalists tried to disregard religion in the national ego, in practice they have been far from doing so. There are purely Turkish Orthodox Christians who were exchanged by the Lausanne Treaty because of their church difference. And it is strange to think that Riza Nour Bey, who was one of the Turkish delegates, signed the treaty although he is a strong nationalist on the basis of origin and language.

The Dardanelles attack passed, but there was trouble on the East Anatolian front. There were rumors about Armenian deportations and their bloody consequences. There was talk of the Armenians having burned Turkish villages at the front and having massacred Turks, and talk of the danger they were creating behind the Turkish army by their revolutionary centers. It was long after this event that the government published a book on the subject exposing the crimes in eastern Anatolia. When the deportations became general public opinion was sincerely against the government. But the country was then in the thick of the fight, and nothing was published on the subject. It was an extremely difficult time for the Turkish population; in spite of the public disapproval of the government's acts, every Turk was deeply conscious of Turkey's danger, and that it would mean complete spoliation and extermination of the Turks if the Turkish army should be defeated. One naturally felt that Armenian revolutionary centers were used as the strategic points to carry out allied policy against the Turks. Besides this political argument, which the Armenians did their best to justify by their own bloody deeds, there was a strong economic one, morally supported by the Germans. This was to end the economic supremacy of the Armenians, thereby clearing the markets for the Turks and the Germans. There is no doubt that the foreign policy which caused the elimination of Armenians and Turks in the vast lands of Turkey took well into account that nature fills up the open spaces of economic value, and that the spaces left empty by the mutual massacre of the peoples in Turkey would be taken up by the European countries with surplus populations.

There are two factors which lead man to the extermination of his kind: the principles advocated by the idealists, and the material interest which the consequences of doing so afford certain classes. The idealists are the more dangerous, for one is obliged to respect them even if one cannot agree with them. Talaat was of that kind. I saw Talaat very rarely after the Armenian deportations. I remember well one day when he nearly lost his temper in discussing the question and said in a severe tone: "Look here, Halidé Hanum. I have a heart as good as yours, and it keeps me awake at night to think of the human suffering. But that is a personal thing, and I am here on this earth to think of my people and not of my sensibilities. If a Macedonian or Armenian leader gets the chance and the excuse he never neglects it. There was an equal number of Turks and Moslems massacred during the Balkan war, yet the world kept a criminal silence. I have the conviction that as long as a nation does the best for its own interests, and succeeds, the world admires it and thinks it moral. I am ready to die for what I have done, and I know that I shall die for it." In 1922 he was shot by an Armenian in Berlin.

In 1916 I spoke to a very large audience, mostly Unionists, in the Turk Ojak on the Armenian question and national economics. I saw the Armenian question quite differently from the way I see it to-day. I did not know about the Armenian crimes, and I had not realized that in similar cases others could be a hundred times worse than the Turks. So I spoke with conviction against bloodshed, which I believed would hurt those who indulge in it more than it hurt their victims. There were some seven hundred present. As I finished, the youth in the Ojak cheered, while a young medical student called Shukri Eflatoun rose and called out to Hamdullah Soubhi: "Mr. President, I want to speak, I want to prove the right to be on the other side." Another member rose and said that the Ojak should not allow Shukri Eflatoun to speak as he wished. They would not hear a word about it. This seemed to me unfair, but the president failed to get a hearing for Shukri Eflatoun. I received the next day a great volume about the massacre of the Turks by the Armenians. What is more I heard that some of the Unionists were furious with me and that they proposed to have me punished, which Talaat Pasha refused. "She serves her country in the way she believes," he had said. "Let her speak her mind; she is sincere." But the number of young intellectuals who came to my house decreased to a considerable degree. Talaat Pasha himself, however, did not change his friendly attitude.

CHAPTER XVII

HOW I WENT TO SYRIA

IN 1916 Djemal Pasha and Rahmi Bey were the two most talked-of personalities; they were both criticized and praised for different reasons. Both very influential figures among the Unionists, they had taken personal views about the administration of the provinces which were under their control. Rahmi Bey was the governor of Smyrna; he had refused to deport the Christians and had guaranteed to keep order in his province. As the area under his administration was out of the war zone he managed to keep order, although there were very serious espionage centers around and in Smyrna, among the very people he protected and kept.

Djemal Pasha in Syria had taken a similarly protective attitude toward the Armenians exiled there. They were not to be molested in any way in the lands under his control. He had hanged two rather notorious old Unionists, Cherkess Ahmed and his companion, for daring to try to start a massacre in Syria. His great difficulty was the famine, from which the Turkish army, the Arab population, and the Armenians suffered equally. It is to his honor that he helped all the charitable organizations for children, for Armenians or Arabs alike, with what he could spare from the army supplies.

Djebel Hauran, which is the granary of Syria, was hostile and made every possible difficulty about supplying Syria with corn; the seas were blockaded, and there was one single railway (and that was not complete at the time) over which the entire military transport and the entire provisioning of the country had to pass. The attack on Egypt may have been a folly, but as the entire war was a folly from every point of view, each campaign had to be carried through as thoroughly as possible.

In the midst of the canal attacks, Djemal Pasha had discovered an Arab plot in favor of the French and had dealt with it with extreme severity. The court martial in Alie condemned forty men to death, and some others to exile. Thus he restored order, which had never been so complete in Syria since he began his constructive policy of building roads, fighting disease, and opening schools. His energies were always most valuable when used for constructive purposes. Wherever he sojourned as governor the people still enjoy good roads and good public buildings and have the memory of a period of great security and public order.

Falih Rifki Bey came to Constantinople to publish the defense of the proceedings of the Alie court martial. He was then a young lieutenant, but in reality he was a journalist and a writer who acted as secretary to Djemal Pasha. (He is at present the deputy for Boli.)

Falih Rifki Bey brought me a letter from Djemal Pasha; the content was this: He had been obliged to close the French schools and monasteries, which used to give education to the Arabs, on political grounds. The schools opened by the department of public instruction were not sufficient. The local governments in Syria, with the aid of the army, had decided to establish a series of schools. Could I go there or send teachers to start the work? This was at the beginning of the year 1916. My sister Nighiar volunteered to go and started with a limited staff. She established the first primary school in Beirut, with six grades. People from all classes went to her school. The Arabs must have loved it, for after the Turkish régime, when there was a great deal of anti-Turkish publication, the Arabic papers spoke kindly of her institution.

In the summer of 1916 I had another letter from Djemal Pasha. He asked me to go with Nakie Hanum and study the situation and draw up a plan for a larger number of schools in Damascus, Beirut, and Lebanon.

As the work would take only the summer months, we accepted, and we started from Haidar Pasha Station for Syria, with Hamdullah Soubhi Bey, who was invited by Djemal Pasha to study the old Moslem and Turkish architecture in Syria and to visit the institutions of the desert. An aide-de-camp of the pasha accompanied us.

As I had not gone beyond Ismidt on the Anatolian line, I left Haidar Pasha with extreme curiosity and interest. I have since traveled so often on that line that the impression of the first trip is somewhat effaced, but I remember well the continual military movement which made one wonder sadly at the unknown future of the men who passed by.

We found out that a Red Crescent commission composed of doctors we knew very well was going to Medina to the army of Fahreddine Pasha, whose defense of the holy place is a pious and chivalrous episode of the World War.

That large stretch of bare yellow land from Eskishehir to Konia was desolate and hot in the extreme. As the train stopped before Konia, near a little village, we spent nearly two hours visiting the place. It was a tiny village with twenty-five houses, and there was hardly a man to be seen. Old women sat at the door of their huts, and little children played about, while a group of young women returned from the fields with their scythes on their shoulders. The heat, the dust, and the sadness of the lonely women were beyond description; the younger ones squatted in the dust and asked us when the war would end and told us the names of their husbands. We were in the second year of the war, and already they looked as if they were at the end of their strength. The end of the war was their concern more than any one's. They not only had their beloved at the front, but they also had to supply Turkey and her army with the means of living. Somehow though they struggled on six more years in their barren fields, with a hopeless wait for their men, which in most cases was in vain.

In Konia the station greeted us with a scene of misery. A large number of Eastern Anatolians, mostly refugees and Kurds, were crowded with their families and few belongings in the station. They were the remainder of the Armenian victims, running from the Armenian massacres. Under the glare of the station lights, huddled together in their bright-colored but tattered costumes, their faces hopeless and entirely expressionless, as refugee faces usually are, they waited for the train. There was that smell of misery peculiar to a human crowd, unwashed, and in physical as well as moral suffering.

At Pozanti Station a series of new buildings had been begun. In fact in every station which came under the authority of Djemal Pasha there were new buildings, good hospitals, a guest-house, a military casino, and all over the country good roads either finished or in the making.

In Mamouré we procured a lorry to go to Islahie, where we were to take the train to Aleppo. The scarcity of transport was so painfully felt that we meant to share this truck with as many people as we could put into it. It was a difficult matter for the aide-de-camp, who not only wanted room for himself (he was very fat) but also feared the cholera and typhus which were raging in the country. Besides, as we were the guests of the pasha, he wanted us to have more comfort than under the circumstances we really cared to have.

We crammed the truck, and after he had in a military tone declared he could not take any more and had seated himself beside the chauffeur, we helped those who came running after us to climb on the truck. They were a Turkish tradesman and an Armenian merchant who were going to Islahie. As we had smuggled them on board when the truck had started without the knowledge of the aide-de-camp, we sat close to these last two unwelcome travelers, like two fierce hens sitting on their newly hatched chickens.

At the foot of the Taurus Range, before we began to climb the giant mountains, we heard a desolate cry and halted. On the road sat a half-naked old woman. Her vest was torn, her white locks were unkempt under a worn-out fez, her naked toes stuck to the ground, and her face had the infinite pathos and loneliness of a lost child. As the aide-de-camp asked why she was there I remember her lips drooping exactly like a child's, so queerly in contrast with her toothless mouth, which kept the appearance of an empty hole.

"I am from the tribe which has gone to Osmanie," she said. "They were to come and fetch me this morning. They have forgotten me. Oh, son!"

She belonged to one of the numerous Turkish nomadic tribes which live in that region. Was she really forgotten, or was she too much of a burden and left to die, or would they come to fetch her? Knowing the traditional respect and love for the old in those tribes, we could hope for the best. As we had to hurry in order to cross the mountains before dark we could not tarry, and so we provided bread, money, and a jacket to cover her old bones and left her to her fate. We knew that she could crawl back to Mamouré and find some connection with her people. As the truck started and she looked like a speck on the receding lonely road I felt my heart torn with these signs of misery which were to become more frequent as we proceeded, but Hamdullah Soubhi sobbed aloud like a little child in pain. Whenever there are differences of opinion and action which separate me from Hamdullah Soubhi I think of him sobbing like a child over the lonely old woman, and I feel the abyss between us bridged.

We reached Islahie in the evening and took the train for Aleppo. The lamps in the train did not work, so we lighted a candle, and its flickering flame enhanced our sense of sadness, at the idea of being so far from home and in the midst of some of the worst suffering in the country, to which one could see no end.

The compartments opened into each other, and the aide-de-camp went to sleep in the one next to ours after telling us not to let in "any dirty beggar."

At the very next station an Arab walked in, in the tattered common uniform of those who go back home from the army. He had the ordinary brown oval face of the Arab, with its deep burning eyes and a youthful beard. He was evidently sick and walked leaning on a stick, and he begged us in Arabic to let him into our compartment, for he felt too tired to go on to his town, which was near Aleppo. Hamdullah, who had been complaining of the sonorous snoring from the aide-de-camp's compartment, now felt it quite welcome, for it left us free to take in the soldier in peace and tend to him to our heart's content.

On the borders of Arab land, in the sad half-light of the candle, that sick Arab, sitting on the red velvet seat, leaning against his stick, his sensitive eyes full of suffering and fire, his low tired voice that poured out his troubles, remains in my mind like a living portrait. I remember Nakie Hanum watching in the passage leading to the aide-de-camp's compartment, ready to tell us in case he should wake, and us feeding the Arab, talking to him in broken Arabic, and trying to console him now that he was returning to his village. It was a comical situation in spite of its pathos, and as we helped him out at his station, and he was beginning to pray for us in wonderful Arabic, with the rich guttural harmony which only an Arabic throat can compass, the aide-de-camp woke up suddenly and came to see what new mischief we were up to. Looking after the figure of the Arab walking into the darkness, leaning on his stick and praying for our happiness, he said severely:

"I hope you did not touch that sick Arab beggar, Hamdullah Bey?"

Hamdullah Bey sat in dignified silence. The aide-de-camp added:

"Forgive me for worrying you, but you do not know the horrors of typhus."

"I do," said Hamdullah Soubhi, with the oratorical gesture and tone he uses in addressing a crowd, and gazed into the darkness where the Arab had disappeared.

We entered Aleppo at midnight, and in glorious moonlight. It is on the border of the Turko-Arab lands, and it is the city of the bard and of popular songs. I expected a warm place, but the nights in Aleppo are freezing like those of the desert.

It looked like a white mass, with dim shapes and curves under the soft blue canopy where the single gorgeous light of the moon had paled the stars. The white dust, the white streets and houses, the eagle-like effect of the tower brooding over the city, and a strange glare in the white moonlight gave one the feeling of a frozen city. We descended to an Armenian hotel, the best in Aleppo, and near it from an Arab night-bar wild music and ecstatic voices struck our ears. We immediately asked for rooms and went to bed, but Hamdullah Soubhi had gone to see what was going on in the bar.

"*Mout, mout,*" cried youthful voices in an ecstasy which might have been caused by some strong drink.

"Why were the youth in the bar shouting *mout* [die]?" I asked Hamdullah Soubhi the next morning.

"An Arab girl sang," he said. "The youths were so intoxicated with the beauty of her voice and the beauty of her person that they could not bear the idea of such perfection existing on earth, so they asked her to die."

"Were they drunk?" I asked, for I had not yet seen how every emotion shakes an Arab and causes him to express it in the most violent way.

"No," he said, "they sat in their silk gowns and smoked their narghiles, and did not look murderous at all."

The whole day we wandered in the streets of Aleppo. Hamdullah Soubhi, as a professor of Turkish and Islamic art, was sight-seeing very seriously, while we gave ourselves up to the more medieval charm of the narrow streets, and the tottering old *hans* (inns) of wondrous beauty, where all the old Turkish bards had sung, and the great had stayed on their way to Arab lands.

The train started late in the evening. In a few hours

the real Arabic villages rose in the twilight like huge human beehives, standing out against the evening sky, their blue smoke curling up in transparent waves, so different from the thick sooty smoke of the modern cities. The air was getting warmer and warmer. We must have slept for some time when I woke up to a state of things which seemed a dream, so different in sound and feeling from what I have known all my life.

A hundred voices, mostly women, called shrill and guttural, "*Ya Mohammed, Ya Abdurrahman, Ya Abdullah.*" Then a few men's voices joined in graver tones, "*Ya Oummi*" (O mother).

We were in Homs, a real Arab town. The women whose husbands and sons were in the army had come to the station because a military train was passing and there was a chance of meeting their men. They were wringing their hands and calling in inexpressible excitement to the soldiers in the cars. Some had found their men, and there was kissing and love-making going on in its naïvest and warmest form.

Nakie Hanum was fighting at the window, which we had left open, to prevent bundles, water-jugs, and fruit-baskets from being hurled into our carriage. Men and women also who wanted a place in the train were trying to squeeze in through the window. Nakie Hanum was defending the window rather cleverly, and with force and authority, telling them in book-Arabic that there was no place. No one listened till Hamdullah Soubhi Bey woke and joined Nakie Hanum in the defense of our little place, and closed the window. I sat selfishly watching them in the warm and quivering atmosphere, as the women ran up and down the platform, wringing their hands. No woman can wring her hands like an Arab woman; there is the same life and beauty in it which one sees in the inspired art of days gone by.

As the train moved on their shrill voices rose above the whistle of the train, and they ran after us, calling all the time. I can still hear the one who called, *"Ya Adburrahman."* Her passionate personality and the flame of her desert heart enveloped one. Who was Abdurrahman, and who was she? I shall never know, but I feel that I caught a glimpse of the inner meaning of that black-veiled shadow through its gestures and its calling.

I woke once more in Baalbek. A bright moon was glistening through the broken pillars of the ruins.

Djemal Pasha's family were in Lebanon at the summer residence. Their house was one of those beautifully built marble dwellings in Sauffer, with spacious marble halls, and picturesque stairs and balconies, that look out on the wonderful Lebanon chain, a fleeting series of sharp misty blue shadows on bare rocks, with velvety soft olive green on the forest-covered tops.

Djemal Pasha was away at the time. The house was kept by his sister, mother-in-law, and stepmother. The sister was a fine serious old Turkish lady. The mother-in-law, who has become one of the Turkish women I have most loved, was a lady about sixty, thin, energetic, chic, and very capricious. One developed a protective feeling for her immediately. Madame Djemal Pasha had taken her sick child to Switzerland at the time. The members of the household were affectionate, simple, and very kind to their servants and to each other. Djemal Pasha arrived from Jerusalem to stay only for two days, and we talked about the way to prepare our plans. I told him that I wanted to see and study the existing schools, and I wanted to talk with enough Arabs to understand the needs of the country. So I asked to go to Beirut and work our plan out there.

He consented, and asked us to go to the desert and Jerusalem, after our work was over, to see the country. Although his military project of conquering Egypt was no longer realizable, he was proud of his public works all over Syria.

After the extreme measures he had taken to put down the conspiracy in Syria, he was anxious to create a good government and an efficient system of public education. He had seen the strong inclination of the Arabs toward the French, based on the educational efforts of the French, and he was desirous of copying their methods in a less religious and more liberal sense.

The first man I consulted was Hussein Kiazim Bey, then residing in the Lebanon. He was one of the former founders of "Tanine" and had been the governor of Aleppo. He had undertaken to organize and help the Armenian refugees to settle in Syria with real humanity and capacity, but after some difference with the central government he had retired and now lived in a large house in Sauffer. I had several talks with him, which impressed me very much. He knew Arabic well and had broad ideas about the treatment of the Arabs

CARPENTERING CLASS IN AINTOURA

and the other minorities. A convinced Moslem, he cited the Koran and prophesied that all rule based on tyranny was doomed to fail. He seemed to have real influence with Djemal Pasha in his new policy of moderation.

I visited Emin Arslan and his sisters, and listened attentively to their ideas on education. For Emir Emin Arslan was a representative person in Lebanon.

The next day we went down to Beirut. On the olive-green and bluish heights of Lebanon there was snow, and we had to wear thick coats, but as we approached Beirut, there rolled before us a plain with pine and banana groves, palms of extraordinary height and slenderness, and in the distance a rich red beach, stretching out to the brilliant blue Mediterranean, a sea without ships, reaching and blending with the sky in liquid softness.

The poorer population looked haggard and underfed. But women of the richer classes, gorgeously dressed and elaborately painted, drove about the town in luxurious carriages. The famine had not reached its climax, but one felt it coming, and the prosperity of the rich hurt one's eyes.

We went all over the schools. Lebanon and Beirut were literally covered with French monasteries, religious schools, and other institutions. The learning was narrow and very much used as political propaganda for the French, but whatever was taught was taught with thoroughness within those mysterious monastic walls.

We stayed in the Hotel Bassoul on the quay and

worked and received our visitors as well. The headquarters was also in the hotel at the time. This led me to know the chief of staff, Colonel Fuad Bey, of whom I shall speak on a further occasion.

The report was finished in two weeks. The skeleton of it in a few words was this: Beirut, Lebanon, and Damascus should unite and establish one common normal school and college. Beirut should be the place for the school. Each of these provinces should have a model primary school with six grades to prepare students for the college and the normal school. Turkish, Arabic, and French should be the three languages taught.

I little thought that I should come back and apply the plan I proposed only a few months later. What I thought most important was the new spirit the governmental education would have to create.

Arabic nationalism so far had been in Syria a political instrument in foreign hands. Nationalism used for political purposes is an ideal turned into a monstrosity. Turkey must help the Arabs to develop a national spirit and personality, teach them to love their own national culture more than any foreign one; and when the time came for the Arab to have his independence, he would geographically and economically see that he had more common ties and interests with the Turks than with the foreigners.

The Arabs had equal representation in the parliament, but somehow it did not work well, and to me it looked as if it would be far safer for Turkey to work with the idea of a future coöperation with the Arabs in their minds rather than with the idea of ruling them always. Endless blood, endless money, and useless struggle have been spent in the Arab lands. The defense and maintenance of Arab lands by the Turks was not what the Arabs wanted; they wanted the French. They repented of this wish soon enough though.

Colonel Fuad Bey called on us several times, and I had memorable talks with him. He is one of our intellectual soldiers, and I remembered him from his letters from Yemen, where he had gone with Marshal Izzet Pasha and arranged the treaty with Imam Yahia. His letters to "Tanine" describing Yemen and the famous Imam Yahia were realistic pictures. I admired him for his unyielding honesty and hatred of corruption, but he was said to be politically weak and very ambitious. I wanted him to tell me about the doings of the Alie court, and what I wanted to know most was whether the Arab nationalists were working simply for a change of rule or for independence.

He spoke Djemal Pasha's and the government's views rather than his own, for I believe he also was against political executions. He said that success was our ultimate ideal and that if a partial terror had not been instituted the Turkish army would have been obliged to leave Syria in the first months of the campaign. Speaking about the Arab nationalists, he believed that some were genuine patriots. He told me about the death of one which I shall never forget.

"I came to Beirut on the day of the execution," he said. "It was before the government house. There were a series of gallows, and some had been already executed. There was one among them who marched among the condemned. He had been a reserve officer and wore a calpak. He was quiet and seemed entirely above the fear of death. He sat on one of the benches and smoked until his turn came. He chose his own particular gallows, and he passed the knot around his neck and said, 'Born an Arab, I have served the Arabs, and I am dying for the Arabs.' I was so much hurt at the idea of killing this great Arab that I did not even ask his name. But the Syrians would know him. He got hold of me strangely. I used to stop a moment each time I passed by the government place and sent him a greeting of respect. I often sat a year later on the balcony of Der-Nassira and told him in spirit that I would give my very best to the Arab children during my stay in Syria."

When we started with Nakie Hanum for Damascus, Djemal Pasha's family and headquarters had already moved on.

A tall gaunt Arab woman dressed in Turkish fashion entered our compartment. She had a dark face with unusually light brown eyes for an Arab woman. In spite of the bony powerful structure of her body and her very thin face, there was an invisible force in her and an arresting quality in her eyes that were very compelling. Her veil was especially flimsy, and her manner contrasted strangely with her height and bearing.

"She must be the wife of a Turkish officer," I thought. "She is interested in Turkish women, and she seems both willing and frightened to talk." So I began a conversation. Oh, yes, she was the wife of a Turk and trying to learn Turkish, she said. Her simplicity and her lack of paint—almost miraculous for an Arab woman of the city—gave one the feeling that in spite of her timidity and shy ways she had an inward confidence in her charms.

The life was extraordinary on the way through Lebanon to Damascus. No people own their land as the Arabs do; they make you feel it instantly. The life substance of the Arab is much warmer and of more aggressive kind than of any other nation I know. No wonder that whether you enter Arabia as their ruler or as a traveler you are soon completely enveloped in its atmosphere. You not only speak their language and live their life, but you actually acquire their looks! It is for the savant to say if it is all owing to the internal and contagious warmth of the people or to geographical influences.

The night was dark and gloomy, but as we neared Damascus an extraordinary harmony of water thundered and echoed in the valley, and among masses of willow-groves the river Bereda coiled with silver brilliance like the movements of a supernaturally white and transparent snake.

The valley is equally wonderful in sunlight with its rich olive-groves and tall poplars, while the same Bereda flows in gigantic sweeps through it all, sending its fresh sparkle to travelers who come from the heat and the dust and the endless desolation of the desert.

It is said among the Arabs that Mohammed's frequent description of paradise in the Koran, "with rivers flowing under its feet," is inspired by the freshness and the force of the Bereda, which he had seen as a child, and again after his march of long days through the desert.

After we handed in our report we prepared to go to the desert, where Hamdullah Soubhi had already gone. It was of supreme interest to me to see the desert, but I also wanted to see a young comrade from the Ojak, Dr. Hassan Ferid, who had organized the Red Crescent hospital in the desert. The hospital was spoken of as one of the best, and so it was one of the attractions as well.

We stayed three days in Damascus before we started for the desert, during which the Damascus ladies entertained us. I also saw the Armenian orphanages in Damascus, which were opened and helped by Djemal Pasha, but which were run by Armenians, mostly women. The Armenian world seemed to consider Djemal Pasha as a godsend, and the women showed me handkerchiefs with his pictures which they carried around their necks.

A trustworthy simple Circassian who had been with me in Syria came, after the occupation of Syria by the French, and told me a very characteristic story. The French had brought in a large number of Armenians with them, and one of them was swearing loudly against

Djmal Pasha in the market-place. A poor Armenian woman spoke to him saying, "He was very good to us and gave us food during the famine and protected our lives when every one was dying in the street."

To which the man answered, "It is an Armenian's duty to swear at all Turks, the more so against the good ones, for it is the good ones who make the world like the Turks."

The last night before we left Damascus the ladies gave a musical evening in the Arab fashion. There was no end of sweets and delicious fruit and of Arab women dancing and singing. The singers and the dancers were in tight European clothes, which rather reminded one of the ordinary Armenian dancing-girls in Constantinople. However, there was an old Bedouin dance performed by two girls, covered in loose and long *mashlaks,* only their eyes showing, and their bodies undulating under the silk draperies, moving with the agility and grace of the desert people. Toward the end a great excitement arose. "She is coming; she is coming; I have arranged it at last," said the lady of the house.

"Who is she?" I asked.

"She is Hedie, the great Arab singer," said my hostess. "Men ruin themselves for her. She is the mistress of an ex-official and war profiteer, who does not allow her to sing in public, but he let her come as a favor for this time, because there are no men."

And she came. She was evidently a Christian Arab, for she came in European clothes and unveiled. Her gaunt thin silhouette had that force and life which no amount of European clothes or lack of paint could disguise, and she had the typical Arabian swing of the body. Although her sleek dark head and light brown eyes had no veil, still I recognized her immediately. She was the lightly veiled woman I had seen in the train from Beirut to Damascus. The unspoken gratitude of her eyes as I calmly acted as if I had never seen her before was marvelous. And the same adoration of the great artiste was as much in evidence in this feminine party of Damascus as it would have been in a salon in Paris.

The ladies sat around her and served her with fruit, delicious apricots and grapes, such as one gets only in Damascus. Hedie had a whimsical smile, very clear eyes, a small head, with hair very simply arranged in a knot at her neck. She looked somehow more genuine, even more honest, than some of the jeweled and elaborately painted ladies who spent all their energies to beautify themselves and keep their husbands to themselves, while Hedie turned the head of every man she met without taking any trouble or pains. Her large hands with their long fingers played with fortunes and let them slip through their tapering ends with utmost unconcern.

After a great deal of begging and urging, which she took as the natural thing, she sang the famous desert song, "Although I am a great chief of the desert, I am thy humblest slave."

The power and force of art are beyond environment.

In that cheap European imitation costume, in that cheap and badly made European dress, she managed to render the song with the soul, the passion of a real Arab. She had a low contralto, pure and deep and powerful, which got the guttural catch of the Arab's emotional tones as she pronounced the word *"zalim"* (cruel), with which epithet the great chief addressed his beloved.

When her song was over I realized with the rest that we had given ourselves to the beauty she expressed in her voice, and we breathed freely as one does after the strain of some strong emotion.

Externally she was not a beautiful person, but she had an unaccountable passionate significance. She breathed it, she gave it out about her to such a degree that one did not wonder at the weakness and folly of men.

The next morning we were on our way to the desert.

Djemal Pasha's mother-in-law also came with us. She was as happy as she could be and promised to stay quietly in Beer-Sheba when we moved about. We were to go on to Jerusalem after visiting the desert.

There was nothing particular about the Arab towns we touched during the first part of our journey. They were bare, hot, and dusty with a yellow sand waste as a background to them all. Women and men walked in the stations, and the scene at Homs repeated itself with more or less noise and excitement. In Toul-Kerem people brought immense watermelons cut in two; they were bright red and deliciously juicy.

The evening set in, and we arrived at Vadi-Sarar, where I witnessed a curious scene from the window of the train. Another military train was being loaded at the station. Every usual human activity plus the tremendous bustle caused by military exigencies was going forward on that single line, so that the jostling and cramming were appalling. Most of the cars were open ones, and the soldiers were carried on these. As the engines used wood, the smoke, which seemed to be composed of myriads of fireflies, spread into the dark air. It was beautiful, but those who sat on the top of the piled wood had to be careful of the sparks. The Arab soldiers, who hated the war and the hardship anyway, made a great fuss, all talking and complaining. A tall Turkish sergeant, erect and hard as an iron bar, stood by the train and tried to squeeze in as many as he could. I could see that his patience was tried to the utmost and his Turkish stoicism exasperated at the Arabs, for the Turkish soldiers all marched through the wilds of Anatolia on foot for days and months without a murmur.

When the sergeant thought he had loaded enough and passed to the next car, a queer and weird wail began, accompanied by the dropping over the edge of the wagon of all the human load, one by one, like ripe fruit falling from a shaken tree. Then the sergeant grew angry, and raising his whip he struck a few. In the metallic, short, and clear command of the sergeant I felt at last the roused anger of the mild and kindly Turk, which is something to be avoided by those who rouse it.

I jumped down and went near the sergeant. I could hardly see his face, but I touched his sleeve.

"Countryman," I said, "they are as weak as women. Don't strike them."

I shall never forget the sudden drop of his powerful arm. He turned to me instantly. He must have been homesick for his mother-tongue, for he broke into a confidential tone at once.

"I start with two hundred, and by the time they reach the next station they become less than forty. They have no endurance, and they give one no end of trouble. I do not like it. They are always after their women; they would rather be shot as deserters than fight; and I would rather go to the firing-line than transport Arabs."

"How many years since thou hast been home?"

"Six."

He suddenly began his work again, his voice sharp and his commands metallic; but he did not use the whip. As I moved back to our train, he cried without stopping his work: *"Allah selamet versoun hemshire!"* which means, "May Allah give you peace, sister!"

Our train started. In that mellowed darkness, illuminated by the sparks of the smoke and the station, the Arabs and the Turkish sergeant melted away.

We were to pass at 2 A. M. through Galilee, and I wanted to see the lake; so I asked Lieutenant Arif, who was the military escort sent by Colonel Fuad Bey, to call me when we arrived.

I woke with a strange noise of falling water and lay

awake for a moment. Then suddenly some one tapped at the window of our compartment. It was Arif Bey, and we hurried with Nakie Hanum, putting on long coats. It was a strange still night; the place smelled of jasmine. We walked through a narrow lane and then through a passage leading to the lake. The whole place was covered with yellow jasmine, which gleamed in the moonlight, and the stillness was such that it disturbed and stirred one more than any imaginable sound could have done. At the end of the passage the lake leaped into one's eyes like a study in black and white. It had a brilliant white sheen, cast by the moon, and on the shores the sail-boats seemed like huge black shadows, falling sharply into the mirror-like transparence of the lake.

It must have been just like that when Christ so often crossed it. He must have sat on the shore and talked to the fishermen, perhaps on the selfsame old stones under the boards that were meant for a landing. We hurried back, all three silent and stirred by the beauty, the sweetness of the jasmine, and the historical significance of the place.

"We have now reached the desert," said Arif Bey the next evening. I was watching and trying to see the desert and expecting a new emotion. But the first contact had no meaning for me. There was a black waste on one side and Beer-Sheba on the other, lighted brilliantly with electricity. Arif Bey jumped down and fell into that sudden-turning-into-stone sort of military attitude, which means the saluting of a superior officer.

"Colonel Behdjet, the commander of Sinai," he introduced himself, as he helped us down. The title and the position sounded grand, but he was as mild and as human as a philosopher in the middle ages.

It was almost uncanny to go through the streets of Beer-Sheba, so well lighted, and all the roads arranged on a plan, with new white houses and the mass of military buildings. Besides the martial figures that moved about, I caught sight of single Bedouins crossing the street, with that strange swing of their slim bodies, leading a string of camels, turning a corner.

There was a square with a green garden and a fountain in the middle of the town, and opposite the fountain there was a large white building kept for the guests, which was prepared for us also.

The house was simply but tastefully arranged with green ferns in pots and flags, and Behdjet Bey took his meals with us. All the officials in Beer-Sheba, especially the doctors, seemed pleased to see people from the outside world, and they tried to entertain us.

The very next day Behdjet Bey started us on our sight-seeing according to the plan he had worked out. It was a well ordered little town, with hordes of Arabs and camels and very efficiently managed hospitals. There were Catholic Arab sisters nursing, dry small women in black veils and with very smooth movements. Among the black shadows of these religious women a sister in white attracted my attention. She had a favored position; the men seemed to have an affectionate dependence on her; while the doctors treated her with tender respect. Her round face and clear gray eyes had not lost their freshness amid all the suffering of the place, and she talked Turkish with a familiar accent. She was known as Sister Anna, and she was a Protestant Armenian. She was the only Armenian who had sensed the double tragedy of the Armeno-Turkish massacres and simply brought her lovely heart to the service of the sick. That suffering has no race, sex, and class, and that the appeasing of it is the only human act which brings a lasting satisfaction, she seemed to have learned by experience.

After the hospitals we went to the German aëroplane station. A German air officer called Erlinger showed us round. I had heard about his wonderful feats in the air, and also of his turning somersaults in the air whenever any ordinary Turkish land officer, curious for the experience of an aëroplane ride, came his way. There was a great deal of humor in his face which justified his reputation, and I felt tempted all of a sudden to go for an air drive. So I said in a conversational tone, "I wonder how it feels to be in the air." Hardly were the words out of my mouth before Erlinger began to shout commands in German, and German soldiers began to pull an aëroplane out. Erlinger stuck a cap on my head and put a fur jacket on me, which he seemed to have got hold of in a mysterious way.

To-day the anxiety and the nervousness of the old lady and Nakie Hanum seem out of place. But then there was a feeling of distrust about aëroplanes. Fortunately we were flying over the desert in no time. The first sensation was of delight caused by that miraculous sense of speed, but I soon became absorbed and thrilled by the yellow vastness of the desert and its wonderfully smooth mounds, flying at a terrible pace under us in an oblique vision.

When the aëroplane, which had been flying smoothly for a time, began to shake and jump, I felt that the time for fear had come and wondered how one held on to an aëroplane when it turned upside down.

Just then Erlinger looked back at me with a quizzical expression. I believe that he wanted to see the effect of it all on my face. In spite of my internal anxiety, his wicked joy at the idea of frightening the Turks, even when they are meek-looking little women, amused me. I smiled understandingly, and that very instant the aëroplane steadied itself. I think that any sign of fear would have led him to the wickedest feats; what was humor and amusement in me he took for courage, and that saved me. As I came down I saw the old lady sitting, with her hands up shutting her ears, and her eyes tightly closed, and she was calling to Nakie Hanum, "Is she alive?"

To which Nakie Hanum answered, "Very much so."

The old lady seemed very nervous, reproaching me with heartlessness, declaring that the fear she felt was going to kill her very soon.

There are strange coincidences in life, and when she began to grow feverish and developed pneumonia, I came to feel repentant, though I knew well enough that no amount of fear could have caused it. She could not be removed for ten days at the very earliest, and the fighting was causing some anxiety to the commander of Sinai. The English aëroplanes had begun to visit Beer-Sheba, and the outlook was not pleasant with a sick old lady in bed.

Sister Anna came to nurse for a few hours in the night, but she would not come in the daytime. "I cannot give up my poor soldiers. She is a great lady and can have every possible care." This was so fine that the old lady, who was pining to have her every minute, almost cried over the beauty of the girl's sentiment.

"It is her show of will which pleases me more than the moral side of it," she said, laughing. "I always did what I wanted. I will tell you an incident which you will never forget. Once I had a toothache, and my husband took me to a dentist, but I was determined not to have my tooth extracted. My husband always spoiled me shamefully, and he actually sat and had his own tooth extracted—to encourage me, you know. 'I will let my tooth be taken out if the dentist also pulls his own tooth out,' I said. The dentist was furious at first, but finally he did extract his own tooth. Whether he wanted to get me off his hands at all costs, or whether my husband paid him very high, I cannot tell, but I took a displeased air and said that I would never allow such a silly dentist to touch my tooth, and I walked out."

Every evening we sat out with Nakie Hanum in the garden. The desert sky is so low and the stars so near that you feel it would be possible for any tall person to

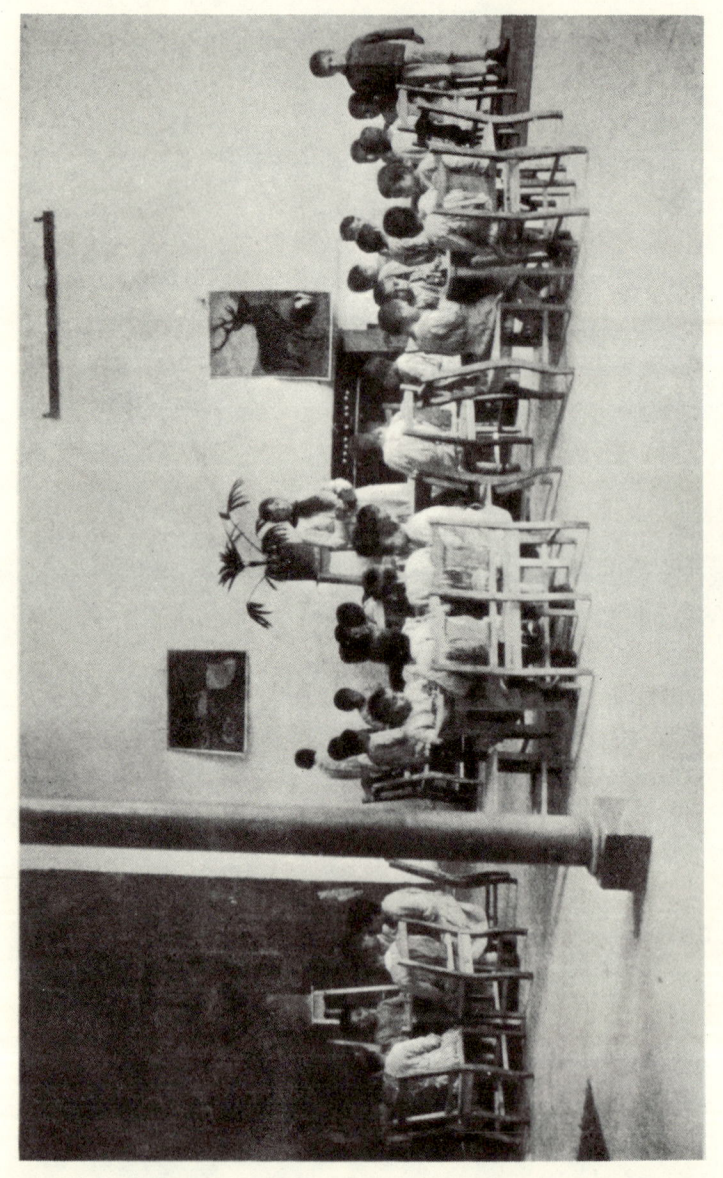

MONTESSORI CLASS IN AINTOURA

stand up and gather them. The moon rose late, but the luster of those near stars, ever so much larger and brighter than the stars I had so far known, illumined the desert with a soft and clear light. The camels and the men stood out in full outline, colorless but mysteriously and softly enveloped in light.

Opposite the garden there was a wooden mosque, where a boyish voice called out for prayers. In no part of the world is the muezzin call so perfect and harmonious as in the mosques of Constantinople. So he must be from Constantinople, I said to myself.

After the call to prayers, the Armenian cook, Artin, a dark Constantinople lad, stood by the door and sang "Aida" in a grave barytone. Somehow I had a feeling that both the young Turkish muezzin and the Armenian cook were suffering from a great longing for Constantinople.

At the fifth day, when we felt that the old lady was out of danger, Behdjet Bey took us for our longest drive in the desert. It was already dawn; the morning light had no warm hues yet; a most delicate lilac and an imperceptible greenish white enveloped the town; the camel-strings and the drivers passed on, with those light steps that made no noise on the sand, and the graceful swing that stays ever in one's mind's eye. We rode into the desert feeling how unfamiliar an auto sounds and how out of place a railway line looks in a desert. In ten minutes we were in absolute wilderness.

It is no use to describe the sense of one's nothingness and almost religious ecstasy that the dawn in the wilderness inspires. It was not connected with any particular religion to me, and I had no historical feeling. The perfect blue of the inverted canopy over the unutterable gorgeous red blaze on the horizon which warmed the tops of the vast golden sand-mounds; the unlimited span of the desert which caught the blaze and reflected it in a ruby veil; the loneliness and the eternal silence of it all! No wonder the Deity of the white man was discovered in this place of miraculous beauty.

Behdjet Bey, who was collecting historical data, told me that the trail we followed was crossed by Moses and Selim the Grim. But this also gave me no historical sensation. I was utterly disconnected with the past and the future; I was as insignificant and as nameless as one single grain of sand among the myriads.

Of course we stopped at every ordinary and orderly little station, each having a well arranged guest-house, a factory for small repairs, a blacksmith, and some water arrangements, as well as some little growth of green. But I was subdued and awed and did not care for civilization or civilized tools. I was impatient to plunge more and more into the desert. It became hotter, the colors madder and more flame-like, and the mountains more frequent. At last the colors all resolved themselves into a glistening and burning gold, and the sky turned into blue fire, burning into one's very brain. I saw no sign of life for so many hours that I could very well imagine the desert to have been created that very day.

On the sides of the trail Behdjet Bey pointed to modest mounds which were the graves of the unknown soldiers who had died on their way to the canal. The humble trace must be lost by now. Let it be lost. The Turk never had a proper grave or a proper memorial for his brave deeds. He knows beforehand when he marches on that what he suffers, however sublime, what he gains, however grand, belongs to sultans and pasha commanders. He has no Perpetual Flame or Arch of Triumph to make him remembered. But the perpetual flame and the arch of triumph are within him, and it is he who constitutes the continuity, the vitality, and the higher meaning of his race. His sultans and his pashas will be but paltry effigies and his race will lose its higher meaning if that sacred fire ever leaves his soul!

We tried hard to reach Haffir station at noon. Dr. Hassan Ferid's hospital of the Red Crescent was there. The white tents blazed in the sun on a mildly raised sand plateau. Dr. Hassan Ferid had gone with Hamdullah Soubhi to Jerusalem, where he would wait for our arrival. The order and the cleanliness was excellent in spite of the enormous difficulties of the place. We took some light lunch and rested for more than an hour. The heat was at its highest; one's feet could hardly touch the burning sands without being scorched; and one's breath burned one like fire.

When we started in the afternoon, I can hardly understand how we bore the heat, till evening came with another series of lights and beauty and spread all over the desert. We reached Kusseime at sunset. It was a pleasant place with a green garden and clear water from which a sparkling fountain rose.

The sheik, a sad-looking man with an enormous sword hung over his burnoose, received us, his little boy clinging to his arm. Behdjet Bey's grave face lighted with something which might have been a smile, and he whispered to me: "He means no mischief with that enormous sword. It is Djemal Pasha's gift, which he carries proudly. It is too heavy. I am sorry for the poor fellow." I wonder what kind of a new toy the present rulers have supplied to the children of the desert.

The little boy of the sheik had his hair shaved, and a tuft of long hair was left on the top of his head, which looked queer. A horde of delightfully brown children in short blue chemises, under which their lithe brown bodies were entirely naked, each with the same shaved head and the tuft of long hair on the top, played before the garden. Their movements were like lightning, and their gestures and talk like flames. The sheik's son stood apart and looked at them wistfully, from the separating human borders which one calls class.

The hospital contained the newly arrived and gravely wounded soldiers brought that very day from El-Arish. One heard their low moan, and their eyes held the far and strange vision of the dying.

We walked out silently and sat by the water, watching the little dark heads popping up and down in spasmodic dancing movements. The Armenians were singing

Turkish songs in one corner of the garden, and the water joined in with its cool melody, while the evening colors faded in the desert. Then we plunged once more farther and farther into the desert.

As we turned homeward the comfort of the night with its cold breath set in. The sky grew brighter, and the stars once more lowered themselves. The distant outlines of the yellow mounds and the endless stretches settled down into the night, while the silence was broken by the long and distant sobbing and howling of the jackals. It was a strange and persistent sound. At times we saw the eyes of the jackals, which approached like golden flash-lights. I could hardly believe in its reality when Beer-Sheba with its lights magically lit our way. I felt that the motion of the car was only a sham and that it would lead us no more to any inhabited land.

Three days later the old lady could be taken back to Damascus, and we started with Nakie Hanum for Jerusalem in the car of the chief engineer of the desert roads, accompanied by Lieutenant Arif Bey.

Once more I fell under the spell of the wilderness, but this time more with its historical sense. The Jerusalem road passed through these low half-rocky hills, all covered with hundreds of old hermit cells, the openings mostly banked up with sand. Every opening drew me and made me wonder at the sort of life the hermit in the past had lived there. What was he thinking of, buried in that desolation, parched by day under the sun, and watched by night by the freezing silver stars of the low heavens?

The first moment that the machine went wrong and had to be attended to, I longed to go out and climb up to those dark cave-mouths and peep into their mystery. We were in a hurry to reach Jerusalem before night. But I did get to one which was low enough, in a moment of machine repairs, and looked in. I had to bow my head down and walk a few steps. All at once I perceived something white and hard lying in the semi-darkness of the cave. I stepped out again and took matches from Arif Bey, who stood by the mouth of the cave.

It was a young Arab lying still, a white chemise covering his body, his face in the dark and his bare feet swollen and purplish. Struck by the sight and the strange smell I left the cave swiftly, and before Arif Bey went in to see, I knew that he must have been dead for some time. The grim reality of the body robbed me of my historical musings instantly. I could now only notice the tremendous number of camel corpses, and infer from them that a far greater human effort had been put forth for the canal invasion than we in reality knew.

It was evening when we entered Jerusalem. The sky of Jerusalem has a violet tinge, and the stars are more distinctly single, each hung by an invisible silver chain on which they seem to tremble and flash.

We were to stay in Augusta Victoria House, something between a religious house and a hotel. It was most beautiful, and wonderfully kept by the noble German matron called Sister Matilda. The building was surrounded by thick pine-groves and looked out to the distant hills of Jerusalem. Its garden and its corridors were covered with rich clusters of red and white flowers.

It had been the headquarters of the Turkish army for some time, but the headquarters had moved on to Damascus when we arrived.

Sister Matilda came forward to receive us in the long glass corridor. When I saw that tall and austere figure with the stately bearing of the fine face I did not wonder any more at the perfect taste, cleanliness, and order of the establishment.

She had genuine affection for the Turkish soldiers, and Djemal Pasha had more than admiration for her; it was veneration. She told me that the staff of the Turkish headquarters never smoked in that building, and the orderlies always took off their shoes when they walked on her polished floors. Some of the younger members had told me that they rather suffocated in her holy atmosphere, being deprived even of smoke, but each and all spoke with sincere respect for her. Djemal Pasha said to me:

"No man has inspired me with the respect with which she inspired me. I should love to appoint her as governor of one of the largest provinces here. She would bring order and prosperity in no time."

She returned his admiration with interest, for she also told me that the order and cleanliness which the Djemal Pasha régime had created was beyond anything she remembered in Jerusalem, although she had been there many years. Of course order was the dominating characteristic of Djemal Pasha everywhere. Speaking of Jerusalem, he said jokingly to me, "I am glad I was stopped by Djemil Bey from creating too much order." He had invited Zuercher to study the place and had drawn up a plan for the general improvement of Syria. The result is an artistic work by Zuercher published after the World War.

The mosque of Omar is one of the supreme things I remember best in Jerusalem. It glistened on its unparalleled terrace, overlooking the medieval and Jewish architecture which surrounded it on a lower plane. Its graceful dome added something to the old town. As I went up the stairs of the terrace, a saying of Mohammed ran in my mind: "All tall men are fools except Omar; all short men are perfidious except Ali!" How rare in history is a man like Omar! I simply gloated over the entry of his army, and his wonderful justice and simplicity—a man of the street, a rare democrat and idealist who had given to the inhabitants such free and happy moments as they had seldom known.

We stood and looked at the opposite hill, which had a steep dark valley at its foot; and on the top of the hill there was a small square Jewish tomb covered with stones. Not only the tomb but also the valley and the hill were covered with piles of stones.

"What is it?" I asked.

"It is the tomb of Absalom," said Djemil Bey. "The Jews go on stoning it."

Because Solomon was once angry with his son, the

poor fellow had to be stoned in his tomb forever. I never liked Solomon much; he was too wise and in a way too much like the wise men who are the leaders of to-day—beautiful maxims for others and a bad selfish life for himself.

I went over the places where the life of Jesus had been played out—first, in Bethlehem, the church of the Nativity, and the stone cave where the manger was. In the church, the Catholic priests, in gorgeous gowns, chanted a service; and beautiful women of Bethlehem, costumed just as they were in Christ's day, knelt on the stones, lost in meditation, while a huge organ played on, making the very stones vibrate.

There is something wonderful about the associations of a great man's life, especially if he has been crowned with martyrdom. The satisfaction of the human being seems never quite complete unless the man who loves and serves does not finish by allowing himself to be tortured and torn to pieces. Then lasting sanctuaries are erected, and he is made an emblem of love and eternal greatness.

Opposite the manger, carved in a massive rock, was the cell of Jerome, where he had lived thirty-two years and had breathed his last. Outside and opposite the place was a house where Paula, a pious Italian woman, had watched that cell for sixteen years. It hallowed the place for me; a heart that keeps a human image for sixteen years is a haunting heart which beats in one's memory!

More even than the church of Calvary and the place

where Jesus was tried, the road called Via Dolorosa captivated me with the sense of Passion week. Those old Roman arches, which covered the winding road to Calvary, cast wonderful shadows, and in the open places the lights blazed over the Jewish crowds, holding their markets, buying and selling, clutching, screaming and gesticulating; surely the setting was the same when He passed on to Calvary!

The garden of Gethsemane belonged to the Italians. It was a garden of chrysanthemums of lovely colors. The two-thousand-year-old olive-tree was there, and the story of the Crucifixion was represented in small wax images of a particularly charming Italian kind. I sat on a wooden bench and watched the brothers moving about and the flowers waving in the breeze.

Churches with Catholic pomp of mystery and music; churches with Orthodox smell of incense and monotonous chants, old tombs of prophets and biblical women; the narrow and medieval streets; the grandiose archways, and the Semites of all types, tongues, religions, sects, and classes!

But those ancient churches and consecrated and historic spots had no peace. One felt that all these many creeds and peoples were trying to have them to themselves, and were ready to jump at each other's throats at any moment. There was a hot and unwholesome atmosphere, mixed with a religious passion verging on hysteria. The Turk alone had a calm, impartial, and quiet look. He divided these spots justly among them all, and stood calmly watching, stopping bloody quarrels and preventing bloody riots in the holy places.

The full extent of this force and tranquillity I realized in a church connected with the Virgin. From a huge and high window the light blazed on a square red carpet. Djemil Bey carefully walked out on the marble, not touching the holy carpet with his feet. From the stairs leading down to a subterranean region a voice that was not Arab, a clear and low voice, was chanting the Koran. We found the owner, sitting on the step, protecting his head from the sun, and leaning over a large Koran opened on his knees. He had a pleasant and serious face and told us that he was the guardian of the carpet marking off the place of one particular creed. The guardian had to be on the alert, and one saw that he was brave and experienced enough to stop any brawls that might arise in this connection.

"Are they very particular?" I asked.

"They would murder each other in an instant if they saw that one crossed the boundary as much as a hairbreadth. See that window?" pointing to the sunny big one. "It was black with the dirt and cobwebs of ages. None dared to touch it. Each asserted the right of cleaning it. But an attempt to do so on the part of any would have meant a wholesale massacre."

"Who washed it at last?" I asked.

He smiled as he answered.

"Enver Pasha came two months ago. He saw the dirty state, and he called the heads of the creeds and asked them to wash it. There was an instant row as to who should hold the brush and who should carry the water. Then the pasha said, 'The Turkish soldiers as the guardians of the place shall wash it,' and it was cleaned in half an hour."

Before we started for Constantinople, Djemal Pasha took us, Nakie Hanum, Hamdullah Soubhi, and myself, to see an orphanage in Lebanon called Aintoura, after the place. It had been an old Jesuit college composed of a series of solid stone buildings, and it had very fine grounds. It was run by only a few women and two men, although there were already about four hundred children. The fact that Djemal Pasha was coming with some visitors was known, and the place had been put reasonably in order, but the children looked dejected, miserable, and sick beyond description. They were Turkish, Kurdish, and Armenian. Each child had a drama, and each had had its parents massacred by the parents of the other children, and now all were stricken with the same misery and disaster. Each child had a Turkish or Moslem name.

None of us spoke during the visit, and as we left the place we seemed to have brushed the inner ugliness and horror of the World War.

I had a conversation in the car with Djemal Pasha which was really illuminating. I said: "You have been as good to Armenians as it is possible to be in these hard days. Why do you allow Armenian children to be called by Moslem names? It looks like turning the Armenians into Moslems, and history some day will revenge it on the coming generation of Turks."

"You are an idealist," he answered gravely, "and like all idealists lack a sense of reality. Do you believe that by turning a few hundred Armenian boys and girls Moslem I think I benefit my race? You have seen the Armenian orphanages in Damascus run by Armenians. There is no more room in those; there is no more money to open another Armenian orphanage. This is a Moslem orphanage, and only Moslem orphans are allowed. I send to this institution any wandering waif who passes into Syria from the regions where the tragedy took place. The Turks and the Kurds have that orphanage. When I hear of wandering and starving children, I send them to Aintoura. I have to keep them alive. I do not care how. I cannot bear to see them die in the streets."

"Afterward?" I asked.

"Do you mean after the war?" he asked. "After the war they will go back to their people. I hope none is too small to realize his race."

"I will never have anything to do with such an orphanage."

He shook his head. "You will," he said; "if you see them in misery and suffering, you will go to them and not think for a moment about their names and religion. You speak as if I am doing something inhuman. I am taking the bread out of the mouths of the Moslem orphans who would have the money spent on them if I did not keep such a large number of Armenian children."

I had not decided on the right and wrong of the question when we started for Constantinople. It was September 16, 1916.

CHAPTER XVIII

EDUCATIONAL WORK IN SYRIA

THE *evkaff* schools, which we had modernized through the work of Nakie Hanum, passed to the ministry of public instruction that very month. Hairi Effendi, the sheik-ul-Islam, who had remained in the war cabinet because of his constructive work in *evkaff,* resigned. I followed with Nakie Hanum.

The two months from September to November, 1916, were to me the most painful during the war. I was in utter despair; the great calamity and hopeless misery which overwhelmed my country seemed to be everlasting. The war seemed endless and human suffering unlimited. I was unable to write a line, and if there had been a monastic life for women in Islam I should have entered it without hesitation. I was in this state of mind when Falih Rifki Bey came once more from Syria with a letter from Djemal Pasha urging me to undertake the organization of the schools in Syria, among which was the orphanage of Aintoura. The number of children in Aintoura had gone up to eight hundred, and they were in a deplorable state.

I accepted the organization of the schools, but still

refused Aintoura. I promised, however, to find a good man to become the director and said I would undertake its inspectorship. I found a fatherly and kind-hearted man who was already doing excellent work in the Red Crescent. He himself had children, and he seemed very tender and kind to helpless things. His wife, who was an old friend of mine and a successful teacher and organizer, undertook to choose the staff.

The college and the normal school for the three provinces were to be in Beirut, where I was to live and spend most of my time.

In Lebanon and Damascus two primary boarding-schools with six grades were to be opened on a modern footing. The staffs for all the three institutions were mostly chosen from among my old pupils who had modernized the *evkaff* schools in Constantinople with great success, and so I started with about fifty women and a few men for Syria, toward the end of December, 1916.

Two days before I started I went to visit my father in Broussa. An incident that happened at the station in Galata illumined me both as to my own nature, in its most angelic and resigned mood, and as to the ways of governments in war.

A strict examination for gold was made of every passenger during the war. The Turkish population somehow never feels real confidence in paper money, and there was enough secret dealing in gold to justify the application of strict measures. There were a great

A GROUP OF GIRLS IN AINTOURA

many Anatolian women who traveled over the country for trading purposes, and they managed to smuggle all sorts of things, the discovery of which would have baffled any government. I saw them waiting their turn before the barrack where the examination was made. As I walked with Nakie Hanum toward the place, a rather dirty-faced but highly painted woman with a German accent came toward us and asked us to follow her.

"I am the government examining inspector for gold smuggling. Come with me to this office," she said, and opened a door to a very big room.

"I would rather go and be examined with the crowd," I answered.

"Now no jabbering; no Turkish ways," she said, with a ridiculous assumption of authority. "I represent the government and do what I please."

I made an instant decision to keep my temper under control and go through the disagreeable process with extreme *sang-froid*, so we walked in. At the end of the room stood a tall man with his hands in his pockets. Although he wore civilian clothes, he was the commissary of the station.

I waited for a moment, expecting the man to leave the room, but he did not do so, though the woman was getting ready to examine us intimately.

"The gentleman must leave the room before you begin," I said quietly.

Evidently she was a woman picked from the worst and lowest classes, and she spoke as her class would speak.

"He is a great man," she shouted. "It is an honor to be examined in his presence. You Turkish women are unbearable—"

"You leave out the Turkish women," I said.

The man then spoke in a jeering tone. "She is a noble Austrian, and I am in command. Be careful about the way you talk to her."

"If you were the sultan, and she an Austrian royal princess, I would not be examined till you leave the room."

I am, generally speaking, a mild little person and keep my temper under control, but I was now struggling with something within me as I had never struggled before. I last remember the woman laying hands on me and trying forcibly to undress me. . . . Then a complete gap. I have never understood this gap, but I am afraid of it as showing incalculable possibilities within me.

The next thing I knew three policemen were entering the room. The man and the woman were not in the room any longer, while Nakie Hanum was smiling queerly.

"Will you please walk to the police station in this building?" said one, while I thought that all the three looked at me with open sympathy.

"What for?" I asked.

"For slapping a woman."

I looked at Nakie Hanum with surprise, but she nodded her head confirmingly.

There was a long table with five policemen sitting in

a row, while the tall man, termed the great man by the woman, dictated with much gesticulation. The room was full of large mirrors. In one of them I caught the image of the woman.

"She has left her finger-marks on my cheek," she shrieked in a sort of refrain.

I caught my own image also in one of the mirrors, and it frightened me with its ferocity. I was crimson to the whites of my eyes, and I seemed to look like an angry tiger.

Part of the report he dictated was in this sense: "As she seemed to belong to a high class, we took her to the room of the commissary, and with due respect the woman inspector tried to make the usual examination for gold. She immediately made seditious and rebellious utterances against the government, used most abusive language, and finally beat the inspector, who is a noble Austrian."

I remember him walking up and down, pleased with his eloquence.

"Sign," he said at last.

"I will not," I said.

"I will arrest you if you don't."

"You may. I can only sign something which is true, and if you allow me to dictate my own statement I will sign."

The policeman sitting in the middle had a long fair face with very kindly eyes. He said something in low whispers to the "great man" which made him consent with some reluctance.

I told the story shortly and simply, and finally added that if those they thought entitled to special treatment were exposed to this sort of thing it horrified me to think of the treatment which the common people must receive. This I signed.

Writers always enjoy a certain consideration, and the idea of this story possibly appearing at some future date in the Turkish newspapers was probably not a welcome prospect to the bully, but to his honor he did not flinch. On the contrary he added a new threat: "I shall say that you have attacked me with an umbrella, and if this lady"—pointing at Nakie Hanum—"had not been present you would have beaten me." I had no umbrella, and if we two, Nakie Hanum and myself, were put together, lengthwise and crosswise, we should still not have been as large as his powerful frame.

I went home that evening realizing sadly and fully the meaning of "seditious and rebellious utterances," which I so often saw given as reasons for delivering over people to courts martial.

The next morning Ahmed Bey, the chief of the police, apologized through the telephone, and thanked me for enlightening them about the undesirable process used in gold examination without the knowledge of the government. As I went to Broussa the next day I found both the process and the woman inspector changed.

We reached Beirut late one evening in the pouring rain. The director of Aintoura took the secretaries and the accountants (who were men) to the hotel, and I with my fifty women teachers found places prepared in the girls' primary school, which, as I have already said, was run by my sister.

The governors of Beirut, Damascus, and Lebanon set to work to help, as did the army headquarters. For us it meant nearly sixteen hours of work each day, but before the end of January the schools opened, the pupils arrived, and the work began in all of them.

The normal school and college, which was to be in common for the three provinces, began in Der-Nassira (Ladies of Nazareth). The building was long and three-sided, perched on a high terrace which overlooked the orange and banana groves, the tall date-palms of the lower terraces, and the magnificent blue expanse of the Mediterranean.

The buildings used to contain a religious and rather fashionable school for Syrian girls, which was run by sisters. The sisters were in the building when we arrived. I drove up to the school the very next morning as the rooms were being whitewashed, cleaned, and prepared. The mother superior received me and went over the place with me.

Djemal Pasha had a convent prepared for them in Jerusalem, and she, Sister Freige, the superior, and the thirty sisters under her were to leave soon. But as we sat with her in the simple sitting-room and a sister offered me coffee, I tried hard to think of some arrangement by which it would be possible to keep them with me. I knew that Djemal Pasha was always kind about finding comfortable quarters for the large number of homeless religious women in Syria, and for Sister Freige and her people he would be especially so. Still they fitted in so well with the whole surroundings that I wanted to make some practical arrangement which would benefit us both. Sister Freige herself was a distinguished personality, with a remarkable presence and face. Her long, dark, oval, clear-brown eyes and the firm mouth with its lines of pity and understanding fascinated me.

In half an hour we came to a complete understanding. She was to stay on with her staff and undertake the entire housekeeping. The left wing, which had an odd arrangement and was unfit for school accommodations, was to belong to them. I remember the affection and the sincerity of her voice as she said, "We will pray for your soul, my child." And they did remember me in their daily prayers in that mysterious church of theirs.

Among the feverish activity of the school days I could rest only at tea-time, when Sister Freige used generally to drop in and give me her views about education and school management. I am afraid that I took none of her advice, but I loved to hear her talk. I think of her now saying, "Weekly baths lead to vanity; freedom breeds saucy girls; friendship between two girls is wrong."

The first month I had trouble concerning the sisters which might have become grave. I was told by a faithful man who was given us as a guard that the sisters were signaling and acting as spies for the French. He told me that there was a wireless apparatus on the roof. I went over the roof very carefully with him and saw that there was nothing at all. I knew the simple women in this monastery to be far removed from all political activity. Sister Freige was perhaps personally pro-French, but she had enough sense of honor to refrain from actually doing anything which might be called treachery. On the other hand, I loved my country too much to allow any sentiment to cause me to protect the sisters if I found any act of treason going on. But in any case I did not want to act on impulse. One day the man came to me and told me that every night after midnight a man entered the sisters' part of the building and left the place before morning. The man was dressed in priest's clothes. On inquiry I found out who the man was. He was a Catholic priest who had to conduct the prayers, as in their ritual women could not conduct them. Then I told Sister Freige frankly that I could not allow it and that they must pray alone. I do not know whether she understood that I was acting in their own interest, but she was sad. Inquiries which were conducted without her knowledge confirmed in every case her statements about little matters which were brought to me, and for which I had to be responsible to my government. However, after some six months both the government and myself felt at peace about them, and Sister Freige never knew my troubles in the matter.

The entrance examinations were exciting. For twenty vacant places in the higher classes, we had 175 applications. It was mostly from Lebanon and Beirut that the applicants filled the school. Fortunately the Damascus students were chosen by our institution in Damascus. Lebanon mostly sent Christian girls, Beirut sent both Moslems and Christians, while the Damascus students were all Moslems. As Jessir Effendi, the Arab inspector of the public instruction, translated the examination questions into Arabic, he smiled. "If you were an Arab you would be accused of Arab nationalism and given to the court in Alie." As a true Nationalist myself I thought that every one ought to know his own country's language and culture. As a fact the girls, who were mostly from French schools, knew nothing about the country they lived in and despised their own language as inferior to French. The new schools which we had opened took the teaching of Arabic very seriously.

We had almost completed the dormitories and the class-rooms when Djemal Pasha came to the school with Azmi Bey, the governor. They went all over the school and finally asked to see the church. It was an enormous place, with no end of statues and images and rather badly lit. Djemal Pasha thought that there ought to be no church in a secular school and that the place ought to be turned into a dormitory or a public hall. I had the dormitories ready, and as for the public hall there was a white-walled rectangular chapel with a beautiful light which suited my purpose better. The church door was closed to the main building, but the sisters entered it from a side door. In this case I insisted that they ought to be allowed to have their church. As we went on discussing the matter I caught sight of an old sister kneeling behind a chair and watching us with furtive eyes. I was not surprised, for it was in their system to know all.

I was rather taken back by a scene that day which made me wonder a great deal. A short fat man who was doing the furnishing of the school came to Djemal Pasha and said that there were crosses on the graves of the sisters in the lower garden, and asked if the pasha desired them to be removed. I was glad to hear Djemal Pasha say furiously: "What do you take me for? Should I ever allow graves to be touched?"

We soon opened classes for sewing and for languages, mainly French and Turkish. The waiting-rooms were filled with Arabic women, anxious to attend these classes. All had pleasant, wide-awake faces and proved to be very apt pupils.

It was at this period that a man called Dumani came to see me. He brought samples of washable home-made stuff which seemed excellent for use as uniforms for the students. He had a weaving factory where he made use of waste silks in Syria. He offered it very cheap, but his condition was that half of the money must be paid in wheat. Azmi Bey took him under his protection, and he furnished all our schools with that wonderful stuff from his factory. When I learned from Sister Freige his history I was more than glad to have introduced him to Azmi Bey. His father, the richest man in Syria, had gambled away all his fortune and died, leaving an enormous amount of debt. Dumani had sold all he could from their property, paid the debtors, and started to work like a simple working-man. He and his brave mother, a noble woman in every way, are among those for whom I have a deep respect.

In the meantime I was not satisfied with the state of things in Aintoura. I had installed the director and his staff in the very first week of January. The place was in a state of incredible filth and misery. Out of the eight hundred children over five hundred were sick. There was no order whatever, and the personnel consisted entirely of a few good but incapable women, a few men, and half a dozen soldiers who were supposed to do some work. The women and the men were overjoyed to see the arrival of a larger staff. Each child, each bed, and each piece of furniture was covered with vermin, and most of the children had mouth disease. The children themselves looked like little wild beasts and acted as such. There seemed to be no human decency or cleanliness left among them. The smell, the dirt, the din, and the sickly sight quite overcame the new staff. They had not imagined such a state possible. Loutfi Bey asked for boilers at once and set to boil every possible boilable thing and to disinfect the furniture and the place thoroughly, for typhus was one of the worst epidemics of Syria. A new doctor also called Loutfi arrived from the front and really worked wonders in establishing a

EDUCATIONAL WORK IN SYRIA

decent hospital and better hygienic conditions. The vermin were destroyed, and the worst of the dirt and filth removed. But in spite of this there seemed to me on my weekly visits to be little or no progress.

The director, Loutfi Bey, was becoming more and more depressed. The complete degradation of the children frightened him. There were a few big healthy-looking children who seemed to dominate the whole place. Loutfi Bey told me that they took the bread of the smaller children and sold it in the village, gambled in all sorts of ways, and did other things which could not be told. I talked with those children, and I talked with the teachers, stayed and observed for a little time, and finally decided to come up to the institution myself and set to work. Der-Nassira was well started in all its branches and was in reliable hands, so that I could absent myself from it for some time.

As Loutfi Bey was too much depressed to go on with the work, he and a few of his staff decided to leave. Dr. Loutfi accepted the direction of the school—[1]an appointment which proved a blessing to the establishment. I wired to headquarters in Damascus, gave notice of the change, and settled down to work.

I began my work by going into the dining-room to see the terrible ordeal of feeding the children, which had so appalled the director and the staff.

The dining-room consisted of three very long and

---

[1] Both the first director, who stayed only for a short time, and the Dr. Loutfi who stayed and worked wonders had the same name.

very large halls opening into each other. Only four hundred and fifty children were on their feet and came to meals. Even the greater part of these looked as if they would be much better in a sanatorium. Two soldiers stood by the door with two large sacks full of bread and distributed it to the children as they passed in. Makboule Hanum, the matron, with a few other teachers were trying to pour out the soup.

Before all the children had got into the hall, a tremendous uproar and fighting began. It was a scene for students of anthropology to see, for it illustrated the terrific struggle for existence among the lowest kinds of animals. The stronger boys were snatching the bread from the weaker ones, and the weaker ones were struggling to keep from giving up their bread. It was a wild fight, with all the children wrestling and tearing each other, crying and screaming. The accountant of the school, a sturdy man, was trying to establish order with a stick but in vain. Some children were still on the floor, and the matron was wounded, blood running down her hands and neck. It seemed this was the worst they could do, and I was glad to see the limit, although it filled one with unutterable sadness to see the quick deterioration of human nature in misery.

The old director was to be our guest till the end of the week, and I remember his pardonable satisfaction as he saw me enter. "I am glad you saw with your own eyes the impossibility of the task," he said.

"They will be eating their dinner in peace in one week," I said. I believe the order and the quiet of the teachers' dining-room hurt me at that moment. That evening I went all over the depots and noted the amount of raw material in the form of piles of yarn, cotton, leather, and wool. There was also a considerable amount of strong stuff which could be turned into bedding. Loutfi Bey had got nearly three hundred suits and some hundred shoes ready; his idea was to dress and organize when all the material should be ready. My plan was to begin at once and get the boys to weave, to carpenter, to make shoes, in short throw this enormous mass of grown-up children into work and make them to a certain degree self-sufficient.

The first night, after working till twelve in my office, which was in the first floor, I quietly wandered into the school. The corridors were full of bigger children laughing and talking with the Arab soldiers who were supposed to be keeping guard. The dormitories were in a wretched state, little ones and big ones all huddled together. I went back to my room at two and made additional notes on what I was going to do.

One of the women from Constantinople who decided to stay on was a good dressmaker. I called from the village several women and with the bigger girls began to prepare the dresses and the bedding of the smaller ones. I had asked headquarters for a good carpenter, shoemaker, and a director to organize a brass band, and procured two very good weavers and a few simple looms to start the weaving of the yarn into stuff for children. The masters arrived in three days, chose the necessary big boys, and set to work feverishly. I owe the quickness of the establishment of order to those bigger boys to a very great extent, the very ones who seemed so impossible and degenerate at the beginning. I had very serious talks with them, and through personal contact I chose also those I wanted for other purposes than weaving and carpentering.

At the end of the week the smaller ones had their dormitory ready with their new bedding; their dresses and a part of their shoes were ready. Each ten small children (boys and girls below seven) had an *abla,* that is, an elder sister from among the bigger girls, who was to mother them, and to help them to dress and wash and go to their classes. One teacher had to sleep in the little room which opened into the dormitory. The first day when each ten marched into the bath-house with their *abla* was a memorable day. When the first ten had had their baths and were dressed in clothes which it was a pleasure to look at, they sat on a bench in the hall of the bath-house, and leaning against each other, they slept with such a happy expression as I had thought was impossible for them. As each ten walked out with their *abla,* dressed and combed and clean, the entire school, which had come down there to watch the change, stood and let them pass with something like awe. That night I went three times to that dormitory to watch the sleep of the little ones.

At the end of two months all the children were well dressed and well shod, all from their own weaving and shoe-making. Their dormitories were clean and well ordered. The young carpenters had made three hundred wooden beds, and were now making bed-tables. Besides they were getting ready a whole Montessori outfit for the small ones, who were having something like Montessori classes. The entire program of teaching, which was divided into five grades, was fully applied. The boys also had their bigger brothers, each twenty-five having a big boy as sergeant. This was an honor, and they enjoyed such consideration as co-workers with the teachers that each sergeant tried to keep his crowd in the best training. The blessedness of work, cleanliness, and interest in games and music kept them in much better humor, and the general harmony among the children was surprising. I remembered the first days when the Kurdish and Armenian children almost tore each other's throats daily and felt very thankful at the speedy change. The two Kurdish boys, who were now the best weavers, had come to me during the first week after I came to Aintoura; both had their heads in white bandages, and both spoke at once:

"We want permission to go to Damascus."

"What for?"

"We want to kill the Armenians."

"Why?"

"The Armenians killed our parents, and they beat us daily."

"It was not those boys who killed your parents. Besides their parents also were killed by other people. Now tell me; how did you get those cuts on your heads?"

I sent them to the hospital and told them that they

must postpone going to Damascus for the time. What I liked about them was that although they expressed so much hatred of the Armenian children, they did not tell me the names of those who wounded them. Now these same boys were weaving the clothes of all their comrades and going about as peacefully as lambs. The Kurdish children possessed the qualities of honesty, truth, and affection to a surprising degree, but unless always treated with firmness and justice they were very hard to manage. They lacked the quality of leadership of the Turks and the Armenians. The Turkish children were the easiest to manage. Besides their first-rate capacity for discipline and leadership, they were mild and kindly and formed the pacifying element of the school. When it came to hard work with self-sacrifice one could always depend on the bigger Turkish boys, and it is through their firmness and goodness that I was able to bring order into the mealtimes. Now orderly children, clean and well combed, marched into the dining-rooms with their *abla* and their sergeant and sat down and had their meals in quiet. But sometimes in the middle of the meals, when the children seemed happiest, one of the little ones would suddenly begin to cry. It was a searching cutting cry which lasted for hours, no doubt caused by some association with their home. Sometimes in the middle of their play in the garden when they seemed happiest, hundreds of the young throats would begin to thunder a Turkish song, "Whither are my own brooks?" The words were An-

THE ARMENIAN CHILDREN WERE GOOD MUSICIANS

atolian, and the music had infinite yearning. One felt that these children whatever happened would carry something crippled, something mutilated in them.

The Armenian children were good musicians, and the brass band which was formed became the joy and the pride of the school. The Armenian children were nearer to the Turkish children than to the Kurds in certain qualities, although nearer to Kurds in race.

How relieved I felt when I could take off my shoes and put my swollen feet on a chair and work at the intricate correspondence which one had to carry on with headquarters and the provinces in order to keep the establishments supplied with food and other necessities!

I had never hoped to hear laughter in Aintoura; the most I looked for was less tears and less sickness. Yet I saw sturdy legs and chubby faces, and I often heard laughter and sounds of gaiety. The comparative friendliness and good health was very cheering after two months of killing work. I never realized how killing it was till one morning as I looked in my glass it became covered with a gray cloud, and I fell on the floor, feeling that I was being overtaken by death before I could start properly all I had to do in the establishment.

The event was in April, the weather was intensely hot, and I was told by the doctor that it was a case of cerebral anemia. I stayed in bed for a week before I went to inspect our school in Damascus.

It was during this week of utter sickness that I made an important decision concerning my own life. I decided to marry Dr. Adnan.

He was in Constantinople and I was in Syria, and our marriage took place in Broussa, to which he was able to go. My father was to represent me, with my letter to him which clearly asked him to give my consent. The marriage took place on April 23, 1917. When I received my father's telegram and that of Dr. Adnan that I was married, I was creeping back to life and work again.

I was getting glimpses into the many-sided lives and peoples of Syria. There were the rich Lebanon and Beirut Christian nobility, an Arab imitation of the Parisian world; the dresses, the manners, the general bearing were of French importation. Strange to say, they still had something of their own which they tried hard to hide. There were the Moslem and Druse nobility, who fiercely, proudly kept their own way and personality. There was a great deal of profiteering and war wealth, all made on wheat. Among the Syrian masses, famine in its cruelest form was fast approaching. In the rich streets of Beirut, men in rags and with famished faces, solitary waifs and strays of both sexes, wandered; lonely children, with wavering, stick-like legs, faces wrinkled like centenarians, eyes sunken with bitter and unconscious irony, hair thinned or entirely gone, moved along. There is an endless vista of road in my mind's eye where these nameless little figures move on and on. There is a vision of rich marble steps before stately mansions, where on a skeleton baby arm one of those miserable little heads rests in unutterable abandon and longing to die.

The first time I heard the cry it echoed and echoed through my brain and heart. It was after a concert in the American College, where I had gone with some teachers, and I had given myself up to the bliss of music. I was driving home through the streets of Beirut back to Der-Nassira when I heard it: *"Dju-an."* It was a solitary cry piercing and insistent and cutting the air like a knife. I have heard that *"Dju-an"* so often since. As time went on, the shrill passionate voices of women, the grave guttural tones of men, in colorless and passionless pain, little children's weak throats which hardly seemed to have a breath left, all gave forth that cry in a single sharp note, like a sword-blade which pierces through the heart.

Syrians, the intellectual ones, often spoke to me about a certain Vedi Sabra, their great musician.

Vedi Sabra's name I had heard in 1908 as the composer of a national song, the words of which belonged to Tewfik Fikret. It began with, "We are a nation of brave men . . . we are Ottomans," and it had been sung by eighty thousand men and students in the garden of Taxim, with Sabra leading the orchestra. In those days race hatred in Turkey had not come into being. In 1915 Vedi Sabra was connected with the conspiracy in Beirut in the French interest, and he was exiled to Erzeroum.

I wrote to Djemal Pasha asking him to let us have Vedi Sabra as the head of our music department, which we meant to make into a model for Syria. Before long we had him at the head of our music classes. In a place where there is moral and physical suffering, after hygiene and order, music comes next as a comforting and reviving influence.

I promised the authorities of Syria to come back for one more year, and if the victory was ours, I hoped that those humble schools of mine, outcome of infinite labor and love, might be the nucleus of the constructive and peaceful institutions which my government meant to start in Syria. So I went back to Constantinople to spend my vacation. Dr. Adnan, who was inspecting the hygienic condition of the Turkish armies, came to Syria in June, and we traveled home together.

In September, 1917, I came back to Syria to serve one one more year, as I had promised. The splendid effort and the capacity of the teaching staff in the preceding year had enabled us to begin the work of teaching without much difficulty in all the institutions. Aintoura had progressed to a surprising degree, for it had continued through the summer months with a lighter program. The number of children had gone up to twelve hundred. There was a neighboring convent for nuns; Dr. Loutfi had rented a part of it from the nuns and had placed there all the girls and some teachers with their handwork classes. I remembered having gone to visit the sisters the previous year. The order was so strict that only the matrons could appear, and only behind an iron railing. We had exchanged polite inquiries about our mutual health through the railings. It had appeared to me like a mythological play on the German stage. Now they also were to accept contact with the outer world, led by the necessity of a livelihood.

The most useful change was the new arrangements in drainage, water, and the installation of electricity. The general cleanliness, the harmony among the inmates, and the progress in the various crafts were great. The young shoemakers now had commissions from the outside world.

Dr. Loutfi's greatest concern was the little ones. There were eighty small children who somehow did not thrive as the bigger ones did, in spite of all the care he lavished on them. The little Montessori classes were furnished with pretty little chairs and tables, brightened by palms, bathed in the sun, where the teachers and the children worked and played. The little ones had a different régime, plenty of sun-baths and the best of everything; still there was a look of depression and fragility about them all. Bad or good humanity has not yet discovered a better place than a family nook, or a better caretaker than a mother. No institution, no matter how scientifically run, can replace these. If the family system is replaced by large governmental institutions, the nature of the human race is bound to undergo a fundamental change, and I believe it will be for the worse.

There was one child among the small ones for whom I was destined to take a keen, even painful interest. She was the youngest there. I had seen her first as one of the sickly tattered crowd of children during the previous year. She had a dirty chemise which covered only a part of her little body; shaking her unkempt curls, she was looking about her with intense curiosity in her little eyes, blazing with passion and will-power. She hardly spoke any language well, but she jabbered in a mixture of Turkish and Kurdish, putting in Armenian and Arabic words now and then. Her name was Jale, which means Dewdrop in literary Turkish, but the name had evidently been given to her by some one in the school; no such name could be given to an Anatolian child. She had been immediately taken up by Sister Ismet, the Turkish nurse, who gave her all her spare moments, and the little girl had conceived a great passion for her in return. She was now one of the gayest and the healthiest children. I knew the reason: she had found in this way a human kinship; if all the rest could each have been adopted by one special woman, Dr. Loutfi's task would have been easier.

There was greater misery the second year, but a readier spirit of helpfulness. Azmi Bey had opened an orphanage with seven hundred Arab children, all gathered from the roads of Beirut and Lebanon. Ali Munif Bey had opened several soup-kitchens for the waifs and the street orphans. His successor, Ismail Hakki Bey, who because of his liberal administration was very much liked by the Lebanon people, was augmenting them. Americans also were doing a great deal. There was one excellent orphanage which was supported entirely by Mr. Dodge, the son-in-law of Dr. Bliss. The self-sacrificing life of the Dodge family in Beirut during the years I stayed there was a thing to be proud of.

There was a growing sympathy and harmony between the governmental and American institutions. I am specially grateful to Dr. Bliss for his encouraging friendliness and help in finding the teachers of Arabic; it was through him that I also got an excellent teacher of physical culture, a young American woman, Miss Fisher, who was a valuable addition to our staff.

The fashionable and rich ladies of Beirut and Lebanon were also active the second year. A fine workshop for embroidery and lingerie was opened and most ably run by them. They employed a great number of young orphans.

Another admirable instance of humanity was that of Dr. Smith in the lunatic asylum of Asfurie. He was protected and helped by Djemal Pasha (he was English), but some persons insisted that in the days when the sane were starving the mad should be allowed to die first. This was a cruel argument, against which poor Dr. Smith struggled hard, and he managed to keep his helpless patients alive to the end. I visited the asylum. It was admirably kept and was the best of its kind in Syria.

I should like to give a picture of my old friend Selim Sabit, an interesting and an unusual personality. I had met him in 1916 when I went to draw up a plan for the schools. He was an Arab copy of Napoleon III in dress and beard. I have often seen young Arabs in higher society affecting the fashion of that particular French period. I cannot really tell whether it was out of admiration for Napoleon III or a fancy that the fashion was becoming. Selim Sabit said that he was seventy-six, but those who disliked him for his eccentric and outspoken character said that he was eighty-four. But his pointed beard he managed to keep coal black, and his small eyes, nearer together than any other eyes I have ever seen, had a shrewd, piercing, and very youthful light. His long oval face had a skin finely wrinkled into thousands of lines. He spoke in rhetorical tones, made such bows as one never sees in this workaday world, wore the brightest of waistcoats, and had dazzlingly colored ties. My first impression was that of a vain old man, and I forgot him. In 1917 I heard him talked of as criticizing the callousness and the indifference of the higher classes to the sufferings of the masses. It was aristocracy offended at the shortcoming of the true aristocracy which prompted him.

Then he became very much interested in the school and often called and offered his services. I soon found that under that travestied exterior a true and loyal heart and an unbounded courage were hidden. His great attachment to the school was founded on its respect for Arabic and on its tolerance. This nationalism was outwardly contradictory in a man who dressed as he did, but it was very sincere. After the first months he tried hard to persuade me to stay in Syria and to run the schools. I refused firmly.

It was with him that I went up to see the Maronite patriarch, our neighbor in Aintoura. The eagle-like house of the patriarch perched on a very high rock, looking down over a steep precipice into waters which had an especially deep blue. The atmosphere of the house seemed to be an imitation of Rome. Cardinals, who had cultivated Italian faces and looked like the pictures of cardinals in art galleries, politely received us and talked perfect French to us. The old man himself looked a genuine mountaineer. Although more than eighty, he still was erect and robust, with the clear eyes of Lebanon. He spoke French with the accent of his countrymen, and in his gorgeous red robe of a flaming pomegranate, he gave one the feeling of a sturdy Lebanon peasant. I had often heard of him as favoring French domination, and I see to-day that the Maronites are upholding the French claims. My own impression is that once the artificial difference of the Moslem and Christian Arab is removed (a feeling nursed and made the most of by the Western powers in the East), all the Arabs, including the Maronites, will unite in no time.

My Arab friends filled my rooms with violets and crimson carnations, which looked like piles of fire in the large trays or baskets in which they were sent. If an Arab likes you in Syria, you receive poems and flowers, and you also receive his confidence unconditionally over a cup of coffee. If you are an official they bribe, flatter, and corrupt you, and so subtle are their ways that it is very difficult to resist them. So even those flowers in the first days made me say to myself, "Am I being corrupted?" But I was soon assured. Flowers cost nothing, and poems addressed to friends are different from those addressed to the great of the land. A man belonging to a rich family did try to bribe me, although clothed in the language of flattery. I was so near the sort of anger I had shown to the gold inspector in Constantinople that I ended the interview as soon as possible and with a suddenness he will not forget. Any one in Syria who is in a position to employ people so as to exempt them from military service must be prepared for such offers.

"It is about Ruffat Effendi, your accountant at Lebanon, than I want to speak," he began.

"What about him?"

"The fact is that I want to be your accountant at Lebanon."

"I am perfectly satisfied with Ruffat Effendi."

"I am ready to make a great sacrifice in gold, thousands in fact, to procure the place."

"To me?" I said as I suddenly rose.

"No, no," he said hurriedly. "I mean to the institutions, and I am going to give Ruffat Effendi two thousand pounds which will make his fortune."

"Did he consent?" I asked, coldly walking to the door.

He was muddled and ashamed and began to beg to be taken in, no matter in what capacity; he would die, he said, if he went to the army.

I opened the door and beckoned him to walk out. And as I went up with the feeling of shame that I had been offered a bribe, I thought of a passage in the "Hull House" of Miss Jane Addams where she tells how she was also exposed to the same thing, and wondered if there was anything in her bearing which made any one dare to offer a bribe, even in the shape of a contribution to her institution.

Vedi Sabra asked to be allowed to put "The Shepherds of Canaan" into a musical play, and after arranging the libretto with me, he set to work. He did the first act in Syria, organizing an orchestra of twenty-five, composed of the best amateurs and professionals in Beirut. Doumet, the Syrian pianist, who had broken his front teeth in order to look like Beethoven, was to accompany the orchestra, and Sabra began to get ready. We would give it before we left Syria.

By November the reverses at the front had begun. I was so absorbed with my work that I had hardly realized that Syria could be taken any moment by the enemy and that the whole place could be turned into a battlefield. I had an anxious letter from Saime Hanum, the head of the Damascus school, asking me to come and make a decision, as there was considerable fear among the people of Damascus.

I started as soon as I could, and it was only in Reyak that I heard very serious news. Djemal Pasha's family had left the day before, and he himself was leaving quite soon; a German commander, Falkenheim, was coming. The military activity on the line had stopped ordinary transport, but I traveled in a carriage full of cartridge-boxes.

After a serious talk with the teachers that evening, I went next day to see Djemal Pasha at his headquarters. He was extremely sad and not in the best of humor with his colleagues in Constantinople. He thought that his removal would upset the entire organization and order, in which he was not mistaken. But as it was war time he felt bound to keep the peace and obey orders. He proposed to take with him the teachers of the schools, which had been opened mainly through his initiative, for there was a possibility of anarchy. I thanked him and told him that until the moment came when the government closed the schools in Syria we should not leave our posts. He was insistent on possible and imminent danger, but I told him that the honor of Turkish women demanded that they should stay till they were officially authorized to leave the schools. Another Djemal Pasha, called the Second at the time, was to be in Syria and at the head of the forces. He and Colonel Fuad, the governors of the provinces, would help us to go on to the end of the year if . . .

I told all my staffs of the immediate danger and frankly admitted the possibility of greater danger and hardship, so that any one who wished was to go with Djemal Pasha. From the first to the last all refused to leave their posts. The sublime sacrifice and the confidence of these women and men I can never forget, although this same confidence gave me moments of difficulty which I can never fully explain.

A series of sleepless and anxious nights followed. Supplies were becoming rarer and rarer; to get the necessary provisions for a fortnight necessitated no end of correspondence. My idea was to get supplies which would last the schools till they closed, and for Aintoura for at least five months. It was after this that I began to follow the military movements with anxiety and interest. In the campaigns in Syria there was at the beginning one soldier's name which shone with special brilliance, that of Colonel Reffet. Fuad Pasha shared the luster in the last months.

The first week of February I started for Damascus. I wanted the provision question settled safely for Aintoura. There was talk of closing the schools in Syria in March on account of military operations, which were not in any way reassuring. Organization and order were hard to maintain under the circumstances. There was almost no transport. It was with difficulty that I could get a carriage with good horses and a reliable driver. Although one had to use a fan in Beirut, a snowstorm was raging on the tops of the Lebanon. Brigandage had begun during the last few months. I started at four from Beirut, and soon the night set in. I found to my great annoyance that there was no oil in the carriage lanterns, and it was not procurable on the way. We had to go nearly ten hours over high icy mountain passes, and all the time in the dark. It was a nightmare, and the brave guard who was on the carriage told me that he had one of the most anxious nights of his life. We reached Zahle, the town before Reyak, half an hour after midnight, and I went to the house of the governor, whose wife was an old friend of mine. I was to proceed to Damascus the next day.

In the morning before I started Major Kemal, the new chief of supplies, came to see me. He had heard of my arrival that night. He promised to send the supplies without my going to Damascus, and solemnly declared that Aintoura should have provisions enough for four months. The order for the closing of the schools in March was confirmed during my stay in Zahle. I went back relieved.

The young Arabs on my return gave me a surprise entertainment. They had translated parts from my works into Arabic and some into French, and they acted them with surprising capacity. I almost cried over the "Folly of Handan," acted by a beautiful Arab girl. She became quite the vogue and acted the part at teas, which are grand affairs in the high life of Syria.

EDUCATIONAL WORK IN SYRIA

I heard Sauda, the native Arab musician, sing and play on that occasion. He accompanied his own songs on the *oud* (a kind of Oriental lute). The rhythm at the end of each verse as he sang was wonderfully striking, and at the end of each he looked with a flash of languid questioning at his audience, and the audience responded with a masterly concert of sighs, as if they were fainting at the very beauty of the music. It was done with such perfect finish, and the entire rhythm of the song, the movement of the musician, and the sighs were so in tempo that my attention was almost called away from the real beauty of the music.

Several other entertainments in Arab schools followed, and the schools finally got up an exhibition of Syrian artists, most of whom I had come to know. The paintings did not amount to much, for the best painters were not in Syria, but there was a small group of statuary by an amateur which was instinct with the inmost significance of Syria's suffering in its clumsily executed stone figures. The group represented an Arab mother feeding a baby at her emaciated breasts, with two small children, one lying dead at her feet, and the other agonizing, clutching her torn skirts, while the woman, with her fallen unkempt hair and dying eyes, was the very emblem of the starving women in Syria. It brought instant tears to my eyes, and it is a pity the young artist had not been trained in the technique of his art, or he would certainly have passed to posterity as having rendered in marble the image of his country's suffering.

Again in the early days of February I was going through the classes in Aintoura. I had gone to stay for a longer spell in the little Montessori class. This time the little ones looked brighter and better, except one little girl who was morose, sickly, and miserable beyond description. All the other children held each other's hands, sang, and turned round gaily, while she walked listlessly. It was months since I had met such a sickly child in Aintoura, so I went to her and taking her thin cheeks gently in my hands, I lifted her face to mine. It was that of Jale, the happiest and healthiest child some months ago.

"Why don't you sing, Jale?"

"I have no more a mother."

Sister Ismet had caught a bad form of malaria, and as it had affected her lungs for the time being, she was removed to a higher place in Lebanon. And it was that separation which had brought Jale into this shocking state. Fortunately I had known to the full in my own life the effect of moral distress on childish sensitiveness.

"You come and be my guest in Beirut sometime. Your mother will be getting well before long," I said.

"You will be my mother," she said, as if deciding on something which depended only on her.

As I was taking leave of the teachers I heard a series of unearthly shrieks which followed each other in rapid succession.

"It is Jale's voice," explained Dr. Loutfi. "The child is a wonderful, almost uncanny creature, who will have her own way absolutely."

SHOEMAKING CLASS IN AINTOURA

I remembered strangely the night in the house of Yildiz when I had forced Mehemmed Effendi to take me into Abdul Hamid's palace where my father was. It was the same case; some one had told Jale that I had forgotten her and gone away.

As she came holding Dr. Loutfi's hand and hugging the tiny bundle containing her belongings, I realized that her little hooked nose was red with crying, and the rebelliously determined look of her eyes was different from that of other children.

She took possession of me, of Der-Nassira, of the sisters in no time. She used to have her little bed laid out in the room where I worked from which my bedroom was separated by a thin partition of boards.

"Are you there, mother?" cried a shrill voice at night several times, and she only left me in peace after I had assured her of my presence.

She chiefly occupied my mind as she sat in the evenings on my homely sofa, sniffing at the flowers with epicurean joy, and singing a song which she herself had made, words and music: "Send us Helva [sweets]. let us eat it, emin, aman, emin, aman." The last words were made up for the sake of the rime.

Vedi Sabra came to my room and played some of the airs from "The Shepherds of Canaan" and asked about the Turkish of the songs, while the school was feverishly preparing for the play. Some of the airs of the musical play were taken from the popular Arab songs, which I thought were charming. And it was usually those airs which Jale also enjoyed. She seemed to love the mild and gentle manners of the Arab musician, and affected a most protecting air toward him, ordering coffee for him whenever he came in. Sabra himself seemed intensely interested.

It was on one of those evenings a strange thing happened. Sabra was telling me in French that he often wondered about the nationality of the little girl. She had Eastern Anatolia written all over her person; the hooked nose, the dominating will, the passion all denoted it; but what was she? Who had made her cover that tremendous space and thrown her into the very heart of Arab lands? Whether it was the effect of our curiosity on her sensitive mind, or the influence of that song of the revolution of 1839, an air of thundering, bloody terror, and the cry of a wild mob which Sabra had adapted to the words of Joseph's brothers, in their murderous mood, "Let us kill him, let us kill him," which Sabra played and sang after we had talked about her, I cannot tell. But before Sabra had struck the last note, she was on her feet, running hither and thither, in extreme excitement, and enacting the bloody scene which had hitherto lain in her subconsciousness.

"We run, we run," she said, running as she spoke. "There is Saïd, Saïd who pounds meat; so and so"—pounding—"who cuts the throats of the sheep"—imitating the action on her little throat. "There is Hadije; she holds my hands and runs; the men from the church must not hear us"; she tiptoed with intense earnestness. "They are coming out, the Armenians are coming out, they take Saïd, they cut his throat, so and so, they put the knife through Hadije, they turn and turn the knife, all her bowels are out."

She was perspiring with emotion and passion, but she did not cry. We were spellbound with horror; she had at last revealed her identity. She was evidently a Kurdish girl who had seen Saïd and Hadije, her parents, who were trying to run away, murdered by the Armenians coming out of a church. Neither Sabra nor I shall ever forget the words and the acting.

I took her on my lap and tried to make her sing the little song of Helva,[2] and I tried to sing with her and gently rock her to oblivion of the vision of horror which she held in her tiny head.

"Saïd who pounds meat is my father; Hadije with the bowels on the earth is my mother," she said before she began to sing the song of Helva.

In connection with another Kurdish child I have another dramatic but happy picture fixed in my mind. It happened in one of my last visits to Aintoura. After the announcement that the parents able to prove their identity could take their children away, some Armenian women had appeared. But as there are very few Turks and Kurds in Beirut and Lebanon, none of these nationals had turned up to claim their children. On that

[2] We took Jale to Constantinople. I meant to adopt her, but as she had trachoma in her eyes, Dr. Adnan thought that I should be exposing my own boys to the incurable disease if I kept her. Makboule Hanum, our matron in Aintoura, had her in the orphanage of Tchaglian. In 1919 the international commission for the separation of the children pronounced her Armenian, with quite a number of other Turkish children. "Ask Mother Halidé," she had said to the commission; "she will tell you I am not Armenian."

day as I walked out of the orphanage, I saw a man and a woman standing by the door and looking very different from the natives of Syria, although they were dressed in a way that was familiar to me. The man was tall with a long black beard, and he had the picturesque and colored costume of the Kurds, although in rags. The woman was his wife. He asked me if this was an orphanage and if it contained Kurdish children. Then he took from his breast a carefully folded but very worn and torn paper. It was his identity card and was going to pieces. He was from near Erzeroum, and in the emigration when the Armenian General Antranik had come, his child Hassan was lost. The pair had walked all about Anatolia going from one orphanage to another in search of little Hassan. The paper was marked all over with red ink by the institutions he had passed with this sentence, "The child Hassan not being in this orphanage." This was the last orphanage they were to come to. As Dr. Loutfi went into the buildings with the precious paper in his hands, my heart was beating as much as those of the old pair. In half an hour Dr. Loutfi walked back holding by the hand a rather delicate-looking child in a clean apron and shoes. The huge pair seemed framed in the ruddy blaze of the mountain evening; at the sight of the child they fell on their knees and opened their long arms, and the child crept hastily into their broad bosoms. Thus Ramazan, the son of Abdullah, found his little son called Hassan in Aintoura.

I asked Dr. Bliss and Mr. Dodge to come to see me and begged them to take Aintoura under the protection of the Red Cross as soon as fighting began in Beirut. The children were supplied for four months, thanks to Major Kemal, and the director with some of the staff was going to stay till the last moment. I also begged them to pass the Armenian children to the Armenians through the Red Cross, and the Moslem children to the Red Crescent in Constantinople, if the necessary moment came. They promised, and they kept their promise. They sent up Mr. Crawford in the name of the Red Cross when the Allied armies entered. This was my last service to Aintoura.

On the twentieth of February the school gave "The Shepherds of Canaan."

Children all over the world are good actors, but the Arab children beat them all in certain ways. They work themselves into an absolute belief of reality. Any play which has dramatic passion, tragedy, and romance can be trusted to Arab children, and in most cases they will perform it to perfection. Ellen, a girl of thirteen, with a contralto that dominated the orchestra, most strange for her size and age, acted Judas. Her face, one of those fair ovals with starlike, warm blue eyes and golden complexion, had wonderful dramatic expression. Her sister, only eleven, a milder and gentler copy of Ellen, looked like a very picture of the Christ-child.

The stage had a real palm-tree and thick red sand.

The children in their gorgeous robes, in brilliant reds and blues and orange, their feet bare, imagined themselves in the desert, feeling the murderous jealousy of Joseph's brothers plotting to sell or kill Joseph. In the last scene when they sang out the air that all Syria knew, "Let us kill him, let us kill him," I felt really anxious for the life of the little girl Joseph. The fierce contortions on their Semitic faces, their murderous hands playing around Joseph like lightning, and poor Joseph running and trying to escape in real and unutterable horror brought down the house. Then the performance passed to the audience. Some one got up and began to thunder in oratorical Arabic. "Feyad, Feyad," went in a whisper through the public. Syria's great poet and speaker so far had kept away from everything connected with the Turks. Now he was not only there but was paying the greatest tribute, and at a moment when the rule of the Turk seemed surely at an end. Speech after speech followed his, and it was a thoroughly Arabic audience. It was dark before they began to go, and they sang Fikret's "We are a brave nation . . . we are Ottomans," with a sincerity that reminded one of 1908.

Thirteen times Beirut forced the school to give that play. As we were only to remain a few days more, we gave it twice a day, and the audience always left singing some familiar air, mostly that of little Joseph, "For all times." On the lamp-posts in the streets of Beirut the name of Ellen was written, and Sabra was lionized and the Arabs quite happy over the little play, "The Shepherds of Canaan," which became theirs. My friend Selim Sabit always had tears in his shrewd little eyes. "The one who reads between the lines has unveiled our hearts," he said.[3]

I put my little actors in a lorry and took them to Aintoura for a night. The boy musicians of Aintoura used to come and play for Der-Nassira, usually on Fridays. This was the turn of Der-Nassira to entertain them. In the carpentering hall, where a stage was improvised, the little actors sang and acted to Aintoura and kept them in delight.

On the fourth of March, thanks to the help and kindness of Djemal Pasha the Second, we left Syria for Constantinople. Thus ended our work in Syria, and we left the Arab lands amid very sincere farewells and some tears.

[3] Selim Sabit always called me "the one who reads between the lines." In 1919 he had opened a competition in the Arabic papers of Beirut. He was to pay ten pounds to the writer who would express best what "the one who reads between the lines" means. I received two letters from him in Angora in 1921. One was full of pictures. It was marvelous how he had managed to put in water-colors the entire Arab land with palms, sands, tents, bananas, and palms. Before I could answer I heard of his death.

EPILOGUE

Of the events during the interval between March and the armistice, signed in Mudros in October, there is not much to tell. It was a historical entr'acte. The curtain had fallen on the Ottoman empire and its last representatives, the Unionists.

There was expectation behind the sense of great loss. The Unionist régime had begun with a bloodless revolution promising liberty, justice, equality, and fraternity. It had brought both the sublime and the infernal to Turkish lands and Turkish people. And after it had passed away, the Turkish people were waiting for the curtain to rise again and reveal a new and pacific Turkey in which the great achievements of 1908 should stand forth, cleansed and purified by the blood and sacrifice of Turkey's great sons.

How the new era began, and what was the scene enacted must be told as a separate tale—the tale of one of the greatest epics of modern Europe!

WORLD AFFAIRS: National and International Viewpoints
An Arno Press Collection

Angell, Norman. **The Great Illusion, 1933.** 1933.

Benes, Eduard. **Memoirs:** From Munich to New War and New Victory. 1954.

[Carrington, Charles Edmund] (Edmonds, Charles, pseud.) **A Subaltern's War.** 1930. New preface by Charles Edmund Carrington.

Cassel, Gustav. **Money and Foreign Exchange After 1914.** 1922.

Chambers, Frank P. **The War Behind the War, 1914-1918.** 1939.

Dedijer, Vladimir. **Tito.** 1953.

Dickinson, Edwin DeWitt. **The Equality of States in International Law.** 1920.

Douhet, Giulio. **The Command of the Air.** 1942.

Edib, Halidé. **Memoirs.** 1926.

Ferrero, Guglielmo. **The Principles of Power.** 1942.

Grew, Joseph C. **Ten Years in Japan.** 1944.

Hayden, Joseph Ralston. **The Philippines.** 1942.

Hudson, Manley O. **The Permanent Court of International Justice, 1920-1942.** 1943.

Huntington, Ellsworth. **Mainsprings of Civilization.** 1945.

Jacks, G. V. and R. O. Whyte. **Vanishing Lands:** A World Survey of Soil Erosion. 1939.

Mason, Edward S. **Controlling World Trade.** 1946.

Menon, V. P. **The Story of the Integration of the Indian States.** 1956.

Moore, Wilbert E. **Economic Demography of Eastern and Southern Europe.** 1945.

[Ohlin, Bertil]. **The Course and Phases of the World Economic Depression.** 1931.

Oliveira, A. Ramos. **Politics, Economics and Men of Modern Spain, 1808-1946.** 1946.

O'Sullivan, Donal. **The Irish Free State and Its Senate.** 1940.

Peffer, Nathaniel. **The White Man's Dilemma.** 1927.

Philby, H. St. John. **Sa'udi Arabia.** 1955.

Rappard, William E. **International Relations as Viewed From Geneva.** 1925.

Rauschning, Hermann. **The Revolution of Nihilism.** 1939.

Reshetar, John S., Jr. **The Ukrainian Revolution, 1917-1920.** 1952.

Richmond, Admiral Sir Herbert. **Sea Power in the Modern World.** 1934.

Robbins, Lionel. **Economic Planning and International Order.** 1937. New preface by Lionel Robbins.

Russell, Bertrand. **Bolshevism:** Practice and Theory. 1920.

Russell, Frank M. **Theories of International Relations.** 1936.

Schwarz, Solomon M. **The Jews in the Soviet Union.** 1951.

Siegfried, André. **Canada:** An International Power. [1947].

Souvarine, Boris. **Stalin.** 1939.

Spaulding, Oliver Lyman, Jr., Hoffman Nickerson, and John Womack Wright. **Warfare.** 1925.

Storrs, Sir Ronald. **Memoirs.** 1937.

Strausz-Hupé, Robert. **Geopolitics:** The Struggle for Space and Power. 1942.

Swinton, Sir Ernest D. **Eyewitness.** 1933.

Timasheff, Nicholas S. **The Great Retreat.** 1946.

Welles, Sumner. **Naboth's Vineyard:** The Dominican Republic, 1844-1924. 1928. Two volumes in one.

Whittlesey, Derwent. **The Earth and the State.** 1939.

Wilcox, Clair. **A Charter for World Trade.** 1949.